A History of the Sudan

A History of the Sudan

*From the Coming of Islam
to the Present Day*

Sixth Edition

P. M. Holt
and
M. W. Daly

**Longman
is an imprint of**

PEARSON

Harlow, England • London • New York • Boston • San Francisco • Toronto
Sydney • Tokyo • Singapore • Hong Kong • Seoul • Taipei • New Delhi
Cape Town • Madrid • Mexico City • Amsterdam • Munich • Paris • Milan

Pearson Education Limited

Edinburgh Gate
Harlow CM20 2JE
United Kingdom
Tel: +44 (0)1279 623623
Fax: +44 (0)1279 431059
Website: www.pearsoned.co.uk

First published 1961 by Weidenfeld and Nicolson
Second edition 1963
Third edition 1979
Fourth edition 1988 published by Longman Group UK Limited
Fifth edition 2000 published by Pearson Education Limited
Sixth edition 2011 published by Pearson Education Limited

First and Second Editions © 1961, 1963 by P.M. Holt
Third Edition © 1979 by P.M. Holt and M.W. Daly
Fourth Edition Longman Group Limited 1988
Fifth Edition © Pearson Education Limited 2000
This Edition © Pearson Education Limited 2011

The rights of P.M. Holt and M.W. Daly to be identified as authors
of this work have been asserted by them in accordance
with the Copyright, Designs and Patents Act 1988.

Pearson Education is not responsible for the content of third party internet sites.

ISBN: 978-1-4058-7445-8

British Library Cataloguing in Publication Data
A CIP catalogue record for this book can be obtained from the British Library

Library of Congress Cataloging in Publication Data
Holt, P. M. (Peter Malcolm)
    A history of the Sudan : from the coming of Islam to the present day /
    P.M. Holt and M.W. Daly. -- 6th ed.
        p. cm.
    Includes bibliographical references and index.
    ISBN 978-1-4058-7445-8 (pbk.)
    1. Sudan--History. I. Daly, M. W. II. Title.
    DT156.4.H64 2011
    962.4--dc22

                                        2010043487

10 9 8 7 6 5 4 3 2 1
15 14 13 12 11

Set by 35 in 10/12pt Baskerville
Printed in Malaysia, CTP-KHL

Contents

Maps

Preface to the First Edition

The first steps towards the making of the modern Sudan were taken, nearly a century and a half ago, when the soldiers of Muhammad 'Ali Pasha, the Ottoman sultan's viceroy in Egypt, brought under their master's rule the Muslim cultivators, merchants and tribesmen of Nubia, Sennar and Kordofan. A common administration, the shared glories and disasters of the Mahdist Revolution and renewed experience of alien rule under the Anglo-Egyptian Condominium welded the Sudanese peoples together, and stimulated the development of Sudanese nationalism. On New Year's Day, 1956, the Sudan emerged into independent statehood.

This is in brief the story which the following pages attempt to tell in more detail. Three factors predominate in modern Sudanese history. The first is the indigenous tradition, itself the product of the intermingling of Arab Muslims with Africans. The fusion began over a thousand years ago and, as allusions to the problem of the Southern Sudan will show, is still a continuing process. This lies at the base of Sudanese nationality, religion and culture. I have therefore dealt at some length with the earlier stages of the fusion in the Introduction, and have returned to the theme of the indigenous tradition in the Conclusion.

The two other factors are the influence of Egypt, which in its earlier phases was late Ottoman rather than purely Egyptian in quality, and the influence of Britain. The effect of these two influences upon the Sudan is seen in its history from the time of Muhammad 'Ali's conquests until the present day. Egyptian rule ended with the Mahdist Revolution, British administration with the coming of independence, but the modern Sudan is politically and materially very largely the heir of these earlier régimes. The cultural influence of both Egypt and Britain is unaffected by the transformation of their former dependency into a sovereign state. The play upon each other of these three factors is the theme of this book.

In the difficult problem of the transliteration of Arabic words, I have adopted a compromise. For the place-names of provinces and larger towns, I have used conventional forms, e.g. Khartoum, Kordofan, El Obeid. The conventional Kassala and Bahr El Ghazal have, however, been slightly modified to the more accurate forms Kasala and Bahr al-Ghazal. Personal names (except for Neguib and Nasser, which have a firmly established conventional spelling) and technical terms are rigorously transliterated, but diacritical marks have been omitted for the sake of simplicity. Ottoman titles which are not purely Arabic in origin, e.g. *defterdar, hükümdar,* are spelt according to modern Turkish conventions.

In conclusion, I wish to express my gratitude to all those who have helped me in the preparation of this book; in particular the General Editor of this series, Professor Bernard Lewis; my former colleague, Mr A.B. Theobald, and Sayyid Osman Sid Ahmed Ismail of the University of Khartoum. All these read the book in draft, and assisted me with their comments and criticisms. Dr G.N. Sanderson, also of the University of Khartoum, kindly provided information on the diplomatic background to the Reconquest. While acknowledging their very real help, I accept, of course, all responsibility for the statements and opinions expressed in my book. Material for the illustrations was generously provided by Dr J.F.E. Bloss and Mr F.C.A. McBain from their private collections of photographs, and by Mr R.L. Hill from the Sudanese archive of the University of Durham. Sayyid Mohamed Kamal El Bakri, First Secretary of the Sudan Embassy in London, was most helpful in making available, or obtaining, further photographic material. I am grateful to the following publishers for permission to reprint short passages from copyright works: Oxford University Press for *Egypt in the Sudan* by R. Hill, Messrs D. van Nostrand Inc., New York for *Diplomacy in the Near and Middle East* by J.C. Hurewitz, and Cambridge University Press for *Sudan Arabic Texts* translated by S. Hillelson. Lastly, I am forever indebted to the Sudanese people for the many happy and formative years which I spent in their land.

1961   P.M. Holt

Preface to the Sixth Edition

Since the appearance of the fifth edition, there has been increasing interest in the history of the Sudan. The civil war and the agreement that ended it in 2005, the Darfur crisis, the emergence of the Sudan as an oil exporter, the elections of 2010 and the referendum scheduled for 2011 have captured the world's attention. These and other recent developments are treated in this new edition. The opportunity has been taken to adjust the coverage of earlier periods and to update the bibliography. The death in 2006 of P.M. Holt, the leading historian of the Sudan, was itself a notable event: he is greatly missed; his work lives on.

June 2010   M.W.D.

Abbreviations and Acronyms

ALF	Azanian Liberation Front
ASG	Anyidi State Government
CPA	Comprehensive Peace Agreement
DUP	Democratic Unionist Party
GONU	Government of National Unity
GOSS	Government of South Sudan
HEC	High Executive Council
IBRD	International Bank for Reconstruction and Development
IGAD	International Authority on Development (formerly IGADD)
IGADD	Inter-Governmental Authority on Drought and Development
IMF	International Monetary Fund
JEM	Justice and Equality Movement
NCP	National Congress Party
NDA	National Democratic Alliance
NIF	National Islamic Front
NPG	Nile Provisional Government
NUP	National Unionist Party
OAU	Organization of African Unity
OLS	Operation Lifeline Sudan
PDP	People's Democratic Party
RCC	Revolutionary Command Council
SACDNU	Sudan Closed Districts National Union
SAF	Sudanese Allied Forces
SANU	Sudan African National Union
SCP	Sudanese Communist Party
SPLA	Sudan People's Liberation Army
SPLM	Sudan People's Liberation Movement
SRWU	Sudan Railway Workers' Union
SSIM	Southern Sudan Independence Movement
SSLM	Southern Sudan Liberation Movement
SSPG	Southern Sudan Provisional Government
SSU	Sudan Socialist Union
SWTUF	Sudan Workers' Trade Union Federation
TMC	Transitional Military Council
UNMIS	United Nations Mission in Sudan
WAA	Workers' Affairs Association

Publisher's Acknowledgements

Picture Credits

The publisher would like to thank the following for their kind permission to reproduce their photographs:

Sudan Archive, Durham University: Durham University, plates 1–8

All other images © Pearson Education

Every effort has been made to trace the copyright holders and we apologise in advance for any unintentional omissions. We would be pleased to insert the appropriate acknowledgement in any subsequent edition of this publication.

Introduction: The Land and the People

The Territories Comprising the Modern Sudan

The medieval Muslim geographers gave the name of *Bilad al-Sudan*, 'the land of the Blacks', to the belt of African territory to the south of the Sahara Desert. In the more restricted sense of the territories lying southwards of Egypt, which formed the Anglo-Egyptian Condominium from 1899 until 1955, and which now constitute the Republic of the Sudan, the term is of nineteenth-century origin, a convenient administrative designation for the African empire acquired by Muhammad 'Ali Pasha, the viceroy of Egypt, and his successors.[1] The Sudan in this sense excluded the vast regions west of Darfur which in the late nineteenth and early twentieth centuries were to pass under French and British colonial rule; on the other hand it included territories which did not form part of the Sudan as traditionally understood – Nubia, the land of the Beja and the Ottoman ports of the Red Sea coast.

Traditionally the name of Nubia was applied to the whole riverain region from the First Cataract to the Sabaluqa Gorge, not far north of the confluence of the Blue and White Niles. It fell into two portions, which had separate histories from the early sixteenth to the early nineteenth century. Lower Nubia, called by the Ottomans *Berberistan*, 'the land of the Barabra',[2] extended from the First to the Third Cataract, and thus included territory both north and south of the modern Egyptian–Sudanese frontier. It was, nominally at least, dependent upon the Ottoman viceroys of Egypt. Upper Nubia, above the Third Cataract, was under the suzerainty of the Funj rulers of Sennar.

East of Nubia, in the Red Sea Hills, were the Beja, recognized by medieval Muslim writers as a distinct ethnic group, not Nubians, nor Arabs, nor *Sudan* ('Blacks'). Suakin and its sister-port of Massawa (which was annexed by Italy in 1884) looked to the Red Sea and Arabia, rather than to the Nile Valley, from which they were separated by the barrier of the Red Sea Hills and the intractable Beja.

The area of the present-day republic is very nearly one million square miles – about one-quarter the size of Europe. Geographically, the greater part of the country is an immense plain. This may be divided into three zones: in the north is rocky desert and semi-desert; south of this is a belt of undulating sand, passing from semi-desert to savanna; south of this again a clay belt, which widens as it stretches eastwards from the south of Darfur to the rainlands and semi-desert lying east of the Blue and main Niles. The Red Sea Hills, a northerly prolongation of the Ethiopian highlands, separate the great plain from the narrow coastal strip.

The Sudanese plain is drained by the Nile and its tributaries. Both the White and Blue Niles rise outside the country. The White Nile enters the Sudan (where its upper reaches are known as Bahr al-Jabal, 'the Mountain River') at Nimule, and after a course of a hundred miles, passes into the clay plain. Here it is obstructed, and enlarges into an enormous swampy area, known as the Sudd (Arabic: *sadd*, 'barrier'). After a winding course of four hundred miles, it is joined by its western tributary, the Bahr al-Ghazal, which collects the waters of a multitude of smaller rivers, draining the south-western plain and originating in the ironstone plateau which forms the Nile–Congo divide. About eighty miles further on, it is joined by the Sobat from the east.

A broad, slow river, the White Nile emerges from the swamps into a region of acacia forests which at one time fringed its banks as far as Khartoum, but now the last part of its journey lies through open, almost treeless plains. From the confluence of the White Nile and Bahr al-Ghazal to Khartoum is a distance of about six hundred miles. The Blue Nile is a shorter, swifter and more beautiful river. Its course within the Sudan covers nearly five hundred miles. The region between the Blue and White rivers, as they converge at Khartoum, is known as the Gezira (Arabic: *jazira*, 'island' or 'peninsula'). Once the granary of Khartoum, the Gezira is now the site of the principal cotton-growing area of the Sudan.

The main Nile flows in a generally northward direction from Khartoum through increasingly arid country. Two hundred miles below Khartoum, it receives the seasonal waters of the Atbara, its last tributary. About a hundred and fifty miles further on, at Abu Hamad, it makes a great bend to the south-west before resuming its northerly course by Dongola to the Egyptian frontier.

The Tribes of the Sudan

There exists a broad distinction between the Northern and Southern parts of the modern Sudan. The North is, with certain important exceptions, Arabic in speech, and its peoples are largely arabized in culture and outlook. Its indigenous inhabitants are universally Muslim; a minority of Arabic-speaking Christians is composed of the descendants of immigrants from Egypt and Lebanon since the Turco-Egyptian conquest. The Southern Sudan contains a variety of ethnic groups and languages. Unlike the Northerners, its peoples are not generally Muslims, nor do they claim Arab descent; although there has been some degree of islamization and arabization. These tendencies were restrained during the Condominium period, when European and American missionaries effected a limited christianization of the region.

Three Southern tribes will appear fairly frequently in the following pages. The Shilluk now occupy a comparatively small area on the western bank of the White Nile, but formerly their range was much more extensive. As late as the mid-nineteenth century their northern limit was the island of Aba, thirty years later to be the cradle of the Mahdia. Until the early years of the Turco-Egyptian régime, they raided the Arab settlements down the White Nile, and one such raid is said to have led to the foundation of the Funj kingdom by a band of Shilluk warriors.[3] Until the coming of firearms and steamers, they were able to meet their northern neighbours on equal terms.

The Dinka occupy a much more extensive territory than the present-day Shilluk, but lack their unity: they are a group of tribes, some of which dwell on the eastern bank of the White Nile, others, the majority, in the grassy flood-plains of the Bahr al-Ghazal, where they herd their cattle. Further south, on the higher land of the Nile–Congo divide, live the Azande, now divided by the international boundary between the Sudan and Congo (Kinshasa).

The arabization of the Northern Sudan resulted from the penetration of the region by tribes who had already migrated from Arabia to Upper Egypt. The process will be described in the following chapter. With certain comparatively minor exceptions, those Northern Sudanese who claim Arab descent belong to one or other of two extensive, if somewhat artificial, divisions: the arabized Nubians, mainly sedentaries of the main Nile, composed of the Barabra and the Ja'ali Group; and the mainly nomadic or semi-nomadic Juhayna Group.

The Barabra, as we have seen, inhabit Lower Nubia. Their representatives in the modern Sudan are the Sukkut and Mahas, who still speak related Nubian dialects. South of them are a series of tribes, inhabiting the old Upper Nubia, who belong to the Ja'ali Group. These tribes claim as a common ancestor an Arab named Ibrahim Ja'al. Whether this eponym is historical or not, the traditional pedigree indicates an element common to all these tribes. Since the Arab irruption into this region, Arab descent has been a source of pride and distinction: hence it is not surprising that stress is laid on a common Arab ancestor. A further genealogical sophistication makes Ibrahim Ja'al a descendant of al-'Abbas, the Prophet's uncle. Thus the epithets Ja'ali and 'Abbasi have become virtually synonyms in the genealogies of the eastern *Bilad al-Sudan*. In spite, however, of the anxiety of the genealogists to provide the Ja'ali Group with a common Arab ancestor, it would be more realistic to regard the submerged Nubian substratum as the common ethnic element among these tribes. This hypothesis does not, of course, reject the undoubted historical fact of Arab ancestry as such: the result of intermarriage between Arab immigrants and the older Nubian population. From this intermingling the present Ja'ali Group derive their markedly Arab characteristics and their Muslim cultural inheritance.

The name of Ja'aliyyin (plural of Ja'ali) is specifically applied to one tribe of this Group, dwelling between the Atbara confluence and the Sabaluqa Gorge. The Ja'aliyyin in this restricted sense formed from the sixteenth century until the Turco-Egyptian conquest a tribal kingdom, dominated by a royal clan known as the Sa'dab. North of them, the region of Berber is the homeland of the Mirafab, another tribe of the Ja'ali Group, who also used to form a tribal kingdom. Further north still are other tribal members of the same Group, the Rubatab and Manasir, inhabiting the banks of the Nile down to and beyond the great bend at Abu Hamad.

The reach of the Nile between the Fourth Cataract and al-Dabba is the homeland of a tribal confederacy, the Shayqiyya, which does not claim Ja'ali origin. Many observers have noted what their history confirms, the difference between their character and that of their neighbours. In the eighteenth century the predatory, equestrian aristocracy of the Shayqiyya dominated Nubia. In 1821, they alone of the riverain tribes resisted the Turco-Egyptian invasion. Their subsequent service to the new régime as a force of irregular cavalry led to the establishment of Shayqiyya colonies around the junction of the Niles and elsewhere.

The most northerly tribes of the Ja'ali Group lie downstream of the Shayqiyya, between al-Dabba and the country of the Barabra. Their homeland is the historical region of Dongola (Arabic: *Dunqula*), whence these tribesmen are known collectively as *Danaqla* (singular: *Dunqulawi*), i.e. 'men of Dongola'. Among them there is far more consciousness of Nubian origin than among the tribes of the southern Ja'ali Group, and a Nubian dialect continues to be spoken.

The arabized Nubians are primarily sedentary cultivators, inhabiting the narrow strip of riverain land and the islands (some of which are very extensive) watered by the Nile flood or irrigation. Their territories lie outside the normal rain-belt. Hence the pressure of population on the land has always been heavy, especially among the Danaqla and Barabra. This economic limitation, in association sometimes with political instability, has made temporary or permanent emigration a recurrent feature of the history of these peoples. The Barabra have provided Egypt with its 'Berberine' servants. In the sixteenth century, Mahas migrated to the confluence of the Niles and established themselves as religious teachers.

Various ruling groups, basically neither Nubian nor Arab, have claimed a Ja'ali (or synonymously, an 'Abbasi) ancestry. The royal family of Taqali, a small Muslim state in the Nuba Mountains, derives its origin from the marriage of a Ja'ali holy man with an indigenous princess. A similar story is told of the origin of the Nabtab, the dominant clan of the Beja Banu 'Amir. The royal Kayra clan of the Fur claimed 'Abbasi ancestry, as did the neighbouring rulers of Wadai. The rise of the Shayqiyya in the eighteenth century produced an emigration of Danaqla to Darfur, which seems to have led to increasing trade between that state and Egypt. In the nineteenth century Ja'ali *jallaba* (petty traders) were ubiquitous in southern Kordofan and Darfur, on the southern fringe of Arab territory, while Danaqla and other members of the great Ja'ali Group played a prominent part in the opening-up of the White Nile and Bahr al-Ghazal. Al-Zubayr Rahma, the merchant-prince of the western Bahr al-Ghazal in the reign of Khedive Isma'il, prided himself on his 'Abbasi descent.

Mention should also be made of several tribes, outside the confines of ancient Nubia, which claim membership of the Ja'ali Group. These are probably synthetic tribes, formed by the accretion of heterogeneous fragments around Ja'ali leaders. It is significant that five of them have names derived from the Arabic root *jama'a*, 'to collect'.

In Sudanese genealogical usage, the term *Juhayna* is practically a comprehensive term for all tribes claiming Arab descent but not asserting a Ja'ali–'Abbasi origin. Arabs of the Juhayna of Arabia, who had migrated to Upper Egypt, played a leading part in the breakthrough into Nubia in the fourteenth century,[4] and there has been a tendency for elements of varied (and non-Arab) origins to link themselves with this successful tribe.

Even the confused and sometimes tendentious genealogical materials available today make it clear, however, that at least two important sub-groups can hardly be linked ancestrally with the Juhayna. The Rufa'a of the Blue Nile preserve some memory of a distinct origin. Their ancestors lived in geographical proximity to the ancestral Juhayna, both in the Hijaz and in Upper Egypt; and this has probably led to their inclusion in the Juhayna Group. In the late fifteenth century an Arab population, probably of varied origins, became sedentarized at the junction of the Blue and White Niles under a chief from the Rufa'a named 'Abdallah Jamma'. He and his successors, the 'Abdallab, became prosperous from the tolls levied on the desert Arabs during their annual nomadic cycle, and were recognized by the Funj rulers of Sennar (1504–1821) as paramount chiefs of the Arabs.[5] The bulk of the Rufa'a were almost entirely nomadic until the nineteenth century, when the northern section became partly sedentarized. The town of Rufa'a on the Blue Nile was originally a tribal settlement. The southern section, on each side of the upper Blue Nile, is still largely nomadic.

A second sub-group which can hardly belong to the Juhayna by descent is the Fazara. This term, now obsolete in Sudanese usage, included until the nineteenth century most of the camel-nomads of northern Kordofan and Darfur. The historical Fazara tribe was of north-Arabian origin, whereas the Juhayna were south-Arabian.

Among the numerous tribes of the Juhayna Group, two have played a sufficiently important part in Sudanese history to be given specific mention. The leading tribe of the southern Butana (i.e. the quadrilateral bounded by the main Nile, the Atbara, the Blue Nile and the Ethiopian foothills) is the Shukriyya, camel-owning nomads. They rose to importance during the eighteenth century as Funj power declined, under the leadership of the Abu Sinn family. Ahmad Abu Sinn (*c.* 1790–1870) lived on good terms with the Turco-Egyptian régime, was given the rank of bey, and for ten years was governor of Khartoum. Their territory included the grain-producing rainlands of the Qadarif, where a tribal market developed. This place, originally called Suq Abu Sinn ('Abu Sinn's Market') has now taken over the name of the region, anglicized as Gedaref.

Another important nomadic tribe is the Kababish. These inhabit a region suitable for sheep and camel rearing in the semi-desert north of Kordofan. They are a synthetic tribe, formed from diverse elements by a common way of life, which is reflected in their name (from Arabic: *kabsh*, 'a ram'). Their wide range, across the north-western trade-routes, made the tribe a factor of some importance in the commercial and political history of the Sudan, especially during the nineteenth century.

An important sub-group of tribes claiming origin from the Juhayna is the Baqqara of southern Kordofan and Darfur. As their name (from Arabic: *baqar*, 'a cow') implies, these are cattle-nomads: the frontier-tribes of Arabdom, inhabiting regions where camel nomadism is climatically impossible. The route by which they arrived in their present habitat is a subject of controversy, but broadly speaking they seem to be a southern offshoot of the great Arab irruption into the lands west of the Nile. The furthest wave of these immigrants was carried as far west as Lake Chad, whence a return-movement towards the east deposited the ancestors of the modern Baqqara tribes.

Between the Baqqara in the South and the camel-Arabs of the North were enclaves of non-Arab sedentaries. From one of these, the Fur, protected by the mountainous bastion of Jabal Marra, developed the important Muslim sultanate of Darfur ('the land of the Fur'). The non-Arab tribes to the south of the Baqqara country were frequently raided for slaves, and intermarriage has considerably modified the physical type of the Baqqara, although they have preserved their Arabic speech and tradition. Two tribes played a particularly important role in the history of the nineteenth century: the powerful Rizayqat of southern Darfur, athwart a principal route from the Bahr al-Ghazal to the north; and the Ta'aisha, an unimportant tribe until the Mahdia, when they were used by their kinsman, the Khalifa 'Abdallahi, as an instrument of his domination in the Sudan.

The Beja are Hamitic-speaking tribes, now inhabiting the Red Sea Hills and parts of the plains sloping down to the main Nile. Their ancestors confronted and, to some extent, intermarried with the Arab immigrants into Upper Egypt in the early Middle Ages. They were camel-nomads, although there has been some degree of sedentarization, especially in connection with the modern agricultural development of the Gash and Tokar deltas. Like the riverain Nubians, the Beja became Muslims, and have undergone varying degrees of arabization. In its lightest form, this amounts to little more than claiming an Arab pedigree; the early Muslim heroes, Khalid ibn al-Walid and al-Zubayr ibn al-'Awwam being preferred as adoptive ancestors.

The most northerly of the modern Beja, the 'Ababda, now divided between Upper Egypt and the Sudan, are, however, Arabic-speaking. As protectors of the route across the Nubian Desert, from Sudanese territory to the Nile at Kurusku, a clan of the 'Ababda played a part of some importance before the construction of the railway, and their chiefs were in close relations with the Turco-Egyptian administration. The more southerly and less arabized Beja underwent a period of expansion in the eighteenth century, moving south-westwards from their mountainous habitats towards the plains of the Atbara and the Gash. The most aggressive of these tribes, the Hadendowa, had established itself in the Taka, the region of the Gash, by the early nineteenth century.

Of the other non-Arab peoples of the Northern Sudan, the Fur have already been mentioned. Although surrounded by a flood of immigrant Arab tribes, they succeeded in establishing a dynastic Muslim state which was not finally extinguished until 1916. Between Darfur and the White Nile, the hilly region of the Nuba Mountains provided a refuge for another indigenous people as Arab tribes gradually occupied the plain of Kordofan. The name of Nuba is applied in Arabic both to these people and to the historical Nubians of the main Nile. The nature of the relationship between these two homonymous groups has long been a matter of controversy. Here it is enough to note that the hill-Nuba never succeeded in asserting themselves against the Arabs, as did the Fur. Their hill-top communities were divided and isolated. They remained for the most part pagan, although the twentieth century opened the way both to organized Christian missionary activity and the more amorphous but effective influence of contact with Muslims. In the north-eastern foothills lay the kingdom of Taqali, whose rulers encouraged the immigration of settlers and established their suzerainty over a considerable area. The kingdom continued to exist in semi-autonomy after the Turco-Egyptian conquest and was integrated into the local government system of the Condominium.

The Ancient Trade-Routes

The territories which now form the Northern Sudan were traversed by a number of trade-routes. These found their outlet mainly through Upper Egypt and the Red Sea. The commerce of the eastern *Bilad al-Sudan*, extending to Darfur or a little further west, was thus quite distinct from that of the central *Bilad al-Sudan*, which found an outlet by way of the Fezzan to North Africa.

The routes of the eastern *Bilad al-Sudan* lay along two main axes. One, running roughly from south to north, linked Sennar with Egypt. The other, roughly from west to east, linked Darfur with Suakin. Commercial relations existed between Sennar and western Ethiopia, centring on Gondar. From Sennar a route ran along the western bank of the Blue Nile through the Gezira to the ancient market-town of Arbaji.[6] Further to the north, the river was crossed, and the way continued along the eastern bank of the Blue and main Niles by al-'Aylafun and Halfayat al-Muluk ('Halfaya of the Kings'), the later capital of the 'Abdallab chiefs.

Beyond Qarri, the old 'Abdallabi capital, there were alternative routes to the north. The western route was apparently the more used in the earlier Funj period. The Nile was crossed near Qarri or al-Diraya (i.e. either above or below the Sabaluqa Gorge), and travellers then struck across the Bayuda Desert in a north-westerly direction, cutting off the great bend of the Nile and avoiding the country of the predatory Shayqiyya. Before the rise of the Shayqiyya, in the late seventeenth century, caravans may well have followed the river all the way. The desert route met the Nile again at Kurti, and continued along its western bank, through the vassal-kingdom of Dongola, to the frontier-post of Mushu, some way south of the Third Cataract. Here the caravans turned into the desert.

At the Salima Oasis, the Nile route was joined by the great artery of trade between Darfur and Egypt, the *Darb al-arba'in* ('the Forty Days' Road'). This began at Kubayh, the principal commercial centre of Darfur, ran to the frontier-post of Suwayna, and thence went north-eastwards across the desert to Salima. From Salima the route went by way of the alum-producing watering point of Shabb to the Kharja Oasis, which was an outpost of Ottoman Egypt. Thence it ran to the Nile at Asyut.

The eastern route seems to have developed during the eighteenth century, in consequence of increasing political instability in the riverain territories downstream of Berber. From Qarri it went along the eastern bank to Shendi and El Damer, and over the Atbara into the territory of Berber. It then left the river, and crossed the Nubian Desert until Ottoman territory was reached in the neighbourhood of Aswan. After Muhammad 'Ali's conquests, a shorter desert-crossing was usual, from Abu Hamad, at the great bend of the Nile, by the wells of al-Murrat to Kurusku in Lower Nubia. The line of the modern railway, between Abu Hamad and Wadi Halfa, is a variant of this historic route.

The routes of the west–east trade axis were also liable to vary in accordance with political conditions. Kordofan was a debatable land between the rulers of Sennar and Darfur, and the situation of the untamed Shilluk on the White Nile combined to render unsafe the direct route from Kubayh to Sennar via El Obeid. Caravans therefore took a more northerly route from El Obeid to Shendi. From Shendi caravans went to Egypt by the desert route described above. Merchants travelling from Shendi to Suakin went up the river Atbara to Quz Rajab, a market-town ruled by an 'Abdallabi chief. A direct route from Sennar also ran to Quz Rajab, but this was rendered dangerous by the Shukriyya nomads. From Quz Rajab, one route went direct to Suakin, while another made a diversion into the Taka.

By the early nineteenth century, Shendi, the point of intersection of the two route-axes, had become the principal commercial centre of the eastern *Bilad al-Sudan*. In the years immediately preceding the Turco-Egyptian invasion it was under the strong autonomous rule of *Makk* Nimr,[7] the Sa'dabi chief. Its populace was composed of indigenous Ja'aliyyin and merchant settlers from Sennar, Kordofan, Darfur and Dongola, the last being the most numerous. In spite of the commercial activity over which they presided, neither the Sa'dab nor any other Sudanese dynasty coined their own money. Millet and *dammur*, the local cotton cloth, the staples of local commerce, formed the media of exchange, while foreign silver coins (in Burckhardt's time,[8] the Spanish dollars of Charles IV) were used for larger transactions.

Shendi was a centre both for the internal trade of the various regions of the eastern *Bilad al-Sudan* and for external trade. Among the principal commodities produced and consumed within the region were millet and *dammur*, while slaves were of pre-eminent importance, both in internal and external trade. The slaves were not, of course, taken from among Muslim peoples, but were obtained chiefly by raiding the fringe of Ethiopia and the tribes southwest of Darfur. A certain number came from servile families settled in the neighbourhood of Sennar. Although many slaves were retained permanently in the Sudanese territories, as domestic servants, field workers and armed bodyguards, there was a considerable export trade to Egypt and Arabia. A smaller, more specialized trade, was in horses from Dongola, which were exported to the Yemen.

Although there was little commercial intercourse between the eastern *Bilad al-Sudan* and the countries west of Darfur, a steady stream of Muslim pilgrims, known generally as Takarir, or Takarna (singular, Takruri), passed from the central and western *Bilad al-Sudan* into Darfur, where their numbers were further augmented from the local peoples. From Darfur some went north, to Asyut and Cairo, where they joined the Egyptian Pilgrimage Caravan. Others made their way to Sennar and Gondar, and thence to the seaport of Massawa. The most favoured route in the early nineteenth century was the great commercial artery by way of Shendi to Suakin. This pilgrimage-route, linking the central and eastern portions of *Bilad al-Sudan*, can hardly have been older than the sixteenth century, when Muslim dynasties were established in Sennar, Darfur and Wadai.[9]

Many of the pilgrims were excessively poor, and depended on charity or earnings from manual labour to complete their journey, which in some cases lasted for years. Their successors in the twentieth century, now generally called Fallata, provided much of the labour force for the cotton-fields of the Gezira, and are a permanent element in the population of the Sudan. At some time, probably in the early nineteenth century, a colony of Takarna established a vigorous frontier-state in a district of the Abyssinian marches known as the Qallabat. The name of their territory is perpetuated in the modern frontier-town of al-Qallabat, anglicized as Gallabat.

PART ONE

Before the Turco-Egyptian Conquest

At Bujarâs [Faras], the capital of the province of Al-Marîs, which is a well-populated city, there is the dwelling-place of Jausâr, who wore the turban and the two horns and the golden bracelet.

> Abu Salih, *History*
> (early thirteenth century),
> translated B.T.A. Evetts

The Sultan of the Muslims, the Caliph of the Lord of the Worlds; who undertakes the affairs of the world and the Faith; who is raised up for the interests of the Muslims; who supports the Holy Law of the Lord of the Prophets; who spreads the banner of justice and grace over all the worlds; he by whom God corrects His servants and gives light to the land; the repressor of the race of unbelief and deception and rebellion, and the race of oppression and corruption; the mercy of God (praised and exalted be He!) to the townsman and the nomad; he who trusts in the King, the Guide: the sultan, son of the sultan, the victorious, the divinely aided Sultan Badi, son of the deceased Dakin, son of the Sultan Badi.

May God, the Compassionate, the Merciful, grant him victory by the influence of the great Qur'an and the noble Prophet. Amen. Amen. O Lord of the Worlds.

> From a charter of
> Sultan Badi VI (1791)

CHAPTER ONE

The Eastern Bilad al-Sudan *in the Middle Ages*

At the time of the coming of Islam in the early seventh century, there were three territories on the main Nile, south of the Byzantine province of Egypt. The first of these, the land of the Nobadae or Nubians proper, extended upstream from the First Cataract. Beyond it lay the country of the Makoritae with its capital at Old Dongola. Still further south was the kingdom of the Alodaei, the capital of which, Soba, lay on the Blue Nile, not far from the modern Khartoum. Christian missionaries had made converts, including the ruling families; and at an uncertain date before 891 the two northern territories were combined into one kingdom, usually called by its Arabic name, al-Muqurra (i.e. the Makoritae). The term al-Nuba (the Nubians), although properly restricted to the people of the more northerly of the two territories, was generally applied to the combined kingdom, and even extended to the inhabitants of its southern neighbour, known in the Arabic sources as 'Alwa.

The conquest of Egypt by the Muslim Arabs between 639 and 641 brought to the border of Nubia a militant power whose control over Upper Egypt was still precarious. Frontier raiding by both sides took place, and in 651–52, the governor of Egypt, 'Abdallah b. Sa'd b. Abi Sarh, besieged Dongola. The campaign is known to us only from later Arabic accounts, which represent the Nubians as suing for peace, but it is clear that 'Abdallah was unable either to inflict a decisive defeat or to extend Muslim territory south of the frontier-town of Aswan. As the history of the following centuries was to show, invaders from the north were checked both by the resistance of the Nubians and by the long and difficult lines of communications from advanced bases in Egypt. In the end Christian Nubia succumbed to gradual erosion and infiltration rather than to organized military invasion.

Medieval Arabic writers attach to 'Abdallah's expedition the conclusion of a formal treaty of peace, which, we are given to understand, henceforward regulated the relations between Muslim Egypt and al-Muqurra. The story presents some anomalies. In the first place, the alleged instrument is known as the *baqt* – a word unique in Arabic diplomatic terminology, and derived from the Latin *pactum* by way of Graecized *pakton,* in Hellenistic usage 'a compact of mutual obligations and its connected payments'. In the second place, the stipulations of the *baqt* are curious. They are described with increasing elaboration as time goes on, until al-Maqrizi, writing eight hundred years after the event, gives what purports to be the authentic text, signed, sealed and delivered. Since it includes the provision that the Nubians shall maintain in good order the mosque the Muslims have built in the city of Dongola, we may stigmatize this as a medieval forgery. Earlier accounts, however, which go back to the ninth century, indicate that the essence of the *baqt* was an annual exchange of slaves from Nubia for provisions from Egypt. The number of slaves is given (with some variation), and in one source the kind and qualities of provisions are specified. One writer's assertion that supply of these provisions originated as an act of grace may be disregarded as a face-saving presentation of state-controlled barter. Survival of the Hellenistic term suggests that 'Abdallah's invasion re-established, after interruption, a trade of long standing. In the first three centuries of Islam, Muslim jurists had difficulty accommodating within their categories this anomalous relationship with a Christian state; al-Maqrizi's 'treaty' may represent such an adaptation of historical fact to legal fiction.

To the east of Lower Nubia lay barren and mountainous territory, the source of gold and emeralds, known to medieval geographers as *bilad al-ma'din*, 'the land of the mines'. This was a region outside the effective control of Egyptian and Nubian rulers alike, inhabited by sparse and fragmented groups of Beja, and by its nature attractive to adventurers. Clashes between Beja and immigrant Arab miners were inevitable, and led in 854 to a full-scale military expedition from Qus, supported by a supply-fleet in the Red Sea. The Beja chief, 'Ali Baba, was defeated, and taken to the caliph in Baghdad. He was honourably received, and sent home with gifts. Such campaigns, and resultant undertakings to pay tribute, were of transient effect; more significant was continued Arab immigration to the land of the mines.

The career of one Arab adventurer in the mid-ninth century illustrates the state of frontier society. 'Abdallah al-'Umari claimed to be a descendant of the third caliph, 'Umar b. al-Khattab. A man of family and education, he bought a gang of slaves and went off to make his fortune in the gold mines. He built up a following among the miners by exploiting the tribal rivalries of the Arabs. His presence disturbed the Nubians, and hostilities ensued. Finally Ahmad b. Tulun, the governor of Egypt, alarmed at the unrest on his southern frontier, sent to Aswan an expeditionary force, which al-'Umari defeated. His prestige in the land of the mines was now, in 869, at its height, but his authority rested on the unstable Arab grouping in the region. In the end he fell victim to tribal assassins. His head was carried to Ahmad b. Tulun, who was, no doubt, as gratified as the Nubian king to learn of his death.

Al-'Umari's régime died with him, but his career indicates the increasing arabization of the region. One of the leading tribal groups in the land of the mines was Rabi'a, which in the time of al-'Umari had allied with the Beja against him, and suffered from his reprisals. By the middle of the tenth century, Rabi'a, who had intermarried with the Beja, were paramount throughout the region, and their chief was styled *Sahib al-Ma'din,* 'the Lord of the Mines'.

In 969 Egypt was conquered on behalf of a dynasty, the Fatimids, who had set up a caliphate in North Africa in opposition to the 'Abbasids of Baghdad. Shortly afterwards an envoy was sent to the court of Dongola. His name, Ibn Sulaym al-Aswani, suggests that he was a native of Aswan, and hence familiar with the Nubians. The object of his mission was twofold: to re-establish trade, which had been interrupted by the change of régime in Egypt; and to seek the Nubian king's conversion to Islam. Ibn Sulaym returned to Egypt to write an account of the Nubians. Extant portions, transmitted by later authors, are the most important single literary source concerning medieval Nubia.[1]

Ibn Sulaym describes the country through which he passed on the way to Dongola. Five miles upstream of Aswan was the frontier-post of al-Qasr ('the fortress'), the gateway to Nubia. Beyond lay the great province of Maris, the old land of the Nobadae, extending along the Nile to a village above the Fourth Cataract, which marked the boundary between Maris and al-Muqurra. The most northerly part of Maris was open to the Muslims, who held land in the vicinity of the frontier and traded upstream. Intermarriage and conversion to Islam are suggested by Ibn Sulaym's comment that some of the Muslim inhabitants did not speak good Arabic. A narrow strip of land by the river was irrigated by water-wheels turned by oxen, and was cultivated in small patches of one to three acres. The land gave several crops in the year: wheat was uncommon, but barley, millet, sorghum, sesame and beans were grown. There were palm-trees, and upstream, where the cultivated area broadened out, vineyards.

In this northern district of Maris were two fortresses, Ibrim and Bajrash (now known as Faras, the residence of the governor who was styled 'the Lord of the Mountain'). Stationed at the approach to the Second Cataract, he controlled the transit-trade and passage upstream. Muslim merchants bartered goods (sometimes termed 'presents') for the slaves he provided. Taqwi at the foot of the Second Cataract marked the limit for boats coming from al-Qasr, and no one could go further into Nubia without the Lord of the Mountain's leave. Beyond the Second Cataract lay the narrow and barren reach of the Nile later known as Batn al-Hajar, 'the Belly of Stone', which is vividly described by Ibn Sulaym. This region was in effect the military frontier of Nubia. Six stages beyond the commercial frontier at Taqwi was the garrison of the Upper Maqs. Although the district formed part of Maris and was within the jurisdiction of the Lord of the Mountain, the commandant held authority from the king himself; the death penalty awaited those who penetrated further into Nubia without permission. Here no Muslim currency circulated, for there were no Muslim merchants, and trade was carried on by the barter of slaves, cattle, camels, iron and grain. This closed military zone enabled the Nubians to launch surprise raids on their neighbours.

The garrison of the Upper Maqs was separated by another cataract from the town of Say, an episcopal see. The next district, Saqluda, resembled that lying south of Aswan, and produced date palms, vines, olives and cotton, which was woven locally. The governor apparently held office by direct royal appointment, and had authority over a number of sub-governors – Ibn Sulaym tells us that Saqluda means 'the Seven Governors'. Passing beyond this last part of Maris, Ibn Sulaym came to the district of Baqum, 'the Marvel', where the Nile spread out among a number of islands. A succession of villages with cultivation, cattle and dovecots lined the banks, for this was the granary of the capital, and the king's favourite holiday resort. Parrots and other birds abounded in the trees, and crocodiles swam in the streams. A further district, Safad Baqal, was equally fertile and well-populated – the churches and monasteries are particularly mentioned – and equally favoured by the king, whose capital, Dongola, lay at its southern extremity, fifty days' journey from Aswan.

As far as his mission was concerned, Ibn Sulaym had only limited success. A disputation with King George of Muqurra over the rival merits of Christianity and Islam was fruitless, as might have been expected. While Ibn Sulaym was in Dongola, the celebration of the Muslim Feast of Sacrifice fell due, and he organized public prayers for his co-religionists, who were about sixty in number, outside the city, with the king's permission. The incident is evidence that the number of Muslim residents in Dongola was very small, and that there was no mosque in the city, despite the alleged provisions of the *baqt* treaty.

Ibn Sulaym must, however, have been more successful in restoring the slave trade between Nubia and Egypt, since black troops formed an important part of the Fatimid army and played a political role in the history of the dynasty. Earlier régimes in Egypt had similarly recruited black slave-soldiers. In the early Islamic period, the country had been garrisoned by Arab tribal warriors, descendants of the conquerors. But the 'Abbasid Caliph al-Mu'tasim (833–42) ended this system. Henceforward the standing armies of Egypt were recruited from a variety of sources, chief among them white slaves of Turkish origin known as Mamluks, and black slaves brought from (or through) Nubia, called *Sudan* – a term which is sometimes rendered 'Sudanese' but simply meant 'Blacks'. Ahmad b. Tulun, the first autonomous governor of Egypt, himself of Turkish Mamluk descent, reportedly had 24,000 Turkish Mamluks and 40,000 Blacks. The founder of the second gubernatorial dynasty, the Ikhshid (also of Turkish origin), likewise had black slave troops. Under the Fatimids, Berber tribal warriors, Turks and *Sudan* formed the forces of the caliphate, and *Sudan* attained particular importance in the reign of al-Mustansir (1035–94), whose mother was a black slave. During the last century of Fatimid rule the *Sudan* underwent various changes of fortune. In 1169 Saladin, as military governor of Egypt, put down a desperate revolt of the black troops and expelled their remnants from Cairo to Upper Egypt. For several years their risings there necessitated expeditions to suppress them. During one of these, in 1173, Saladin's brother, Turan Shah, penetrated into Nubia and captured Ibrim, which, however, was evacuated by the Ayyubid garrison two years later. An ambassador was sent to Dongola, ostensibly on a mission to the Nubian king, but actually to spy out the country in case Saladin and his brothers needed to retreat there.

Since the tenth or early eleventh century, the chief power in the vicinity of Aswan and the northern part of Maris had been a clan originating from the Arab tribe of Rabi'a, linked with the group dominating the Land of the Mines. Its chief performed in 1007 a notable service to the Fatimid caliph of Egypt, al-Hakim, by capturing a rebel known as Abu Rakwa. He was rewarded with the honorific *Kanz al-Dawla*, 'the Treasure of the State', which later chiefs inherited, and from which his clan was called Banu'l-Kanz. In 1174 an alliance between the rebel *Sudan* and the reigning Kanz al-Dawla was suppressed by another of Saladin's brothers. Banu'l-Kanz were driven out of the Aswan region southwards into Nubia.

The period of the Fatimid caliphate saw the rise of an important port on the Red Sea coast. This was 'Aydhab, near the northern frontier of the modern Sudan, and from it routes ran across the desert to the river ports of Qus and Aswan. 'Aydhab shared in the trade between Egypt and the Indian Ocean, and in the pilgrimage traffic to the holy cities of Mecca and Medina. The older route, passing by way of Lower Egypt and Sinai, presented increasing difficulties in the later eleventh century, particularly after establishment of the Latin Kingdom of Jerusalem. Although 'Aydhab had obvious disadvantages – lack of a fertile hinterland to supply provisions, the hazardous journey to the Nile, remoteness from Cairo, so that revenues and administration were shared with the Beja – the port enjoyed a busy commerce and much prosperity until the late fourteenth century.

Apart from the campaigns of Saladin's brothers, the period of Ayyubid rule in Egypt seems to have been one of peaceful relations with Nubia. The situation began to change in the second half of the thirteenth century, when Mamluk rulers displaced the Ayyubids. Two of the early Mamluk sultans, Baybars (1260–77) and Qalawun (1279–90), began their careers as military slaves. As warrior-kings and converts to Islam, they saw their principal duty as protection of Muslim territory against the infidel – the Mongols, the Crusaders and the Nubian Christians. The Mamluk period saw adoption of an aggressive policy towards Nubia, designed to bring al-Muqurra under the Mamluk sultanate's control. Contributing to this policy was Upper Egypt's long role as refuge of insubordinate Arab tribes and the reappearance of the Banu'l-Kanz who sought to regain their former seat at Aswan. The decline of al-Muqurra was accelerated also by quarrels and rivalry within the ruling family.

In 1268 King David, who had usurped the throne from his maternal uncle, sent a letter to Baybars informing him of his succession. Baybars replied by demanding the *baqt*; presumably trade had again lapsed with the change of régimes in Egypt. That Nubia might still be a dangerous neighbour was demonstrated in 1272, when David's forces carried out a damaging raid on 'Aydhab, Egypt's principal Red Sea port. In 1275 the governor of Qus sent a full-scale expedition including both Mamluks and Arab tribesmen, to install Shakanda, another Nubian prince, in place of David. A battle was fought in 1276 near Dongola, in which the Mamluk force was victorious. This was the first Muslim army to penetrate so far into Nubia since 'Abdallah b. Sa'd, over six centuries before. Shakanda was crowned in Dongola, and for the first time a Nubian king took an oath to a sultan in Egypt as his overlord.[2] From the point of view of the Egyptian chancery, Shakanda had become a provincial governor, and the Nubians had become *dhimmis*, i.e. tributary Christians living under Muslim rule and protection. The fortresses of Ibrim and al-Daw were placed under the sultan's jurisdiction, and their revenues went to his privy purse.

This pattern of events – invasion of Nubia to install a pretender as vassal-king – was to recur on several occasions in the next forty years. At no time did the Mamluk sultan attempt a permanent conquest of al-Muqurra, although for a short time in the reign of Qalawun there was a Mamluk garrison in Dongola. Nevertheless the remote security of Nubia, which had impressed Ibn Sulaym three centuries before, was at an end. In 1292 one of these vassal-kings wrote to al-Ashraf Khalil, Qalawun's son, after interruption of the *baqt*, that the land was wasted 'because of the invasions of the Muslim armies time after time after time', augmented by destruction caused by the king of al-Abwab, the southern neighbour of al-Muqurra.

Another of Qalawun's sons, al-Nasir Muhammad, inaugurated the last stage in the history of al-Muqurra. The last of the Crusader territories had been conquered by Khalil; the Mongol rulers of Persia and Iraq had been converted to Islam, and no longer threatened the Mamluk sultanate. Now the potential danger from Christian Nubia was also brought to an end. An expedition in 1316 installed as king a Nubian prince, 'Abdallah Barshambu, who had been converted to Islam while a hostage in Cairo. The sole significant act of his short reign was to turn the church in Old Dongola into a mosque, an event commemorated in an inscription dated 16 Rabi' I 717 (i.e. 29 May 1317), which still exists. 'Abdallah Barshambu was soon overthrown and killed by a rival, none other than the current Kanz al-Dawla, whose clan had intermarried with the Nubian royal family. After further troubles, and another Mamluk expedition in 1323–24, the Kanz al-Dawla established himself on the throne.

Thereafter little is heard of al-Muqurra in the Egyptian chronicles, and only one further Mamluk expedition (in 1366) seems to have been sent. The Nubian kingdom had ceased to threaten the southern frontier of the Mamluk sultanate. The islamization of the rulers was under way, and Arab immigration into the cultivable riverain areas and the rainlands further south was increasing. It is significant that the expedition of 1366 occurred when a usurper had obtained the throne of Dongola with Arab tribal assistance, and had subsequently fallen out with his allies. Al-Muqurra was rapidly passing into a dark age. Its epitaph was written by the great contemporary historian, Ibn Khaldun, towards the end of the fourteenth century:

Then the clans of the Juhayna Arabs spread over their country, and settled in it, ruling it and filling it with ruin and decay. The kings of the Nubians set about holding them back, but lacked strength. Then they proceeded to win them over by marriage-alliances, so that their kingdom broke up, and it passed to some of the offspring of Juhayna through their mothers, according to the custom of the barbarians by which possession goes to the sister and the sister's son. So their kingdom was torn to pieces, and the Juhayna nomads took possession of their land. They have no means of imposing royal control over the damage which could be stopped by the submission of one to another, and they are faction-ridden up to the present. No trace of sovereignty remains in their land, but now they are wandering bedouin who follow the rainfall like the bedouin nomads. No trace of sovereignty remains in their land, because the tincture of Arab nomadism has changed them through mixture and union.[3]

The history of the southern kingdom of 'Alwa is even more obscure than that of al-Muqurra. It was more remote from Egypt, with which it had little direct contact. An account is given by Ibn Sulaym, who cites as his informant a certain Samyun, crown-prince of 'Alwa. The position of Soba, the capital, is correctly given, and the description continues:

In it are fine buildings and spacious residences, churches abounding in gold and gardens, and there is a suburb in which is a community of Muslims. The ruler of 'Alwa is wealthier than the ruler of al-Muqurra; he has a bigger army and more horses than the Muqurri. His land is more fertile and more extensive. They have few date-palms and vines; and their principal cereal is white millet resembling rice, from which they make their bread and beer. Meat abounds with them because of the abundance of their cattle, and the great wide plains, so that it takes days to reach the hill-country. They have excellent horses and brown Arabian camels. Their religion is Jacobite Christianity, their bishops being appointed by the patriarch of Alexandria, like the Nubians'. Their books are in Greek which they interpret in their own language. They have less understanding than the Nubians. Their king may reduce to slavery any of his subjects he wishes for any offence or no offence, and they do not hold that against him. Nay, rather they prostrate themselves before him, not resisting his order however repugnant, and call out, 'Long live the king! His will be done!' He wears a crown of gold, and gold is abundant in his land.[4]

The northern frontier province of 'Alwa, marching with al-Muqurra, is called by the Arabic writers al-Abwab, 'the Gates', a term still applied to the region of al-Kabushiyya in Ja'ali territory, south of the confluence of the Atbara with the Nile. Here was a governor sometimes referred to as king of al-Abwab. During the thirteenth and fourteenth centuries, the rulers of al-Abwab frequently co-operated with the Mamluks against al-Muqurra. After his defeat in 1276, King David fled to Adur, king of al-Abwab, but was sent as a prisoner to Cairo. Ten years later Adur sent an embassy to Qalawun professing submission and complaining about the king of al-Muqurra. At about the same time, another embassy arrived with gifts from Dongola, presumably to conciliate the sultan and avert an alliance between him and al-Abwab.

The subsequent decline of 'Alwa goes unrecorded in history, but after the collapse of the kingdom of al-Muqurra there was nothing to prevent the steady immigration of Arab tribesmen into the great plains to which Ibn Sulaym refers. Islamization, albeit at first of a very superficial kind, must have accompanied this population movement and the intermarriage of the Arabs with native peoples. Christianity lingered on into the sixteenth century: a Portuguese source, connected with the embassy to Ethiopia in 1520–26, speaks of the recent existence of a hundred and fifty churches in 'Alwa, and witnessed the arrival of a delegation asking for priests. Probably by this time Soba had ceased to exist.

Meanwhile, the Red Sea coastal areas remained in touch with the outside world, although here too there was a decline during the Mamluk sultanate. With reduction of the Latin kingdom of Jerusalem to the coastal fringe of Palestine in the time of Saladin, Muslim pilgrims returned to their old route by Sinai. The vital line of communication for trading caravans between Upper Egypt and 'Aydhab was frequently endangered by the lawlessness of tribesmen, both Arabs and Beja. Sultan al-Nasir Muhammad endeavoured to secure this sector by commissioning a punitive expedition against the desert tribes. In 1317 his force advanced from Qus to 'Aydhab, then along the coast to Suakin and inland in a great sweep to the River Atbara, upstream to Jabal Kasala, then down river to the Nile, returning to Egypt through al-Muqurra. This remarkable achievement failed to repress the nomads. The hazards which they caused to caravans passing between 'Aydhab and Qus on the Nile appear to have ended trade through this port in the second half of the fourteenth century.[5]

CHAPTER TWO

The Eastern Bilad al-Sudan *from the early Sixteenth to the early Nineteenth Century*

The period of Sudanese history from the early sixteenth to the early nineteenth century is for the most part obscure and lacking in firm historical data. Primary sources are few and have hardly been exploited. The oldest literary source extant is a biographical dictionary (a genre characteristic of Islamic historical writing) containing nearly three hundred notices of Muslim holy men. Muhammad wad Dayfallah, the compiler of this work, the *Tabaqat,* came from a family of religious scholars living at Halfayat al-Muluk. He is said to have been born in 1726–27, and he died in 1809–10.[1] The *Tabaqat* contains biographies going down to 1802–03. It is clear from internal evidence that these are not all the work of one hand, since they vary considerably in style, nature and language, some of them amounting to only a few lines, others to several pages, subdivided into chapters. It is therefore reasonable to assume that the *Tabaqat* includes older materials.

The second literary source available to us is conventionally called the Funj Chronicle, and it exists in a number of recensions.[2] The original chronicler was a certain Shaykh Ahmad ibn al-Hajj Abu 'Ali, better known as Katib al-Shuna, 'the clerk of the government grain-store' – an office he held after the Turco-Egyptian conquest. His home was in the eastern Gezira, near the Blue Nile, but all we know of him comes from a few references in his chronicle, the last of which dates from 1838. Internal evidence indicates that the original draft was made before the fall of the Funj sultanate in 1821, but the oldest extant recension goes down to 1838. Later continuations brought the chronicle down to 1871–72, with a good deal of editing and supplementing of the earlier material. The Katib's original version falls very clearly into two parts. The first, much shorter, portion deals with the origin of the Funj, and the rulers from the early sixteenth century to 1724. From that date, the accession of Badi iv Abu Shulukh, the information becomes increasingly copious, as the author draws on his own recollections and those of the generation of his father (d. 1802). The Funj Chronicle is thus a detailed source for events of the last century of the Funj kingdom, although the author's field of vision is practically limited to the Gezira, and he has little to say about the important tribal polities of the main Nile.

A source of a different kind is provided by Sudanese genealogies. A number of these were collected by the later Sir Harold MacMichael, and published in translation in his *History of the Arabs in the Sudan*. These genealogies were compiled in the nineteenth or early twentieth century, and incorporate earlier materials. The intention of their compilers was not historical accuracy but primarily to make a statement about contemporary political and social relationships. These genealogists lay stress upon the descent of the Funj from the Umayyads, that of the Ja'aliyyin tribe from the 'Abbasids, and of more than one holy family from the Prophet. At best the genealogies offer firm historical data for only a few generations before the time of writing. Before that, as with Funj traditions, it is a matter of interpretation.

A further problem is the deficiency of documentary sources. Here some advance has been made in recent years, with the discovery and (to a small extent) the publication of land-charters and related documents.[3] Extant charters, so far as they are known, are of comparatively late date, and none earlier than the eighteenth century; most date from or after the reign of the Funj ruler Badi IV (1724–62). These charters throw light on the social history of the Sudan in the period, systems of land-tenure, the position of religious teachers (who were the principal beneficiaries) and the great officers of state. Like the *Tabaqat* and the Funj Chronicle, they indicate an islamization of indigenous usages and institutions.

The fourth main source of information on the Sudan in these three centuries is travellers' accounts. These are fairly few in number, and were for the most part written by men passing through the region to get to Ethiopia or to Egypt. The earliest is of the Jewish adventurer, David Reubeni, who claimed to have spent time in the entourage of 'Amara Dunqas, the first Funj ruler.[4] The seventeenth-century Turkish writer, Evliya Chelebi, purported to describe a visit to Sennar in 1671–72, but his veracity has been impugned.[5] Reliable information begins in the eighteenth century, and becomes increasingly detailed and valuable as time goes on. Of outstanding importance is the account given by James Bruce of his return from Ethiopia to Egypt by way of Sennar and the main Nile in 1772.[6] A detailed picture of society and conditions in Nubia as far south as Shendi was given by the Swiss traveller, John Lewis Burckhardt, who made two journeys in 1813 and 1814.[7]

The origins of the Funj have been a tantalizing problem for modern students of Sudanese history, and various interpretations have been placed on the scanty data available, not always with due caution. The Funj have been regarded as Shilluk immigrants to the Blue Nile, from Bornu, or from Ethiopia.[8] The White Nile hypothesis has recently been revived, with the immigrants now presented as bearers of ancient Nubian culture.[9] An anthropologist suggests that the enquiry itself has been wrongly formulated, and that the origin of the Funj should not be sought in tribal migrations but in the status and function of the group so designated.[10] Essentially, however, the problem remains unsolved.

The establishment of the Funj kingdom, arabicized and islamicized as *al-Saltana al-Zarqa* (the Black Sultanate), is ascribed to a certain 'Amara Dunqas, and is dated with curious precision to the *Hijri* year 910, i.e. 1504–05. If any reliance is placed on Reubeni's account, 'Amara's court was constantly on the move throughout his domains, and the 'king's city' was Lam'ul, an unidentified site eight days' journey beyond Sennar. The legend of the founding of Sennar given in the Funj Chronicle suggests that 'Amara and his people were cattle-nomads, who, in the early sixteenth century, were moving northwards down the Blue Nile. The permanent settlement of the dynasty at Sennar was perhaps not for another century, since, according to the Funj Chronicle, Sultan Irbat or Rubat (1616–45) founded the mosque there. His son, Badi II Abu Diqin (1645–80), completed it and built a five-storied palace.

While the Funj were establishing their power on the upper Blue Nile, its lower course and the territories of the southern reaches of the main Nile, i.e. substantially the kingdom of 'Alwa, had been overrun by Arab immigrants. Traditionally, the town of Arbaji on the Blue Nile was founded thirty years before Sennar by an Arab named Hijazi ibn Ma'in, which suggests Arab penetration by the late fifteenth century. A greater figure was 'Abdallah Jamma', a leader of the Arabs (*Jamma'* means 'Gatherer'), who is presented in tradition as a champion of Islam. To him is ascribed the capture of Soba, which sank into unimportance: according to Reubeni, in the time of 'Amara Dunqas it was in ruins. 'Abdallah's status as Muslim hero is confirmed by traditions representing him marrying the daughter of a Hijazi holy man, and as the eponymous ancestor of the ruling clan, the 'Abdallab.

The situation these traditions seem to depict is of two immigrant groups, both perhaps nomadic, moving into the former kingdom of 'Alwa, Muslim Arabs from the north, pagan Funj from the south. Katib al-Shuna makes brief reference to co-operation of 'Amara and 'Abdallah to fight the indigenous people, but a tradition transmitted by Bruce speaks of the defeat of the Arab leader near Arbaji in 1504 by a pagan, black nation, subsequently known as the Funj. The chief of the Arabs 'thus became as it were their lieutenant'. This tradition specifies 1504 as the year in which military victory gave the Funj hegemony over the Arabs; the allusion to Arbaji indicates its significance as an Arab frontier-settlement. But Funj dominance did not remain unshaken. 'Abdallah Jamma', whose capital was at Qarri on the main Nile, died in the reign of 'Amara II Abu Sikaykin (1557–69), and the Funj king thereupon appointed 'Abdallah's son, 'Ajib al-Kafuta, to succeed him. Early in the seventeenth century 'Ajib revolted and drove out King 'Abd al-Qadir II, who fled to Ethiopia. His brother, 'Adlan I, regained the throne, and defeated 'Ajib at the battle of Karkoj in 1611–12. 'Ajib himself died in the battle, and his sons fled to Dongola. The mediation of a Muslim holy man, Shaykh Idris wad (i.e. son of) al-Arbab, obtained an amnesty for them. They returned to Qarri, where one of them was duly appointed shaykh.

In other respects the early Funj period was a time of territorial expansion and consolidation. Bruce recorded the conquest of Jabal Moya and Jabal Saqadi, isolated hills in the central Gezira, by 'Abd al-Qadir I, a son of 'Amara

Dunqas, who ruled in the mid-sixteenth century. 'Abd al-Qadir II had apparently accepted Ethiopian suzerainty before 'Ajib al-Kafuta drove him into exile. His successors rejected Ethiopian claims, and relations deteriorated into inconclusive frontier warfare in 1618–19. The reign of Badi II saw a significant extension of Funj power westwards. A defeat was inflicted on the Shilluk, who at this time dominated much of the lower White Nile, and a bridgehead was established at Alays, now called al-Kawwa. Badi then made a difficult crossing of the plain of Kordofan, and besieged the little Muslim hill-state of Taqali, imposing tribute on its ruler.

Far to the north, Funj territory marched with Egypt, which became an Ottoman province in 1517. For some decades, however, much of Upper Egypt was beyond the effective control of Cairo, while Lower Nubia was similarly loosely dependent on the Funj sultan; at first there was no occasion for a clash between the Ottomans and the Funj. Extension of Ottoman rule into Nubia occurred when Özdemir (Azdamur) Pasha, a relative of the former Mamluk sultan, Qansawh al-Ghawri (1501–16), was authorized to undertake an expedition against Ethiopia. On his way from Upper Egypt to Suakin, he intervened in a tribal struggle in Lower Nubia, and captured Ibrim. Garrisons of Bosniak troops were installed there and at Aswan and Say, while administration of the region (primarily collection of revenue) was committed to an official entitled *kashif.* These remote representatives of Ottoman authority developed, during the next three centuries, into an hereditary caste intermarrying with local people. From Nubia, Özdemir proceeded to the Red Sea coast. Suakin passed into his hands; Massawa was taken in 1557, and became his administrative centre; Zayla was conquered from the Portuguese. Özdemir died in 1559–60, during the course of an inland campaign, having thus established the Ottoman province of Habesh, i.e. Abyssinia.

Like Lower Nubia, Habesh in the seventeenth and eighteenth centuries became a weak and remote outpost. The Portuguese threat passed away, and the Red Sea became, in the seventeenth century, a quiet backwater of Muslim commerce. When Bruce visited Massawa in 1769, it no longer had an Ottoman governor but was ruled by a tribal chief with the title of *na'ib* (Arabic: 'deputy'). The Ottoman garrison had intermarried with local people and their descendants formed an hereditary military caste. The *na'ibs* were nominally subordinate to the Ottoman governor of Jedda, but in practice were dependent on the rulers of Ethiopia, with whom they shared the customs revenue, and had ceased to pay tribute to the sultans. In 1814 Burckhardt found a similar state of affairs in Suakin, which was governed by an *amir* chosen from the patrician families of the Hadariba, a tribe of mixed Arab-Beja origin. Descendants of the Ottoman garrison-troops, who claimed mostly Kurdish ancestry, were another element in the population. Ottoman authority was limited to the *amir*'s recognition by the governor of Jedda, and to a customs-officer, who had the title of *agha.*

The Funj king was thus the overlord of extensive territories, from the Third Cataract to the foothills of Ethiopia, and from the eastern desert to

Kordofan. It was not a centralized or highly administered state, but rather a species of high-kingship, in which much power was held by subordinate rulers. Chief of these was the 'Abdallabi shaykh of Qarri, who bore the title *manjil* or *manjilak*, and was viceroy over the north. Within this region were tribal territories along the main Nile, notably of the Ja'aliyyin and the Shayqiyya, which defeated the forces of Badi II, and broke away from Funj suzerainty. Old Dongola was still a town of importance, and a colony of Funj in the vicinity strengthened the king's control in the north. In the southern territories, the heartland of the Funj kingdom, provincial governors were appointed by the king, but there was a tendency for the office to become hereditary. Four of the chief governorates were the march-provinces of the Taka (the modern Kasala); Atbara, on the upper waters of that river; Khashm al-Bahr, controlling the riverain areas upstream of Sennar; and Alays, guarding the crossing of the White Nile into Kordofan.

The conversion of the Funj rulers to Islam seems to have taken place very early. Reubeni's account, for what it is worth, depicts 'Amara Dunqas as at least a nominal Muslim, showing great respect to self-styled descendants of the Prophet. His son and successor bore the Muslim name 'Abd al-Qadir. 'Abdallabi tradition describes the revolt of 'Ajib al-Kafuta against 'Abd al-Qadir II as a holy war, which was followed by the building of mosques far up the Blue Nile and in the Ethiopian marches. 'Ajib is also represented as making the Pilgrimage to Mecca. Bruce, in a significant remark about the Funj invaders, says that 'They were soon after converted to Mahometism, for the sake of trading with Cairo.'[11] No doubt, here as elsewhere, merchants were bearers of Islam. Yet traces of its African origin can be discerned in the Funj monarchy until the end: the Funj Chronicle describes accession ceremonies that have nothing to do with Islam; the ruler continued to use the old, non-Arabic title of *makk*. Bruce even asserted the existence of a custom of king-killing, the licensed regicide being a household officer from the royal clan entitled *sid al-qom* ('the lord of the kindred'), but evidence in the Arabic sources for this practice is not clear.

Islamization of the peoples of the sultanate was largely the work of individual holy men who settled, taught the Qur'an and endeavoured to bring social usages into conformity with the Sharia. Some such teachers were already active before the coming of the Funj: Ghulamallah b. 'Ayid, whose father came from the Yemen, lived in the Dongola region, probably in the early fifteenth century; Hamad Abu Dunana brought the Sufi order (*tariqa*) of the Shadhiliyya to the Berber district in 1445. The marriages (whether real or alleged) of Hamad's daughters are interesting. One was the mother of the holy man Idris wad al-Arbab, while another is said to have been the wife of 'Abdallah Jamma' and the mother of 'Ajib al-Kafuta. There are some indications that 'Abdallah himself was primarily a holy man, although of a more militant character than was usual in the Nilotic Sudan.

The *Tabaqat* of Wad Dayfallah ignores Muslim pioneers before the Funj sultanate, and its geographical range centres upon the main Nile. But it offers a glimpse of the islamization of the borderland between Funj and 'Abdallab in the northern Gezira when, after speaking of the foundation of Sennar and Arbaji, Wad Dayfallah states:

> And in that territory, no school of religious learning or of the Qur'an was known. It is said that a man would divorce his wife, and another marry her on the same day without *'idda*, until Shaykh Mahmud al-Araki came from Egypt, taught people about the *'idda*, and dwelt on the White Nile. He built a castle called the castle of Mahmud.[12]

Thus the Muslim missionary is shown as primarily a teacher of Islamic law, the Sharī'a, and introducing Muslim usages regarding divorce and remarriage. (It is significant that the Sudanese word for a religious teacher or holy man is *faki*, from the Classical Arabic *faqih*, 'a jurist'.) And Mahmud had a fortified dwelling, on the very frontier of Islam, 'between the Hassaniyya and Alays',[13] i.e. between the Arab tribal land in the northern Gezira and the future Funj bridgehead. The precariousness of Islamic institutions is illustrated by the remark that between Khartoum and Alays were seventeen schools, all destroyed by the Shilluk and *Umm Lahm*, the year of famine and smallpox in 1684.

Wad Dayfallah represents the second half of the sixteenth century, the time of the joint rule of 'Amara II and 'Ajib, as a period of active islamization. Holy men coming from Egypt, Baghdad and the Maghrib taught the Sharī'a and religious sciences, and initiated followers into the Sufi orders. Particularly important was the Qadiriyya order, introduced into the Gezira by a visitor from Baghdad, Taj al-Din al-Bahari, in the second half of the sixteenth century. Natives early played a part in these activities. Mahmud al-'Araki studied in Egypt before returning to his homeland on the White Nile. The territory of the Shayqiyya was an important centre of Islamic teaching in the reign of 'Ajib. Four brothers, the Sons of Jabir, three of whom had studied in Cairo, maintained a school in which they taught the Sharī'a, and the succession of teachers continued in descendants of their sister.[14] Establishment of a holy family consisting of the kinsfolk of a religious teacher or Sufi guide was characteristic of Sudanese Islam in this period.[15]

The *fakis* had a distinctive and important role. Some, especially local heads of Sufi orders, possessed considerable political influence. Badi II Abu Diqin granted Bishara al-Gharbawi, a holy man in the Shayqiyya territory, exemption from all taxes and dues; these privileges were confirmed in the following century by Badi IV Abu Shulukh to his successors. Other *fakis* were endowed with grants of land and, perhaps in connection with these, were invested with Funj symbols of authority, the stool and turban, and even in one case with the *taqiyya umm qarnayn*, the horned cap which was the distinctive sign of secular authority. The holder of this exceptional privilege, Shaykh Hasan b. Hassuna (d. 1664–65), the grandson of a Tunisian immigrant, possessed great herds, traded in horses and dominated the country around the village which still bears his name, north-west of Khartoum, like a feudal lord, having a private army of slaves, 'each one of whom bore a sword with scabbard-tip and plate and pin of silver'.[16]

In the eighteenth century, when Funj-'Abdallab control over the main Nile was weakening, the Majadhib, a family of hereditary *fakis*, established a tribal theocracy among the Ja'aliyyin, south of the Atbara confluence. The founder of the state was Hamad b. Muhammad al-Majdhub (1693–1776) who, after studying under Sudanese teachers, made the Pilgrimage and was initiated into the Shadhiliyya order. He acquired enormous prestige among the Ja'aliyyin as a teacher and ascetic, and became the effective ruler of a district centring upon his residence at El Damer.

Burckhardt, who visited El Damer in 1814, described the Majdhubi theocracy in its last phase. Its ruler, *al-faki al-kabir* 'the great teacher', was Muhammad al-Majdhub (1796–1831), a grandson of the founder. Burckhardt comments on the neatness, regularity and good condition of El Damer, which had several schools drawing pupils from a wide area in the Sudan; the teachers had many books on theology and law, brought from Cairo. Many of the *fakis* had studied at Cairo, in al-Azhar, or at Mecca. The religious prestige of the Majadhib was widely acknowledged and served as a passport to travellers on the route to Suakin.

Relations between the *fakis* and rulers were not always harmonious. Holy men frequently acted as mediators or protested oppression. An outstanding example of opposition is provided by Hamad al-Nahlan, called Wad al-Turabi, an ascetic who, while on Pilgrimage at Mecca, declared himself to be the *mahdi.* On his return, he protected the nomad Arabs and the villagers of the eastern Gezira during a great tax-gathering expedition commanded by the *wazir* of Sultan Badi iii al-Ahmar about the end of the seventeenth century. The episode, demonstrating the miraculous power of Wad al-Turabi, is described at length in the *Tabaqat.*[17] Cult officials of the Funj period are comparatively insignificant.

The reign of Badi iii (1692–1716) was troubled in other respects. He was confronted by a revolt of his minister, Irdab, who appears to have commanded the Funj warriors, and who was supported by the 'Abdallabi chief. The rebels appointed a new sultan and marched against Badi. Although their forces were much larger, he defeated them and killed Irdab. Another revolt of the Funj took place under his son and successor, Unsa iii, who was deposed in 1720, and sent away. His successor, Nol, was connected on the female side with the Unsab, the previous succession of sultans. His reign, until 1724, was short and peaceful, but under the son who succeeded him, Badi iv Abu Shulukh, power was finally to pass from the hands of the Funj sultans.

In the meantime, a new state had arisen in the west. The Keira sultanate in Darfur began as a tribal kingdom in the mountainous region of Jabal Marra, and emerges into history about the middle of the seventeenth century. We have no indigenous literary sources to chronicle its development. But since the sultanate survived until 1874, and was restored from 1898 to 1916 by 'Ali Dinar, we are much better informed on Keira institutions than we are on those of the Funj. The first European traveller to reach Darfur was probably W.G. Browne, who was there between 1793 and 1796.[18] A much more informative account is of Muhammad ibn 'Umar al-Tunusi, who dwelt there from 1803 to 1811.[19] Shortly before the overthrow of the sultanate, it was visited by the German traveller, Gustav Nachtigal, who left a valuable record of its historical traditions and its condition in 1874.[20] Another corpus of traditions was recorded by Na'um Shuqayr, the Lebanese historian of the Sudan, his principal informant being the *imam* of the last sultan before the Egyptian annexation.[21] In the last few years, the range of primary source-materials on the Keira sultanate has been significantly extended by the publication of land-charters, a work still continuing. These, like their counterparts from the Funj sultanate, do not antedate the eighteenth century.

In the Keira sultanate we can see more clearly than in the Funj the expansion of a tribal kingdom into a Sudanic empire, accompanied by the evolution of the rulers from African divine kings to Muslim sultans, and by the progressive islamization of their institutions and subjects. The ascendancy of the Keira was preceded by two semi-legendary tribal power structures, traditionally and conventionally represented as the dynastic kingdoms of the Daju and Tunjur. The Keira clan and the rulers of Wadai are represented as the successors of the Tunjur rulers. The original centre of the Keira was in the northern part of Jabal Marra, whence successive waves of expansion made them dominant over the rest of the hill-country and the surrounding plains. The first of their rulers known to us was Sulayman, who probably lived in the second half of the seventeenth century, and whose reign coincided with (or caused) a tribal split, part of the Keira (represented as a defeated faction) moving out of Jabal Marra, eastwards into the plains. This group, the Musabba'at, was to play an important part in the history of both the Funj and Keira sultanates in the eighteenth century. The reign of Sulayman is also traditionally seen as the beginning of the islamization of Darfur.

The principal phase of expansion was concluded in the reign of Sulayman's grandson, Ahmad Bukr, who died about 1730. This brought the sultanate up against neighbours who could make effective resistance against conquest and absorption: Wadai to the west, Zaghawa nomads to the north, the Musabba'at to the east. South of Darfur were non-Muslim peoples who provided the slaves that were an important element in the society of the sultanate and the principal article in commerce with the north. On his deathbed, Ahmad Bukr obtained an oath from his magnates securing the passage of the sultanate to each of his sons in turn. This attempt to regulate the succession was, in the event, productive of a series of struggles during the ensuing decades.

Kordofan was a buffer territory between the Funj and Keira sultanates. The eastern part was to some extent within the Funj sphere of influence. Badi II had reduced the kingdom of Taqali to tributary status in the later seventeenth century, while the Ghudiyat tribe in southern Kordofan was closely identified with Funj suzerainty. Their chief bore, like the 'Abdallabi ruler, the title of *manjil*, and paid tribute to Sennar. Western Kordofan received the Musabba'at immigrants, who established a sultanate of their own.[22] Engaged alternatively in warfare against their kinsmen in Darfur and in attempts to conquer central Kordofan, the Musabba'at were a disturbing element to both the greater sultanates. Shortly before the middle of the eighteenth century, 'Isawi, the sultan of the Musabba'at, defeated the Funj representative in central Kordofan. Meanwhile, a faction of the Musabba'at under Khamis b. Janqal, a son of the previous sultan, had made their way to Sennar, where they formed an element in the forces of Badi iv. Thanks largely to them, an invasion by the Ethiopian ruler, Iyasu ii, was halted at the River Dinder in 1744.

The reign of Badi iv ended in disaster. The reasons for his downfall are implied in the charges made against him by Katib al-Shuna. It seems that he tried unsuccessfully to erect a new monarchy on new foundations. He proscribed the Unsab, the former royal clan his father had supplanted, and granted the lands of the old families to his supporters – the Nuba and the followers of Khamis. It is probable that the earlier risings of the Funj against Badi iii and Unsa iii had been revolts of free-born warriors against sultans seeking a new military power base in slave-troops. When Badi ii returned from his campaign against Taqali, he settled his captives, many of whom were Nuba, 'some of them in the east, and some of them in the west; and they built villages surrounding Sennar, like a wall about it'.[23] So writes Katib al-Shuna; Bruce saw these villages when he passed. Their garrisons and the sultans' slave-troops were no doubt further recruited from the tribute Badi ii imposed on Taqali. A similar shift to reliance upon aliens and slaves characterized the rule of Badi iv's contemporary, Sultan Abu'l-Qasim of Darfur (*c.* 1749–77).

As Badi's reign went on, his arbitrary rule (as the chronicler describes it) became more intolerable. Once more a rising of the Funj took place, but its outcome did not follow the pattern of previous military revolts. The victory of the Musabba'at in central Kordofan had been reversed by a new leader of the Funj forces, Muhammad Abu Likaylik, whom Badi had appointed as shaykh (perhaps meaning governor of Kordofan) in 1747. The commanders of the Funj forces occupying Kordofan were dismayed at the news reaching them of their ruler's behaviour, and agreed with Abu Likaylik to depose him. The army crossed the White Nile at Alays, where they were joined by the sultan's son, Nasir. They advanced on Sennar and surrounded the town. Badi was allowed to leave under an amnesty, and Abu Likaylik installed Nasir as sultan (1762). This was the end of the effective Funj sultanate: as Katib al-Shuna remarks:

> From that time, the Hamaj held the power to loose and bind. They gained the mastery over the Funj. Shaykh Muhammad slew their magnates, and appointed and removed from office among them. The date was reckoned by the period of the shaykhs of the Hamaj, without reference to the kings.[24]

This was the irony of the revolution of 1762, that it redounded to the success neither of the Funj warriors who had plotted it, nor of the 'Abdallab, who for over two-and-a-half centuries had represented the Arab element in the Funj sultanate. Whoever the Hamaj, the kinsfolk of Muhammad Abu Likaylik were, they were neither Funj nor Arab. His and their victory may be seen as the resurgence of an autochthonous group, now islamized and Arabic-speaking. The Hamaj regency was thus inaugurated.

The withdrawal of the Funj garrison from Kordofan under Abu Likaylik in 1762 presaged loss of the province. The power of the Musabba'at revived under their chief, Hashim b. 'Isawi, who defeated the Ghudiyat in 1772 and regained control of central Kordofan. The real danger to Hashim came from the Keira ruler of Darfur, Muhammad Tayrab who, at the end of his reign in 1786–87 invaded Kordofan, and perhaps even reached the Nile at Omdurman. Henceforward until the Turco-Egyptian conquest, Kordofan was a dependency of the Keira sultanate.

Muhammad Abu Likaylik was a strong and capable ruler, although illiterate. Eight years after his seizure of power, he deposed Nasir and banished him from the capital. The ex-king plotted with the Funj against the regent, but Abu Likaylik learnt of the conspiracy, and had him put to death. When Abu Likaylik died in 1776–77 he was succeeded in the regency by his brother, Badi wad Rajab. A political crisis ensued in another conspiracy of the Funj with their new king, Isma'il, against the regent, and once again the conspirators were unsuccessful. Isma'il was deposed and sent to Suakin, and his son, 'Adlan II, was installed as king. A still more ominous development took place in 1780, when sons of Abu Likaylik, resenting their treatment by their cousin, conspired with two other malcontents, the 'Abdallabi shaykh and the governor of Khasm al-Bahr, both of whom had been deprived of office and had joined forces with 'Adlan. In the fighting that followed, Badi wad Rajab was defeated and killed, and one of the sons of Abu Likaylik, Rajab, assumed the regency. 'Adlan was now intent on regaining the full royal power, and in 1784–85, while Rajab was on campaign in Kordofan, he carried out a *coup* against the regent's brother and deputy in Sennar. Rajab, returning from Kordofan, was killed in battle with the king (November 1785), and the Hamaj dispersed in disarray. Their eclipse was brief. Another son of Abu Likaylik, Nasir, became regent, and moved against Sennar. In 1788–89 the royalist forces were defeated in a battle, and 'Adlan died (it was said of grief, poison or witchcraft) a few days later.

The ascendancy of the Hamaj, thus restored, was never again lost until the Turco-Egyptian conquest, but it was an ascendancy over a declining and diminished kingdom. For the weakness of the Hamaj regency in this period there were several reasons. Internal rivalries in the ruling clan recurred frequently and disastrously. The Regent Nasir was opposed by his brothers, Idris and 'Adlan, and after several months of fighting, he was put to death in 1798 by the son of the Regent Badi, to avenge his father. 'Adlan himself became regent in October 1803, but two of his nephews, sons of former regents, conspired against him, and he was killed in an affray at the end of the same year. One of the conspirators, Muhammad wad Rajab, succeeded him, but his regency ended in anarchy in 1808, when he was killed by his cousin, Muhammad, the son of the Regent 'Adlan, in pursuit of a vendetta against his father's killers.

Muhammad wad 'Adlan then became regent himself, his long rule lasting until 1821, when he too fell victim to a rising headed by his cousin, the son and brother of earlier regents. Shortly before the murder of the Regent Muhammad wad 'Adlan, in the words of Katib al-Shuna:

> The approach of the son of the ruler of Egypt, Isma'il Pasha, had been confirmed to him. He had assembled the notable *fakis* and others to make enquiries, and had summoned the king of the Ja'aliyyin, Kunjara and other tribes to war, with their rendezvous at Khartoum.[25]

His death plunged the Funj kingdom into anarchy at the very moment of the Turco-Egyptian invasion.

During these unhappy decades, when the Funj kings were ciphers and the Hamaj regents were destroying themselves in internecine quarrels, their nominal vassals grew in power and intervened in the politics of Sennar. Chief among these vassals were the 'Abdallabi shaykhs, the kings of the Ja'aliyyin and the governors of Khashm al-Bahr. Each of these positions was disputed by rivals within the ruling families, and the kaleidoscopic and transient alliances of their factions with those among the Funj and the Hamaj characterize this last period of the history of the kingdom. One of the most successful was *Makk* Nimr wad Muhammad of the Ja'aliyyin, who established himself as king in Shendi in 1801–02. Meanwhile, the Majadhib theocracy in El Damer controlled the region around the junction of the River Atbara and the Nile, while Berber was the capital of the tribal kingdom of the Mirafab. Further north, the territories controlled by the Shayqiyya had long since been lost to the Funj.

The sultanate of Darfur, by contrast, was at this period at the height of its power. The warrior-sultan, Muhammad Tayrab, died at Bara on his return from his victorious campaign in Kordofan. A succession struggle ensued, in which the successful faction installed their candidate, a pious posthumous son of Ahmad Bukr named 'Abd al-Rahman al-Rashid. 'Abd al-Rahman was sultan at the time of Browne's visit to Darfur, and the traveller describes him as 'a man rather under the middle size, of a complexion adust or dry, with eyes full of fire, and features abounding in expression. His beard is short but full, and his countenance, though perfectly black, materially differing from the negro; though fifty or fifty-five years of age, he possesses much alertness and activity.'[26]

The reign of 'Abd al-Rahman al-Rashid marked the apogee of the Keira sultanate. Territorially, it was now at its widest extent. The royal court, which under previous rulers had migrated to a succession of sites from the original homeland of the Fur, was now permanently settled east of Jabal Marra and gave its name, El Fasher (al-Fashir), to the capital of the sultanate. Islam was striking deeper roots: 'Abd al-Rahman had been a *faki* before he became sultan, and the divine kingship of his ancestors was becoming overlaid with the formalities of an Islamic monarchy. Holy men, among them immigrants from the Nilotic regions, received estates, and supplied the sultanate with religious teachers and clerks in the administration. The country was still almost completely secluded from the lands to the north, although slaves (captured in raids on the pagans of the south) were sent to Upper Egypt. Apart from these regular commercial contacts, the first attempts to establish political communications begin about this time. Browne tells us that 'Abd al-Rahman, on his accession, sent a present to the Ottoman sultan:

> It consisted of three of the choicest eunuchs, and three of the most beautiful female slaves that could be procured. The Othman emperor, when they were presented, had, it is said, never heard of the Sultan of Dar-Fûr, but he returned an highly-ornamented sabre, a rich pelisse, and a ring set with a single diamond of no inconsiderable value.[27]

Bonaparte, when in Egypt in 1799, received a letter from 'Abd al-Rahman, and replied asking the sultan to send with the first caravan two thousand black slaves, over sixteen years old.[28] But this attempt to form an army of black Mamluks came to nothing. Under 'Abd al-Rahman's successor, Muhammad Fadl, the Keira sultanate was at last to be brought into violent confrontation with a superior military power.

The early nineteenth century, before the Egyptian conquest, saw the appearance of new influences in the religious life of the Sudan. These were repercussions of that great wave of revival and reform that arose in the heart of Islam during the late eighteenth century, and that produced, among other phenomena, the Wahhabi movement in Arabia. One aspect of the revival was a new activist spirit in the Sufi orders. The Khalwatiyya order, founded in the fourteenth century, took on fresh life in the eighteenth, when missionaries were sent to propagate its teachings in Africa. One of these, al-Sammani (1718–75), established a new sub-order, which was brought to the Sudan about 1800, by a Sudanese, Ahmad al-Tayyib al-Bashir, who had been initiated in Medina.[29] He won many adherents in the Gezira, particularly along the White Nile, for the Sammaniyya *tariqa*.

Another religious teacher whose followers were to have great influence in the Sudan was Ahmad ibn Idris al-Fasi, who originated from Fez in Morocco but spent much of his career in Arabia, where he died in 1837.[30] Like the Wahhabis, he was a reformer who sought to restore the primitive model of Islam, purged of superstitious innovations. He influenced Muhammad al-Majdhub, when the latter was an exile in Mecca after the Turco-Egyptian conquest. Another disciple was Muhammad 'Uthman al-Mirghani (1793–1853), who was sent by Ahmad as a missionary to the Sudan. He won an enormous following among the Nubian tribes between Aswan and Dongola, and in 1816–17 reached Sennar. Here he seems to have gained little success, and he left the Sudan, never to return. While on his missionary journey, however, he had married a woman of Dongola, by whom he had a son, al-Hasan.

After Ahmad ibn Idris's death, al-Mirghani organized his own adherents, in Arabia and the Sudan, as a new order, the Mirghaniyya or Khatmiyya. Further proselytization was carried out in the Sudan by his son, al-Hasan, and the order was favourably viewed by the Turco-Egyptian rulers. But the coming of the Egyptians had brought an important change into the structure of Sudanese Islam, as will appear.

PART TWO

The Turco-Egyptian Period: 1820–81

You are aware that the end of all our effort and this expense is to procure negroes. Please show zeal in carrying out our wishes in this capital matter.

Muhammad 'Ali to the *Defterdar*
(23 September 1825)

I have granted you ... the government of the provinces of Nubia, Darfour, Kordofan, and Sennaar, with all their dependencies – that is to say, with all their adjoining regions outside of the limits of Egypt. Guided by the experience and wisdom that distinguish you, you will apply yourself to administer and organize these provinces according to my equitable views, and to provide for the welfare of the inhabitants.

Ferman of Sultan 'Abd al-Majid
to Muhammad 'Ali Pasha
(13 February 1841)

CHAPTER THREE

The Inauguration of the Turco-Egyptian Regime: 1820–25

Muhammad ʿAli's conquest of the Sudanese provinces has some similarity to Özdemir Pasha's conquest of Lower Nubia and the Red Sea littoral nearly three centuries previously. Both expeditions were primarily private ventures of ambitious servants of the Ottoman sultan. Their armies fought in the sultan's name, the territories acquired were formally annexed to his dominions, but they lay in practice outside the bounds of his effective control. However differences between Özdemir's and Muhammad ʿAli's status affected the future history of their conquests. In 1820 the autonomous viceroy of Egypt could draw on considerable military and economic resources to secure his rule. Muhammad Ali and his successors held tenaciously to the territories he had acquired, were influenced by current European ideas and sought not merely to acquire territory in traditional Ottoman fashion, but to exploit its resources of men and natural products.

Muhammad ʿAli's primary motive in undertaking the invasion of the Sudan was probably political. In the early days of his rule in Egypt, his most dangerous opponents had been the Mamluks, survivors of the military and governing élite whose chiefs had been, in the previous century, the real masters of Egypt. By massacre and proscription he had in 1811 broken their power, but a remnant of the Mamluks had escaped and established themselves in the petty state of Dongola, then a dependency of the Shayqiyya. Their headquarters, which they called *Ordu* (Turkish: 'Camp', thus the Sudanese *al-ʿUrdi*), is generally known as New Dongola, and stood on the left bank of the Nile, south of the old frontier between *Berberistan* and the Funj dominions. Here they built a walled town, recruited black slaves to replenish their own dwindling numbers and clashed with the Shayqiyya for control of the region.

History had demonstrated the extraordinary vitality and tenacity of the Mamluks; it was commonplace for a defeated faction to withdraw upstream until an opportunity arose for a descent on Cairo and a political revolution. Although the Mamluks of Dongola were perhaps too insignificant in numbers and too remote to follow the traditional pattern, their inviolability was certain to cause anxiety to the viceroy of Egypt.

In 1812, therefore, Muhammad 'Ali Pasha sent an embassy to urge the Funj sultan to expel the Mamluks from the dominions he nominally ruled. Neither the sultan nor the Hamaj regent any longer possessed effective authority in Dongola, as Muhammad 'Ali was doubtless aware. The embassy served a more practical purpose in spying out military weakness and political fragmentation. The situation was also reported by *Makk* Nasr al-Din of the ruling family of the Mirafab of Berber, who sought Muhammad 'Ali's support against dynastic rivals. Political disorder on the middle Nile had almost stopped trade with Egypt, and the desire to revive commerce was one of Muhammad 'Ali's motives in making the conquest.

But the viceroy had greater ambitions than restoring trade relations. Conquest of the Nilotic Sudan would bring under his control a principal channel of the slave-trade. At this time Muhammad 'Ali's military situation was precarious, and the idea of a slave-army, docile, trained in the European manner and personally loyal to him, was most attractive. The Albanian troops who had raised him to power were dangerously insubordinate, and could well be put to the task of conquering and pacifying the remote Sudan. A further attraction of the region was its fabled gold mines which, could they be located and exploited, would provide the viceroy with the means to assure his position in Egypt and his independence of the sultan.

There is no convenient designation for the conquest of 1820–21. The 'Egyptian conquest' calls up anachronistic associations. Today's Arabic-speaking Egyptian state with its national army did not then exist: the government of Egypt was in the hands of a ruling élite of Turkish-speaking Ottoman subjects. But 'Ottoman conquest' is equally unsatisfactory. Although Ottoman suzerainty was recognized, the sultan's power was even more tenuous in the Sudan than in Egypt itself. The clumsy adjective 'Turco-Egyptian' has therefore been adopted to describe both the conquest and ensuing administration. But to the Sudanese the invaders were *al-Turk,* 'the Turks', and their régime was *al-Turkiyya.* These terms, at first linguistically justifiable, subsequently came to include all non-Sudanese members of the ruling and military élites. Thus the Condominium administration set up in 1899 was 'the second *Turkiyya'* and, to unsophisticated Sudanese, its British officials were 'Turks'.

The force that left Cairo early in July 1820 numbered about four thousand combatants. Albanians and 'Turks' of unspecified origin were prominent. Another element was the Maghribis – Arabs of north-west Africa, who had long provided soldiers of fortune for the Ottoman Empire. The most genuinely Egyptian element in an ethnic sense was the Bedouin tribal forces; the Egyptian *fallahin,* as yet unconscripted, had no part in this military venture. Of particular importance, because they knew the Nubian marches, were the 'Ababda tribesmen who provided camel-transport. The expeditionary force's commander was the viceroy's third son, Isma'il Kamil Pasha, then about twenty-five years of age. Three *'ulama'* travelled with the expedition, to summon the Sudanese Muslims to obey the agent of the Ottoman sultan. The officers included George English, a renegade American who served as an artillery officer and wrote an account of the expedition. A much more detailed description was written by a distinguished French observer, Frédéric Cailliaud.

On 20 July 1820 Isma'il and his staff joined the army at Aswan. The timing of the start of the campaign was governed by the flood of the Nile, during which season alone it would be possible to haul the boats over the Cataracts. The *kashiflik* of Lower Nubia had long been autonomous of Cairo, and Husayn *Kashif*, one of the brothers who ruled the region, would have disputed the advance of the expedition but, finding himself unsupported, fled to Kordofan. His brother, Hasan *Kashif*, submitted to Isma'il, and was confirmed in office.

The Second Cataract was passed, and the ruler of Say made his submission, only to revolt later and be killed in the fighting. English was not a little surprised to find the people of Say, descendants of the Bosniak soldiery, 'as white as the Arabs of Lower Egypt, whereas the inhabitants of Nubia are quite black, though their features are not those of the Negro'.[1] The Mamluks of New Dongola made no resistance. A few came in to surrender, but the majority of them fled south and sought refuge with the Ja'ali ruler, *Makk* Nimr of Shendi. The petty rulers of the Danaqla submitted to Isma'il, and were confirmed in their positions.

Destruction of Shayqiyya military power was a principal object of the expedition. A summons sent to their chiefs to surrender their horses and arms was rejected. The Shayqiyya confederacy was at the time headed by *Makk* Subayr, principal ruler of the Hannakab, in the western part of the territory, and *Makk* Jawish, whose capital was Marawi. On 4 November a battle took place near Kurti, in which the Shayqiyya were defeated. The remnant of their forces crossed the Nile and took refuge in a stone fortress at the foot of Jabal Dayqa (now Jabal Ibn 'Awf), where they were bombarded and routed once again. This ended serious military resistance. Subayr submitted, while Jawish fled southwards to the Ja'aliyyin. Isma'il's victory over the Shayqiyya was largely a consequence of superior armament. The Shayqiyya were armed principally with swords and lances, and shields of hippopotamus or crocodile hide, while some of their leaders wore coats of mail. They disdained the use of firearms.

Having concentrated his forces, Isma'il prepared for a further advance. A river column of boats, with a protective escort moving along the bank, was sent upstream, while the pasha marched with the bulk of his troops across the peninsula of the Bayuda Desert on the left bank of the Nile. He set out on 21 February 1821, and reached the river seven days later at al-Buqayr. On 5 March the desert column reached al-Ghubush, opposite the residence of *Makk* Nasr al-Din, the ruler of Berber,[2] who made his submission and was confirmed in office.

Isma'il was in the meantime negotiating with *Makk* Jawish and the fugitive Mamluks at Shendi. All made their submission, with the exception of a small remnant of the Mamluks, who continued their flight and vanished from history. The amnestied Mamluks returned honourably to Egypt. On 19 May *Makk* Jawish made a capitulation no less final than honourable. 'I have fought against you,' he said to Isma'il, 'to the utmost of my means and power, and am now ready, if you will, to fight under the orders of my conqueror.'[3] He was given an army rank and accompanied Isma'il on the rest of the expedition, while Shayqiyya cavalry were enlisted under the command of their chiefs as irregulars.

The two rulers of the Ja'aliyyin, *Makk* Nimr of Shendi and *Makk* al-Musa'id of Metemma, also submitted and were confirmed in their positions. A similar submission was made by the sick and aged chief of the 'Abdallab, Shaykh Nasir wad al-Amin. His son and *Makk* Nimr accompanied Isma'il as hostages. Hitherto the advance had been up the western bank of the Nile, but it was now necessary to cross into the Gezira. The passage of the White Nile took from the early morning of 20 May to the afternoon of 1 June; only nine small boats had been able to pass the Third Cataract. The horses and camels were swum across, or floated with inflated water-skins. Had the kingdom of Sennar possessed an effective army, Isma'il's troops could have been caught at a serious disadvantage, but there was no enemy in the vicinity, the passage was unopposed and the remainder of the advance was a military parade.

The Regent Muhammad wad 'Adlan, who had sent a defiant message to Isma'il, had been killed by conspirators supporting his cousin, Hasan wad Rajab, about the beginning of April. The following weeks were wasted by internecine struggle between the two factions. From this, Hasan emerged victorious only to flee to the Ethiopian frontier on hearing of the approach of Isma'il. Such authority as remained in Sennar was held by the old minister, the *Arbab* Dafa'allah, and the brother of the murdered regent. As the expeditionary force approached, they began to negotiate a capitulation. English describes the arrival of Dafa'allah and his colleague as ambassadors:

> I saw these personages when they arrived. They were two, one a tall thin elderly man of a mulatto complexion, dressed in green and yellow silks of costly fabric, with a cap of a singular form,[4] something resembling a crown, made of the same materials, upon his head. The other was the same young man who had come a few days past to the Pasha. He was dressed today in silks like the other, except that his head was bare of ornament. They were accompanied by a fine lad about sixteen, who was, it is said, the son of the predecessor of the present Sultan. All three were mounted on tall and beautiful horses, and accompanied by about two hundred soldiers of the Sultan, mounted on dromedaries, and armed with broadswords, lances and shields.[5]

On the next day, the last Funj sultan, Badi vi, came in person to Isma'il's camp to make his submission. He was well received and honourably entertained. He apparently obtained recognition of his position from the pasha, like the other Sudanese rulers, but politically this meant nothing. A pension, granted to him and the royal family, continued to be paid until the Mahdist revolution. On the following day, probably 13 June, the expeditionary force entered Sennar. The town was far gone in ruin and decay. Even the mosque had been profaned by the scrawled drawings of pagan raiders. The old royal palace was derelict, and Badi's own residence was a large courtyard containing low brick buildings. The condition of Sennar was visible evidence of the debility of the Funj state at the time of the conquest.

After the reduction of Dongola and the Shayqiyya country, Muhammad 'Ali Pasha had sent out a new expeditionary force of three or four thousand troops and a battery of artillery to conquer Darfur. Muhammad Bey Khusraw, the *Defterdar*, left Cairo to join his troops on 20 April 1821.[6] The force assembled at al-Dabba, on the left bank of the Nile below Kurti and, with the assistance of Shaykh Salim, chief of the Kababish, struck south-westwards across the Bayuda towards Kordofan. The Furawi governor, the *Maqdum* Musallim, was invited to surrender and replied with a letter protesting against this unprecedented invasion of a Muslim country not subject to the Ottoman sultan. At Bara the horsemen of Darfur and tribal warriors of Kordofan were routed by the firearms and artillery of the invaders. The *maqdum* was killed in the fighting, and the *Defterdar* entered El Obeid, the provincial capital.

On hearing of the loss of Kordofan, the sultan of Darfur sent an army to recover the province. This too was defeated. The inhabitants of the plain of Kordofan were soon reduced to submission, and the brutality of the *Defterdar* and his troops was long remembered.[7] But the Nuba hillmen of Jabal al-Dayir, as well as those of the remoter mountains to the south, remained unsubdued. The ultimate objective of the expedition, the subjection of Darfur itself, was also beyond the powers of the invaders. Muhammad 'Ali Pasha later tried to gain his end by supporting the claims of a brother of Sultan Muhammad Fadl, named Abu Madyan, but this attempt to install a puppet sultan in El Fasher also ended in failure.

The first impressions the people of Sennar had of their new ruler were by no means wholly unfavourable. The conquest had been achieved practically without bloodshed, and Isma'il Pasha deliberately presented himself as a mild and accessible administrator. His coming was to mark a new era: he would listen to no petitions concerning events before his arrival. To this rule, however, one important exception was made: Hasan wad Rajab and the killers of the Regent Muhammad wad 'Adlan were pursued and captured. Hasan himself was imprisoned and treated with leniency, but some of his underlings were put to death by impalement – a punishment that was a disagreeable innovation to the Sudanese.

Having attained his military objective, destruction of the independent power of the refugee Mamluks and the Shayqiyya, Muhammad 'Ali Pasha now sought to realize his further aims: exploitation of the wealth of the Sudan, especially its gold and slaves. In late 1821 Isma'il was joined at Sennar by his elder brother, the famous Ibrahim Pasha, as commander-in-chief of the troops of Sennar and Kordofan. Repeatedly urged by Muhammad 'Ali to send slaves to Egypt, the two brothers decided to make expeditions into the pagan territories south of Sennar, but Ibrahim fell ill and returned to Cairo. Isma'il went on and established his authority over the auriferous region of Fazughli, where a levy of gold was laid on the traders.

Meanwhile preparations were going forward for taxation of the riverain districts. A census of slaves and flocks had already been made, but apart from a levy of fodder no taxes had been demanded. During Isma'il's absence the arrangements were completed. The fiscal system was organized by a committee of three: the pasha's secretary, Muhammad Sa'id, the *Mu'allim*[8] Hanna al-Tawil (a Coptic financial official) and the *Arbab* Dafa'allah. Taxes were to be paid at the rate of fifteen dollars per slave, ten dollars per cow and five dollars per sheep or donkey. The burden would thus fall on the settled people, not on the nomads (there was no mention of a camel-tax), who were still virtually outside the control of the régime. It has rightly been said that this taxation appears 'almost unbelievably onerous, and to amount to something approaching confiscation'.[9]

Confiscation was indeed probably the intent. Specie was rare in the Sudan, and taxes could be paid in strong male slaves instead of cash. Thus Muhammad 'Ali's demand for slaves to train as soldiers could be met from the reservoir of slave-labour in the newly conquered provinces, until sufficient recruits could be obtained by raiding the pagan tribes of the upper Blue and White Niles and the Nuba Mountains. This device, if carried out, would however have grave social and political consequences. It would destroy the slave-retinues of the petty rulers who had accepted Muhammad 'Ali's suzerainty, and would jeopardize the livelihood of all but the very poorest families, since slaves were universally employed in the households and fields. The Sudanese rose in rebellion.

The first symptoms of revolt appeared at once with sporadic attacks on Egyptian troops. Isma'il treated the rebellious Sudanese with clemency, and tried to modify the assessment. But the books had already been sent to Cairo. Among his troops, moreover, disease was widespread, and he removed his headquarters downstream from Sennar to Wad Medani, supposedly a healthier site. While Isma'il was at Wad Medani, Hasan wad Rajab escaped from confinement to play a part in the developing crisis. In October or November 1822 an incident sparked off a wider rising: Isma'il left for the north, and at Shendi demanded a heavy contribution of money and slaves from the Ja'aliyyin and insulted their chief, *Makk* Nimr. The following night his quarters were set on fire and he perished among his retinue.

At once revolt flared out among the riverain Sudanese from Shendi southwards to Wad Medani. The small garrisons on the main and Blue Niles, at Karari, Halfaya, Khartoum, al-'Aylafun and al-Kamlin, evacuated their posts and made their way, not without difficulty, to general headquarters at Wad Medani. Here the secretary, Muhammad Sa'id, who had been appointed deputy governor (*kâhya*) by Isma'il before his departure, assumed command. He fortified his position and sent a reconnaissance party to the confluence of the Niles.

Alarming though the situation was, two factors favoured the Turco-Egyptian régime. Its troops, although inferior in number, were superior in their possession of firearms and military experience to their opponents – a mixture of peasants, tribal warriors and the private slave-soldiers of the Sudanese magnates. Secondly, the revolt was never either a general or unified movement. Mahu Bey held the province of Berber against the rebels upstream. Dongola and the far north were totally unaffected. The Shayqiyya remained loyal to their new masters, and their irregulars served in operations against the rebels. Even within the area of the revolt, the garrison of Khartoum was assisted by the people of the nearby village of al-Jirayf, whose chief guided the troops to Wad Medani.

The rebels never had unity of leadership. There were three principal centres of revolt. The Ja'aliyyin were led by *Makk* Nimr and *Makk* al-Musa'id. The 'Abdallab revolted under their chief, Nasir wad al-Amin. In the Gezira, resistance was led by those two survivors of the Funj-Hamaj régime, Hasan wad Rajab and the *Arbab* Dafa'allah. The latter, on the outbreak of revolt, had fled from Wad Medani to 'Ibud, whither the rebels began to muster.

In these circumstances, it was possible for Mahu to hold out in Berber, and for Muhammad Sa'id to undertake local operations in the vicinity of Wad Medani. A cavalry squadron was sent from Wad Medani to 'Ibud, where the rebels dispersed without a fight. The *Arbab* fled up the Blue Nile, and joined forces with his old enemy, Hasan wad Rajab. The deputy governor sent out another force, which included Shayqiyya levies, which defeated them at Abu Shawka, south of Sennar. Hasan wad Rajab was killed. Dafa'allah escaped and made his way to the Ethiopian marches.

Neither Mahu nor Muhammad Sa'id was, however, strong enough to undertake the general suppression of the rebellion. This was the work of the *Defterdar* who, on hearing of the death of Isma'il hastened from Kordofan with a body of his troops and a contingent of Fur warriors. Entering Ja'ali country, he found that Nimr and al-Musa'id were blockading Mahu in Berber, but their sons and a large number of followers were at Metemma. They negotiated an amnesty, but an unsuccessful attempt by a tribesman to assassinate the *Defterdar* provoked him to fury and a massacre ensued. He then marched north to relieve Berber. The Ja'ali chiefs advanced to meet him, crossed the Nile and were defeated in a battle on the west bank. Freed from the blockade, Mahu left Berber and met the *Defterdar* at El Damer.

After their conference, the *Defterdar* advanced along the east bank into the 'Abdallabi country. He found Halfaya deserted, and burnt it. Another massacre took place on Tuti island, at the confluence of the Niles, while al-'Aylafun, which offered resistance, was looted and burnt. Shaykh Nasir had fled, but as the *Defterdar* pursued him up the Blue Nile, he doubled back to Qubbat Khujali, near today's Khartoum North, and crossed to Omdurman, where he was joined by survivors of the battle of Abu Shawka. Having reached Wad Medani, the *Defterdar* sent out an expeditionary force that completed the task of reducing the Gezira to submission. Meanwhile the *Defterdar* returned to Kordofan.

During his absence another force had dispersed the concentration of 'Abdallab and Hamaj at Omdurman, but the rebels fled to Shendi, to which

Makk Nimr had returned. It was clear that further measures would be needed to suppress the revolt among the Ja'aliyyin, and the *Defterdar* again set out for the river. On hearing of his approach the rebels dispersed, but the main body of them under Nimr and al-Musa'id fled to al-Nasub in the Butana, near Abu Dilayq. Here they were defeated. Nimr and al-Musa'id fled, and a vast number of prisoners, including many members of Nimr's family, were taken.

Returning to the river, the *Defterdar* made his camp at Umm 'Uruq, a site now uncertain. A last rebel force under al-Musa'id and Shaykh Nasir was still at large east of the Blue Nile. In September 1823 the *Defterdar* advanced against it. The rebels were defeated at Makdur, between the Rivers Rahad and Dinder. The *Defterdar* now struck north-eastwards as far as Sabderat, just across the present Eritrean border, whence he returned to the Nile.

In January 1824 Muhammad 'Ali Pasha informed the *Defterdar* of his impending recall. In his last few months he ordered all the prisoners of war, whether slaves or freemen, to be sent to Cairo. A new deputy-governor was appointed to Wad Medani, while Muhammad Sa'id returned to Cairo with the remainder of the household and possessions of Isma'il Pasha. At Umm 'Uruq the *Defterdar* awaited the arrival of his successor; then, at the beginning of the new Muslim year (August–September 1824), himself departed for Egypt.

He was succeeded as commander-in-chief (in effect, as military governor) by 'Uthman Bey the Circassian, who was accompanied by five battalions of infantry. These were soldiers of a new type, the *Jihadiyya*, regular troops recruited from the slaves obtained in the Sudan, and drilled on European lines in the training camp established at Aswan in 1821. Muhammad 'Ali's great project of a new model army in place of the motley troops of Egypt was only partially achieved: the slave recruits perished by hundreds in the Egyptian climate, and by 1824 conscription of the Egyptian peasantry had begun. Nevertheless, the black *Jihadiyya* could fulfil a useful function as garrison troops in the Sudanese provinces. Henceforward the military strength of the Turco-Egyptian régime was mainly derived from two sources, the regular *Jihadiyya*, of slave origin, originating from what would now be called the Southern Sudan; and the Shayqiyya irregulars, serving mainly as cavalrymen under their own chiefs.

'Uthman Bey realized at once the strategic importance of Khartoum, the trunk of land[10] at the confluence of the Blue and White Niles. He decided to build a fort and to garrison a regiment there. From this beginning in a few years Khartoum was to develop as the military and administrative capital of the Sudan. As yet, however, army headquarters remained at Wad Medani, whither 'Uthman proceeded. The new commander, an elderly Mamluk, regarded his task with the eyes of a soldier rather than of an administrator. To repress revolt and get in the taxes were his sole aims, and he emulated the *Defterdar* in harshness and brutality. The consequence was a flight of cultivators from the Nile Valley to the remote district of the Qadarif in Shukriyya territory. Here they were pursued by government troops and shot down.

'Uthman's few months in office were made more difficult by natural calamities. An epidemic of smallpox coincided with drought, famine and the migration of refugees to produce severe depopulation. The commander-in-chief was ailing and left the responsibility of government to a deputy, a mere subaltern whom high-ranking officers refused to obey. The army was drifting into anarchy, with consequent suffering for the people of the Sudan, when 'Uthman Bey died on 11 May 1825. The deputy prudently concealed the fact of his death until he had summoned the experienced governor of Berber, Mahu Bey, to take command.

CHAPTER FOUR

Settlement and Stagnation: 1825–62

Mahu Bey, who had been governor of Berber since 1822, was a cavalry officer of Kurdish origin. His fortitude during the revolt had prevented his province from falling to the rebel Ja'aliyyin. He took over the command of troops in the province of Sennar: the command in Kordofan, which had been held by the *Defterdar* and 'Uthman Bey jointly with Sennar, was now detached.

Mahu's brief period of authority marks a turning-point in the history of the Turco-Egyptian régime. He adopted a policy of conciliation towards the frightened and resentful Sudanese. Taxes were reduced, and the licence of the *Jihadiyya* was repressed. The novelty of his approach appeared when he summoned an assembly of remaining Sudanese notables in the Gezira, and consulted them on the means of restoring order and bringing back the emigrants. He particularly approved of the advice of a minor shaykh, 'Abd al-Qadir wad al-Zayn, whom he raised in rank and employed as his adviser on native affairs. 'Abd al-Qadir accompanied Mahu on a tour to the Qadarif, the asylum of many of the refugees. Mahu sent grain from the Qadarif to the stricken Gezira, thereby winning the gratitude of its people. Mahu's rule also marks a stage in the advance of Khartoum to the status of a capital. It was his habitual residence, and he stationed his troops at Qubbat Khujali, across the Blue Nile. Mahu was succeeded in June 1826 by 'Ali Khurshid Agha, whose exceptional ability as an administrator is indicated by his long term of office in the Sudan and the successive promotions and extensions of power conferred on him by Muhammad 'Ali. His appointment seems to have been designed to inaugurate a new period of civil administration, rather than military rule: he bore at first the title of 'governor of Sennar'; his predecessor had been commander-in-chief. His authority did not at this time extend to the northern provinces of Dongola and Berber, nor to Kordofan, but Sennar, including the Gezira and surrounding territories, the heart of the old Funj-'Abdallab dominions, presented administrative and political problems of far greater gravity than those confronting his colleagues.

That his policy essentially continued and fulfilled Mahu's was symbolized when they met:

The Amir Mahu Bey met him in Omdurman, and they conferred together in private there for a while. Then Mahu Bey ordered Shaykh 'Abd al-Qadir to be brought forward, and he presented him with his own hand to Khurshid Agha, saying, 'If you desire the prosperity of the country, then act according to the opinion of this man.'[1]

Restoration of prosperity was indeed the first object of the new governor. To achieve it, the lands abandoned during the revolt and subsequent repression had to be brought back into cultivation, and the thousands of emigrants, many of whom had made their way to the hill-country of the Ethiopian marches, persuaded to return to their villages. In the Ja'ali districts, much riverain land was given to loyal Shayqiyya, who paid no taxes but received a forage ration in consideration of their service as cavalry.

Khurshid's new deal was devised with the assistance of Shaykh 'Abd al-Qadir, who was instructed to convoke an assembly of notables, and to draw up a list of the villages, showing whether they were inhabited or lying waste. Letters of amnesty invited the fugitives to return, and promised freedom from disturbance. One inveterate opponent of the Turco-Egyptian régime, Shaykh Idris wad 'Adlan, brother of the murdered Regent Muhammad, was visited in person by Shaykh 'Abd al-Qadir in the summer of 1826. Idris accepted the offer of amnesty, and accompanied 'Abd al-Qadir to Berber, where he was welcomed by Khurshid and formally recognized as shaykh of the Funj Mountains.

Another assembly of notables subsequently held in Khartoum was instructed to elect one of their own as paramount shaykh and official intermediary with the governor. Their choice fell on 'Abd al-Qadir, who was invested with the paramountcy from Hajar al-'Asal to the further limits of the Funj Mountains, thus regularizing his position as native adviser to the governor. Khurshid also consulted regularly a corps of experienced officers, the *mu'awins* (assistants), who formed a kind of intelligence branch, and his Coptic financial intendant.

In 1828 Khurshid began a serious attempt to bring back the refugees from the Ethiopian marches. Some came in to him when he toured the region. 'Abd al-Qadir advised him to exempt the chief notables and *fakis* from taxation, in order to gain their support. The stratagem proved highly successful. Under the influence of the notables, many emigrants returned, to the great benefit of cultivation and the profit of the revenue.

A particularly important refugee was Shaykh Ahmad al-Rayyah al-'Araki, whose family enjoyed great religious prestige. During the troubles, he had led thousands of his tribesmen, the 'Arakiyyin, from the Blue Nile into exile in the Ethiopian marches. He now came in to submit to Khurshid. After an honourable reception, he was sent back to proclaim an amnesty to the emigrants, and took letters from 'Abd al-Qadir promising freedom from disturbance. The governor warned that he would shortly make an expedition to the region, and kill those who had not submitted. He quickly fulfilled his promise and, freely or under compulsion, thousands of emigrants returned to the Blue Nile. The expedition also extended Egyptian rule over the Qallabat and its colony of Takarir settlers from the western *Bilad al-Sudan.*

Another crisis threatened in 1835. Khurshid returned from a visit to Cairo during which he had been instructed by Muhammad 'Ali to conscript Sudanese freemen for military service. This project, no doubt devised because of pressure laid on Muhammad 'Ali's man-power by his occupation of Syria, seemed merely to extend a system applied in Egypt proper since 1824. The rumour of Khurshid's intention filled with dismay an assembly of officials and Sudanese notables he summoned to Khartoum. After two days of private consultation with Shaykh 'Abd al-Qadir, who insisted that conscription would start a fresh wave of emigration and damage the new prosperity of the country, Khurshid abandoned the project. An alternative proposal was accepted, by which the people of every locality should contribute a quota of their slaves as recruits for the *Jihadiyya.*

Khurshid devoted much energy to the development of Khartoum. Settlers were granted privileges, and the population rose so rapidly that the mosque he had built in 1829–30 was demolished seven years later to give place to a larger one. A barracks and military storehouse were constructed for the *Jihadiyya* garrison, and a dockyard was set up on the Nile. Building materials were provided so that townspeople could build permanent houses in place of their tents of matting and hides. Commerce was encouraged. Khurshid resisted Muhammad 'Ali Pasha himself to prevent exploitation of the revenue and products of the Sudan for the benefit of Cairo. His period of office witnessed a boom in trade, some petty merchants making great fortunes. But the prosperity of the Sudan was always precarious. Khurshid's new deal had been favoured by the good rains of 1826; the difficulties of his last years were increased by drought and famine, beginning in 1836 and accompanied by a cholera epidemic.

Khurshid was less distinguished as a soldier than as an administrator. In the summer of 1827 he led an expedition from al-Rusayris, on the upper Blue Nile, into the Dinka country. As a slave-raid this was no great success, only five hundred captives being brought in, while the Dinka put up a very stiff resistance, using arrows and spears, and routed Khurshid's cavalry. Khurshid pushed on as far as the Sobat, whence he returned to al-Rusayris. In the autumn of 1830 he organized an expedition against the Shilluk, whose raids in canoes were still troubling the Arabs of the White Nile as they had done in the sixteenth century. As Khurshid's ships moved upstream, the Shilluk fled to the interior, and the expedition penetrated to the mouth of the Sobat. On the return journey, the Shilluk attacked. Artillery fire dispersed them and the troops took booty and slaves, but the Shilluk returned, recovered their booty and compelled the expedition to withdraw with a mere two hundred captives.

Khurshid's third great expedition, in 1831–32, was against the Hadendowa of the Taka. After crossing the Atbara at Quz Rajab, the expedition became entangled in the bush, and was heavily defeated by the Hadendowa under their chief, Muhammad Din. Unable to advance, Khurshid established a fortified camp and beat off another attack, but he was glad to be able to extricate himself and return to Khartoum.

The last years of his rule were marked by a series of frontier wars with Kanfu,[2] the Ethiopian ruler of the district of Kwara. The Ethiopian marches were always a critical area, remote from the centres of Turco-Egyptian power and a convenient refuge for malcontents. One of these was Rajab wad Bashir al-Ghul of the Hammada Arabs, whose brother, Abu Rish, had been preferred by the authorities as head of the tribe. Rajab conspired with Kanfu to invade the Egyptian Sudan. Khurshid was alerted by Ahmad *Kashif* Ghashim, district officer of the Qadarif. Khurshid, slave-raiding in Fazughli, sent reinforcements. In the ensuing battle the Ethiopians were completely defeated and Rajab fled. He was, however, betrayed by Kanfu to Khurshid, who had him put to death in Khartoum in the spring of 1836.

Ahmad *Kashif* now took the initiative and raided Ethiopian territory. His first expedition took a number of prisoners, but on his second raid he unexpectedly confronted a large army under Kanfu. Ahmad's own troops had been augmented by reinforcements from Khurshid, but their commander resented his subordinate position and would not co-operate with Ahmad. In April 1837 the Turco-Egyptian troops were heavily defeated at the battle of Wad Kaltabu, but Ahmad escaped with his life, and the Ethiopians withdrew.

Khurshid was now thoroughly alarmed. He believed that Kanfu was seeking to annex the frontier districts around the Qallabat, which would then once more become an asylum for emigrants. He asked Muhammad 'Ali for reinforcements for a counter-attack. The viceroy agreed and, in the meantime, Khurshid gathered his own forces and marched from Wad Medani to the Qallabat. Here he paused, and the campaign came to an inglorious conclusion when the British government intervened to warn Muhammad 'Ali against attempting conquests in Ethiopia. The reinforcements had already been despatched under Ahmad Pasha Abu Widn, who met Khurshid on his return from the Qallabat.

Khurshid's rule was now near its end, although he continued to enjoy the favour of Muhammad 'Ali Pasha. In February 1834 he had been appointed governor (*mudir*) of the four Sudanese provinces, Sennar, Berber, Kordofan and Dongola. The unique nature of his appointment was indicated by the grant of a special title (*hükümdar*, usually translated governor-general), differentiating him from the governors (*mudirs*) of provinces of Egypt proper. In May or June 1838 Khurshid was recalled to Cairo. He was expected to return after medical treatment, but never did so,[3] and some six months later Abu Widn was confirmed in office as *hükümdar*.[4]

Under Abu Widn, the administration continued on lines laid down by Mahu and Khurshid. Shaykh 'Abd al-Qadir was again commended by the outgoing ruler to his successor, and continued as chief native adviser. Abu Widn distinguished himself by a rigorous investigation of the fiscal system, which had been relaxed under Khurshid to the great profit of the financial officials. Several of these suffered distraint and punishment. An edict ordered all tenants of riverain land to bring their holdings fully under cultivation. Derelict land was to become the property of the first claimant who cleared and irrigated it, and land thus brought into cultivation was given a three years' exemption from tax.

Abu Widn's stringency in fiscal matters produced two serious incidents. Shayqiyya settlers had been allowed to colonize the lands of Ja'aliyyin rebels and emigrants; Abu Widn cancelled their forage allowance and demanded payment of land-tax with arrears from the time they had taken possession. The Shayqi chiefs produced their charter, to no avail. They then proposed to abandon their lands, but to pay the arrears of tax if they might still receive their fodder rations. The governor-general rejected this compromise too, and insisted they continue to occupy their holdings. Very reluctantly, the Shayqiyya accepted the order, with the exception of *Makk* Hamad, who with his family and two hundred followers set off from Shendi for the Ethiopian marches.

On the way, the emigrants fell in with Ahmad Abu Sinn, chief of the Shukriyya, who informed the governor-general. Abu Widn set out in pursuit, attacked Hamad and captured his baggage together with most of the women and children. Hamad and a few followers escaped, and raided Abu Widn's camp. The governor-general suspected *Makk* Kanbal,[5] chief of the accompanying Shaiqiyya contingent, of conspiring with Hamad; Kanbal was shot, probably at Abu Widn's instigation, and the Shayqiyya were sent home. Failing to catch up with the refugees, Abu Widn consulted 'Abd al-Qadir, Ahmad Abu Sinn and Shaykh Abu Rish of the Hammada, and offered an amnesty. Hamad submitted on condition that the Shayqiyya be allowed to vacate their lands, while those who wished to remain should pay a fixed annual tax, without arrears. The fodder allowance remained cancelled.

A second crisis over taxes concerned Shaykh Abu Rish himself. When, probably early in 1842, Abu Widn demanded double payment from the Hammada, the chief fled to the Ethiopian marches and joined forces with a band of freebooters. They re-entered Sudanese territory and defeated a district officer. Although it was now the rainy season and movement was extremely difficult, Abu Widn set out from Wad Medani to punish the raiders. Abu Rish was abandoned by his allies and decided to submit. He came to Abu Widn's camp, and was pardoned after the intervention of Shaykh 'Abd al-Qadir and other notables.

The last important territorial expansion of the Egyptian Sudan in the reign of Muhammad 'Ali Pasha was achieved by Abu Widn's occupation of the Taka. Although the area had been invaded by the *Defterdar* and Khurshid, neither had established his authority; Khurshid's campaign against the Hadendowa had been an ignominious failure. In 1840 Abu Widn determined to make a fresh expedition and to obtain payment of tribute by the Beja. The two tribes that formed his principal objective were the Hadendowa under Muhammad Din, in the wooded country of the northern Gash, and the Halanqa further south around Jabal Kasala.

The troops assembled at El Damer, and on 20 March 1840 Abu Widn began an advance up the Atbara. On the way he was joined by Muhammad, son of the *Arbab* Dafaʿallah who, in spite of his father's turbulent career, had been received into favour and was an important notable of the Gezira.[6] He brought with him his private retinue of troops. The expeditionary force halted at Quz Rajab, and then continued its advance in the direction of Jabal Kasala.

Although Muhammad Din had sent his son as an envoy, the first tribal chief to come in was Muhammad Ila of the Halanqa. He was a parvenu, a *faki* unrelated to the old chief, who had fled on news of Abu Widn's approach. On 12 April the Turco-Egyptian force encamped on the Gash near the village of Aroma, and two days later Muhammad Din arrived to make his submission in person. But to extract tribute from the unwilling and elusive Hadendowa was no easy matter, although Abu Widn seized Muhammad Din and other chiefs as hostages.

Finally the expeditionary force moved on to Jabal Kasala and encamped near al-Khatmiyya, headquarters of the Mirghani family. On the campsite the town of Kasala subsequently developed, and became the chief administrative centre of the eastern Egyptian Sudan. Abu Widn now tried to defeat the Hadendowa by stratagem. Muhammad Ila suggested damming the River Gash, in order to prevent its flood from reaching the Hadendowa. Deprived of water for their lands they would, the governor-general hoped, be compelled to submit and pay tribute. The device failed; the floodwaters broke the crudely constructed dam. An advance against the Hadendowa was rendered ineffective by the scrub of the lower Gash. Abu Widn patched up an agreement with his opponents, and returned to Khartoum.

Although Abu Widn had failed to reduce the Hadendowa to submission, his campaign had been much more successful than Khurshid's. Muhammad Din, leader of the Hadendowa, was taken as a prisoner to Khartoum, where he died of smallpox in the following year. More important, the Turco-Egyptian administration had obtained at Kasala a permanent foothold. Extension of the Egyptian Sudan towards the Red Sea inevitably gave new importance to the old Ottoman ports of Suakin and Massawa, at that time nominal dependencies of the Hijaz. Abu Widn raised the question of their status, demanding that the governor of Suakin should pay taxes to the Sudanese treasury. In the face of Ottoman opposition, Muhammad ʿAli Pasha withdrew this claim. In 1846 Sultan ʿAbd al-Majid granted him the ports on an annual lease, which was terminated three years later. It was not until 1865, in the reign of Khedive Ismaʿil, that the two ports were permanently annexed to the Egyptian Sudan.

While Abu Widn was *hükümdar*, an event occurred which was to have consequences of lasting importance for the history of the Sudan: the opening of the White Nile route to the south. This was the achievement of Salim, a Turkish sailor, usually called Salim *Qabudan* from his rank as captain of a frigate. The situation on the river, southwards from Alays, of the fierce Shilluk warriors, and the hazards of navigation, had until now prevented the penetration of black Africa from the north. Khurshid Pasha and Muhammad 'Ali had discussed an expedition up the White Nile in 1836, but it was not until November 1839 that Salim and his boats passed into the unknown waters guarded by the Shilluk. After struggling through the *sudd* and up the Bahr al-Jabal, they returned to Khartoum. Salim led a second expedition in 1840 which, in January 1841, reached the country of the Bari, with whom contact was made near today's Juba. Salim's third expedition, in 1842, reached only a few miles further south.

Abu Widn was a strong and effective governor: the Sudanese chronicler declares his period of office better even than that of Khurshid. He was perhaps too successful: it was rumoured that he sought to make himself independent, or that he was plotting with Sultan 'Abd al-Majid to separate the Sudanese provinces from Egypt. When he died suddenly in Khartoum, on 6 October 1843, the story quickly spread that his wife, Muhammad 'Ali's daughter, had poisoned him. In any case Muhammad 'Ali sent a special commissioner, Ahmad Pasha Manikli, to decentralize the administration. The office of *hükümdar* was abolished. Each province would be autonomous, under a governor corresponding directly with Cairo. Yet a few months later, Muhammad 'Ali changed his mind and Manikli, who had remained in the Sudan to report on the gold of Fazughli, was ordered to reintegrate the administration. He himself was appointed *hükümdar*. His period of office was notable for a punitive expedition against the Hadendowa that won him the nickname of *Jazzar*, 'butcher'.

Muhammad 'Ali's uncharacteristic vacillation marks the beginning of nearly two decades of feeble administration in the Sudan. These are the years of the great viceroy's senility, of the retrogressive reign of 'Abbas I (1849–54), and the capricious rule of Muhammad Sa'id (1854–63). Eleven representatives of the viceroy sat at Khartoum during the twenty years following the death of Abu Widn. Few held office long enough to rule effectively. One of the great pioneers of Western culture in Egypt, Rifa'a Rafi'al-Tahtawi, spent a few unhappy years in Khartoum, nominally organizing a school, in fact a victim of 'Abbas's jealous obscurantism: Bayard Taylor, an American tourist, met him there in 1852 and heard his long tale of woe. In 1856 a cholera epidemic broke out which claimed, among many less distinguished victims, the great counsellor Shaykh 'Abd al-Qadir wad al-Zayn.

At this juncture the Viceroy Muhammad Sa'id himself visited. What he saw horrified him and he resolved at first to abandon the Sudanese provinces. By the time he had reached the capital, however, he had modified his views. The administration was again decentralized: four provinces were established, one combining Khartoum and the Gezira; another uniting Dongola and Berber; Kordofan; and the Taka. These would be linked more closely with Egypt by a camel-post, while a railway from Wadi Halfa to Khartoum was projected. This decentralization lasted until 1862, when Musa Hamdi was appointed *hükümdar*.

It was probably unfortunate that this period of hesitation and relaxation of control followed so closely on the opening-up of the White Nile route to the south. Muhammad 'Ali took no initiative to develop the region, although the *hükümdars* sent small annual trading expeditions from Khartoum to obtain ivory. Monopoly of that trade coincided with the collapse of the general system of monopoly of Sudanese exports, which Muhammad 'Ali had maintained since 1824. The European trading community in Khartoum resented exclusion from this last and potentially most profitable field of Sudanese commerce. Its spokesman was a Savoyard, Antoine Brun-Rollet, who was supported by the Catholic mission to Central Africa. The founding of this mission was a direct consequence of the opening-up of the White Nile, and it established its headquarters in Khartoum in 1848. Its leading figure was a young Slovene Jesuit, Ignaz Knoblecher (or Knoblehar) who, after a short visit to the Bari, returned to Europe, where he gained influential supporters in the Austrian Empire. The recall of the *hükümdar*, 'Abd al-Latif 'Abdallah, by 'Abbas I in 1851, removed the last obstacle to the free entry of both traders and missionaries to the south.

The Catholic mission at Gondokoro had a short and unsuccessful life. Permanently established in 1853, it was abandoned after about a year, the one surviving missionary founding a new station, called Holy Cross, among the Dinka, a hundred and fifty miles down-stream. Knoblecher revived the station in 1855, but the missionaries failed to establish fruitful relations with the surrounding tribes. Frustration, and very heavy mortality, led to the closing of the mission at Gondokoro in 1860. Holy Cross had been abandoned in the previous year. An attempt by Franciscans to resume activity on the Upper Nile in 1862 met with no success.

The resentment and hostility the missionaries encountered was partly due to the rapid deterioration of relations between the tribes and European traders, who had come south for ivory. Their first field of activity was the Bari territory, but a stable trading system proved impossible to establish, and armed clashes ensued. The slave trade played no part in this early friction but developed during the later 1850s as a by-product. Unable to satisfy their demands by peaceful exchange, the traders began to take ivory by force. Accompanied by bands of armed retainers, recruited largely from the Danaqla and Shayqiyya of the north, they set up fortified stations, known (from the thorn fences surrounding them) as *zaribas*. These served as headquarters, entrepôts, and garrison-posts. Slaves were needed to supply the trading-communities, as concubines and porters, and were also used as a form of recompense to their retainers, thereby reducing overheads. Thus, under the auspices of the ivory traders, a secondary slave trade developed, which helped to supply the markets of the north. To obtain slaves, as well as cattle, which were indispensable for bartering for ivory, the traders allied themselves with hostile tribal groups, and promoted raiding.

For about a decade European traders dominated the White Nile, but their prosperity was transient. The real profits of the ivory trade went to those who advanced the capital, and to the middlemen of the north. These were mainly Ottoman subjects – Egyptians, both Copt and Muslim, Syrians and Sudanese

– who were better placed to grasp the secret levers of influence in Khartoum and Cairo. European firms were unable to break into the closed circle of the ivory export trade. A few fortunate European traders on the White Nile made quick profits, and withdrew; the unfortunate were killed by the climate. By the end of Muhammad Sa'id's viceroyalty, Europeans had been almost wholly abandoned the White Nile trade.

A similar sequence of developments was occurring at about the same time in the vast area watered by the tributaries of the Bahr al-Ghazal. Here two lines of penetration, and two types of trader, converged and effected a symbiosis. Northern districts, roughly speaking along the Bahr al-'Arab, had for centuries been the border between Baqqara Arabs and non-Arab tribes. This territory was an old-established slave-producing area, and the typical merchants were *jallaba*, small-scale Muslim traders from the north. In the middle and later fifties, passage up the Bahr al-Ghazal from the White Nile was discovered, and Syrian and Egyptian traders penetrated the interior in search of ivory. The traders constructed *zaribas* on the upper courses of the rivers, clear of the marshy clay plains inhabited by the Dinka. They easily subjugated the docile tribes living between the Dinka and the Azande of the Nile–Congo divide, to which the rivers gave access. Like the Dinka, the Azande did not easily succumb to the newcomers, but they were profoundly affected by them.

Ivory was the original attraction to the traders and their northern retainers, who were known as *bahhara*, because they had come from *al-Bahr* – the River. As on the White Nile, however, the *zariba* system necessitated slave establishments of some size. A special feature of the trader communities of the Bahr al-Ghazal were bodies of slave-troops, known as 'bazingers', which ultimately amounted to half the armed forces of the traders. Many Azande voluntarily joined their ranks. The *jallaba*, who had previously paid tribute to the tribal chiefs, now found protection and opportunities for trade in the *zaribas*. While some remained small, independent merchants, others acted as agents for wealthy operators in Kordofan and Darfur. The *zariba*-owners also began to trade in slaves, like their counterparts on the White Nile. An extensive slave trade developed, channelled through the overland route, northwards from the Bahr al-Ghazal. At its height, this was perhaps six times as great as the river-borne trade.

By the end of Muhammad Sa'id's reign, the Upper Nile and Bahr al-Ghazal had thus been opened to a predatory commerce, and over large areas the traditional tribal structure was in dissolution. European opinion was aroused by the great increase in the slave trade, and the viceroy, more deeply influenced by European culture than his predecessors, tried to stop it. On his accession in 1854 he had instructed provincial governors to prevent introduction of slaves into Egypt from the south, and the public slave-market in Khartoum was closed. The village of Kaka, in Shilluk territory, now became the principal slave-market for the White Nile. In 1855 Sa'id endeavoured to extend his rule over the river. An expeditionary force was sent to establish a post at the mouth of the Sobat, and to search for slaves in boats passing down the river. The project had little success, and in 1857 the troops were withdrawn. The protests of missionaries over the anarchic situation on the Upper Nile stimulated Austrian and British pressure on the viceroy for renewed action. The *hükümdar*, Musa Hamdi, notified the traders in October 1862 that boats would be allowed to leave Khartoum for the south for trade in ivory only. A capitation tax, equivalent to one month's pay, was made payable for each employee, while an officer with a small body of troops was appointed to inspect the traffic on the river.[7] Muhammad Sa'id's southern policy was to be taken up with greater effect (and disastrous consequences for Egyptian rule) by Khedive Isma'il.

The picture of political stagnation in these years is repeated in the field of economic history. Muhammad 'Ali began with an optimistic view of the Sudan's resources. A period of disillusionment followed. Even more disappointing than the slave-soldiers was the gold sought principally in two regions, around Fazughli and at Jabal Shaybun in the Nuba Mountains. European experts, pushed on by Muhammad 'Ali himself, prospected these areas, but to little purpose. The iron deposits of Kordofan were slightly more productive, and provided nails for the government shipyard. An attempt to improve output with the aid of English iron founders was a failure. The copper deposits of Hufrat al-Nahas, between Darfur and the non-Arab peoples, were outside the range of Egyptian control until long after Muhammad 'Ali's time.

Attempts to improve Sudanese agriculture were more successful. In the early years after the conquest, Egyptian peasants were sent to teach their methods to Sudanese cultivators. Something was done to increase the irrigable areas by the main Nile. New fruit-trees were introduced, while plantations of sugarcane and indigo were developed. The spread of cotton-production lay in the future, but Mahu Bey is said to have obtained from the Ethiopian frontier the seed which bears his name, and which was the parent of Egyptian cotton. One of the most valuable exports of the Sudan was, as it is today, the gum arabic of Sennar and Kordofan, while the role of the ivory trade has already been described. Cattle and camels, brought from the Sudan, augmented Egyptian livestock, depleted by epizootics and warfare.

CHAPTER FIVE

The Era of Khedive Isma'il: 1863–81

The reign of Khedive Isma'il (1863–79) marked the culmination of Turco-Egyptian power in the Sudan. Under him the administration regained the vigour it had lost since the later years of Muhammad 'Ali, and the territories of Egypt's African empire were enormously increased. But with all his ability, Isma'il lacked the caution of his grandfather. Moreover he ruled at a time when international interest in Egypt, and in Africa generally, was far more marked, and the issues at stake far greater, than they had been while Muhammad 'Ali lived. The last years of Isma'il's reign were a period of increasing difficulty, ending in his deposition.

Three related themes emerge from the story of the Egyptian Sudan during the two decades that may broadly be called the era of Isma'il. The first is a great expansion of the territory ruled by the khedive. The second is a prolonged struggle against the slave trade. The third is increasing employment in high office of men who were neither Muslims nor Ottoman subjects, but for the most part Europeans and, at least nominally, Christians.

Although Muhammad 'Ali valued his Sudanese possessions largely because they tapped a reservoir of slaves he could use in his army, the lucrative and flourishing slave-trade became increasingly an embarrassment to his successors. Muhammad Sa'id and Isma'il were westernized rulers, with genuine sympathy for the nineteenth-century humanitarianism to which Muhammad 'Ali had paid no more than occasional lip-service. The combination of anti-slavery idealism and schemes for colonial expansion, a frequent feature of European imperialism in the last decades of the century was, at a rather earlier period, characteristic of Khedive Isma'il. To dismiss his measures as a hypocritical pretext for acquisition of territories is an over-simplification. The campaign against the trade was begun years before the khedivial government had made any attempt to extend its power over the great slave-acquiring areas of the Upper Nile and the Bahr al-Ghazal, while the first suggestions of such an extension seem to have come from the British consul in Cairo.

The measures taken in Muhammad Sa'id's reign had been a pitiful failure. The slave trade proceeded as vigorously as ever; the source of the trade lay beyond the control of the administration. Further steps were taken in 1863.

The White Nile province was reconstituted with its headquarters at Fashoda, in Shilluk territory. This to some extent strengthened the hand of the authorities. Of the two merchant-princes who dominated the area, one fled while the other made terms with the administration. At the same time Musa Hamdi tripled the capitation tax on personnel. This action, coming just when the traders' boats were about to leave Khartoum, provoked a great outcry from the European trading community, who suspected that the governor-general was trying to drive them off the river. Within the next few years, in fact, the few remaining Europeans withdrew from their establishments in the south.

A further measure against the slave trade, in June 1864, was the establishment of a force of river police. This was equipped with four steamers and half-a-dozen armed sailing-ships, which intercepted the traders' boats on their return downstream. After the first shock, the river police seem rapidly to have lost their efficaciousness. An official inquiry in 1866 revealed that the traders had quickly learnt to elude or bribe the patrols, and that their operations were continuing on a large scale. The khedive's good intentions were defeated by three factors: the existence of powerful and wealthy vested interests in the mercantile community; the lack of honest and well-paid officials; and the absence of any provision for the future of confiscated slaves. Although in theory these should have been repatriated at the traders' expense, they were in fact brought to Khartoum where many were enrolled in the army. Thus the administration itself connived at a veiled form of slave-recruitment.

Withdrawal of the European traders from the White Nile and the Bahr al-Ghazal was followed by the emergence of a new generation of merchant-princes in the extensive regions outside khedivial control. On the White Nile the most successful of these was Muhammad Ahmad al-'Aqqad, who probably with the financial backing of Isma'il himself, bought up most of his competitors' establishments. He was succeeded, on his death in 1870, by his son in-law, Muhammad Abu'l-Su'ud. To recoup the enormous expenses of the ivory trade al-'Aqqad, like his predecessors, turned to slave trading. A loophole in a khedivial decree authorizing personnel of expeditions to bring their black concubines and children to Khartoum made possible the transport and sale of thousands of slaves annually.

The only answer to this recurrent problem seemed to be further extension of khedivial rule, and the appointment of officials from outside the circle of vested and corrupt interests. The khedive sought to attain both these objectives when, in April 1869, he took into his service the British explorer, Samuel Baker. His tour of duty was to last two years, during which he would lead an expedition to annex all the territories in the Nile basin, suppress the slave trade and establish a chain of posts in the newly-acquired regions. Baker was given a princely salary and equipment, and a flotilla of six steamers and several sailing ships.

If strength of body and force of character had sufficed for the task, Baker would have been an admirable choice. But he was deficient in administrative qualities and blind to his delicate and invidious situation. He was an English-man and a Christian in the employ of a Muslim ruler. His mission was odious to the powerful and entrenched slave-trading interest with its numerous ramifications in the administration, army and Sudanese society generally. He quarrelled with the governor-general, Ja'far Mazher, with the slave-traders and with the tribes he was supposed to protect. Nevertheless, he carried the flag beyond the borders of Uganda, and left garrisons to mark the authority of the khedive along the Upper Nile.

Meanwhile another expedition was attempting to establish the khedive's authority in a different region. The Bahr al-Ghazal was dominated by the merchant-princes, whose *zaribas*, strung out along the routes to the north, were stages for slave-caravans going to Kordofan and Darfur. And about the middle of the century a certain Muhammad al-Hilali had established an autonomous kingdom in the adjacent region of Dar Fartit under the over-lordship of Darfur. Trouble had subsequently developed between the vassal and his suzerain, and Hilali sought asylum with Ja'far Mazhar, who proposed to support him. Seeing in Hilali an instrument by which he might extend his power, Isma'il agreed to his appointment as chief of the Bahr al-Ghazal district, despite protests from Darfur.

The principal opposition Hilali had to fear was not the enfeebled sultanate of Darfur, but the powerful and independent merchant-princes of the Bahr al-Ghazal itself. The most important was a Ja'ali, al-Zubayr Rahma Mansur, who had made himself the principal trader in the western part of the region and sent his caravans into Darfur. Zubayr's relations with Hilali were at first friendly, but soon deteriorated. The difficulties of the slave traders on the Nile worked to the profit of those in the remote Bahr al-Ghazal, who rejected Hilali as an agent of the administration. In 1871 Hilali asked Khartoum for reinforcements, and when they arrived he began to attack and reduce the *zaribas* of the traders. Zubayr marched to the aid of his friends and kinsmen. The unfortunate Hilali was killed in battle. The khedive saved appearances, realizing that Zubayr was beyond his power, by constituting the Bahr al-Ghazal a province and appointing Zubayr as its governor (December 1873).

The Upper Nile and Bahr al-Ghazal had thus been added, at least in name, to Isma'il's African empire. The administrative organization of the territories was the work of another Englishman, Charles Gordon, who had made a name for himself as a soldier in China. Appointed governor of the Equatorial province in 1874, he established a capital at Lado, organized the series of garrisons to hold the region and strove to reconcile the tribes, disaffected by the depre-dations of the slave-traders and heavy-handed methods of Baker. When he resigned in 1876, Egyptian authority was still feeble. Once again, a basic prob-lem was personnel. Although there were advantages in employing foreigners, their salaries were high, and they succumbed to the climate. The Danaqla, on the other hand, who had long been inured to the region and were hardy and intelligent, felt little loyalty to the administration or sympathy for the campaign against the slave trade.

Meanwhile Zubayr, ruling in the Bahr al-Ghazal, made an agreement with the Rizayqat Baqqara in southern Darfur for safe passage of his caravans. In 1873 the Rizayqat broke the agreement. Zubayr complained to their overlord, Sultan Ibrahim Muhammad of Darfur, at the same time invading the territory of the Rizayqat and defeating them. The strained relations that followed, between the sultan and Zubayr, led to further hostilities. Zubayr covered his aggression by informing the governor-general, Isma'il Ayyub, and through him the khedive, of a project to invade and conquer Darfur in the name of the Egyptian government.

While Isma'il Ayyub concentrated his forces in Kordofan, Zubayr struck into Darfur from the south. A Fur army was defeated in January 1874, and in October Sultan Ibrahim was killed at the battle of Manawashi. On 2 November Zubayr entered El Fasher, where he was joined a few days later by Isma'il Ayyub. Thus Darfur became a province of the Egyptian Sudan, over half a century after Muhammad 'Ali had originally planned its conquest. Zubayr's great triumph was followed rapidly by eclipse. A clash with Isma'il Ayyub was inevitable. When it occurred, Zubayr went to Cairo, to plead his cause in person, and there he was detained. The Bahr al-Ghazal thus lost its master, at a time when the khedive's authority in the province was little more than nominal.

The reign of Khedive Isma'il witnessed also an expansion of the Egyptian empire in the east. In 1865 the Ottoman government finally ceded to Egypt the ports of Suakin and Massawa,[1] opening a new phase in relations with Ethiopia. In 1871 Isma'il appointed as governor of Massawa a Swiss, Munzinger, whose authority was later extended over the whole Sudanese coast. Munzinger began to prepare for war against King John IV of Ethiopia. He died in an ambush, but Isma'il's aggressive policy continued. Two Egyptian expeditions in succession were overwhelmed and defeated in the Eritrean highlands in 1875 and 1876.

Isma'il's failure in Ethiopia was the first of a series of calamities. In 1877 Gordon was appointed governor-general of the Sudan, the first Christian and European to hold this post. At the outset he faced the legacy of Isma'il's expansionist policy – an unsettled frontier with Ethiopia, revolt in Darfur and anarchy in the Bahr al-Ghazal. In the course of a few months he attempted to reach a settlement with Ethiopia, pacified Darfur and appointed as governor of the Bahr al-Ghazal the one man who might possibly have served as an instrument of Egyptian rule – Sulayman, the son of Zubayr. These successes were superficial. Gordon's difficulties were partly personal, partly the result of circumstances. He was inexperienced in the routine of administration and contemptuous of bureaucracy. He was impulsive and relied on intuition, while his deeply personal religion tended to invest his decisions and his vacillations with a divine sanction in his own eyes. He was a fanatical Christian. He neither read nor spoke Arabic. But Gordon was unfortunate in assuming power at a time when Isma'il, the one man whom he could trust, was declining in authority. He had neither sound finances nor effective

forces to back him. He mistrusted his Egyptian subordinates, often with reason, but the caprice of his appointments and dismissals indicates a lack of
judgement, while his reliance on inexperienced Sudanese and Europeans, often
ill-equipped for their tasks, weakened an administration already defective in
tradition and *esprit de corps.*

From July 1878 the tide turned against him. He was now solely responsible for suppression of the slave trade, a policy difficult in any circumstances
and impossible in the conditions of those years. Sulayman, superseded by
a rival, revolted in the Bahr al-Ghazal; risings broke out in Darfur and
Kordofan. Gordon, in concert with two Italian subordinates, Gessi in the Bahr
al-Ghazal and Messedaglia in Darfur, succeeded in restoring order, but the
south-west was sullen and unreconciled. To cut off supplies from Sulayman,
Gordon had authorized the Baqqara chiefs to harry the *jallaba* who traded
in their districts. El Obeid and the other towns of Kordofan and Darfur were
filled with survivors and kinsmen of these traders, thus abruptly deprived of
their stake in Egyptian rule. In June 1879, as a result of European pressure,
Isma'il was deposed by the Ottoman sultan. Gordon's administration effectively
ended, although his formal resignation came in 1880, after an unsuccessful
attempt to reach a settlement with Ethiopia. His successor as governor-
general was Muhammad Ra'uf, a man of mixed Nubian and Ethiopian
parentage who had served under both Baker and Gordon. During his administration, in June 1881, the storm broke.

In economic matters, the reign of Isma'il was a period of unfulfilled promise.
The story of the Sudan railway is typical. Muhammad Sa'id had planned
a railway to link Upper Egypt with the Sudanese provinces. The scheme
was abandoned, but Isma'il took it up as a means of assisting administrative
centralization. A British engineer, John Fowler, made plans to open the
First Cataract to shipping, and to construct a railway from Wadi Halfa to
Metemma. Progress was delayed by the khedive's financial difficulties. The
line reached only thirty-three miles south of Wadi Halfa when work was
suspended, and was finally abandoned after the British occupation of Egypt.
Thereafter, apart from an abortive attempt to construct a line from Suakin
to Berber in connection with the campaign against 'Uthman Diqna in 1885,
there was no further railway-building in the Sudan until Kitchener's campaign
in 1896.

Two other grandiose schemes of Isma'il's time were equally unfortunate.
At the beginning of his reign, he encouraged formation of a private
Compagnie du Soudan to develop rail and river transport and assist the export
trade. After an initial buying spree, the company got into difficulties, and in
1868 went into liquidation. When the American Civil War caused a boom
in Egyptian cotton, much to the khedive's profit, the governor in Suakin,
Ahmad Mumtaz, perceived that the Sudan also had areas suitable for cotton
growing, and started an experimental plantation in the Tokar district. This
was a success. Isma'il's interest was aroused and Mumtaz put 2,500 acres of

the Gash delta under cotton, but by this time the Civil War was over and the boom was ending. Although in 1871 Mumtaz was put over the combined provinces of Khartoum, Sennar and the White Nile, where he found wider scope for cotton projects, his financial situation crumbled and he was dismissed from office. In the early twentieth century, 'Mumtaz' was still a synonym for cotton in the rural Sudan.

Against these failures must be set developments in communications. Steamers had appeared on the Sudanese Nile before Isma'il's time, but creation of a fleet of government steamers took place in his reign. Most were sent upstream from Egypt, and had difficulty in passing the cataracts between Aswan and Khartoum. A dockyard west of Khartoum, near the junction of the Niles, serviced the steamers, which played an important part in strengthening the hold of the administration, particularly over the outlying provinces of the south. That was aided also by development of the telegraph system: in 1866 Wadi Halfa was linked with Upper Egypt, and by 1874 the line had been extended to Khartoum; a section completed in 1875 linked this line with the Red Sea coast by way of Berber, Kasala and Suakin; a third line connected Khartoum with the west, running by El Obeid to the borders of Darfur.

PART THREE

The Mahdist State: 1881–98

A Mahdi who since he arose never betrayed or deceived, who guided the blind and codified religious knowledge: who penetrated into the inmost secrets of the divine presence; who every day is revealed in the colour of a new light; who strives not after created things but after the Creator.

> From a verse panegyric by Ahmad Sa'd,
> translated by S. Hillelson

The woe which befell us has now befallen the Ansar; English gunfire, and slaughter, and wretchedness. The Sirdar takes up his quarters in the Khalifa's courtyard. Shaykh al-Din is a prisoner, and Ya'qub carries firewood.

> From anonymous verses circulating
> after the defeat of the Khalifa,
> translated by S. Hillelson

CHAPTER SIX

The Mahdist Revolution: 1881–85

It is still frequently asserted that the Mahdia was due to the oppression and misgovernment of the Egyptians in the Sudan. This hypothesis remains too easily and uncritically accepted, despite ample correction by historians, and fails to explain why the revolution began when and where it did. The savage pacification by the *Defterdar* was a regrettable but abnormal incident of the conquest; thereafter there was, as we have seen, a good deal of association of Sudanese notables and men of religion with the administration. Corruption that shocked nineteenth-century European visitors had long been endemic in Egyptian administration. Failure to see this as part of the pattern of late Ottoman provincial government is unwarranted and unhistorical.

In fact for two years after the declaration of the Mahdi the revolt was practically confined to the southern fringe of the Arab provinces, centring in Kordofan, the conquest of which was the first major achievement of his followers. It spread only gradually to other parts of the Sudan, last of all to those northern riverain provinces with the longest experience of Turco-Egyptian rule. Thus at the outset the reasons for the success of the Mahdia lay in local conditions. Moreover by then the Sudanese had borne alien rule for sixty years; why did it suddenly become intolerable? There is no reason to assume that the burden had suddenly become heavier under the feeble rule of Muhammad Ra'uf – it had, however, become easier to throw off.

To explain the timing of the outbreak, we must look to events in Egypt, which followed to some extent a similar pattern. The khedivial autocracy virtually ended with the deposition of Isma'il in 1879. His son and successor, Muhammad Tawfiq, was a puppet of the great powers. The change of rulers swept away the prestige which had surrounded the viceregal dynasty from the time of Muhammad 'Ali. The forces of opposition gathered around the army leader, 'Urabi Pasha, and effected by gradual stages a change in the centre of power; a genuine revolution was abruptly nullified in September 1882 by British occupation. The collapse of the khedivate in 1879 was as obvious to the Sudanese as to the Egyptians and, by a turn of the screw, revolutionary changes in Egypt made metropolitan control over Sudanese provinces weak and hesitant. No communication has ever been shown between supporters of 'Urabi in Egypt and those of the Mahdi before his declaration, but both movements found opportunity in the power-vacuum caused by the disappearance of Isma'il's autocracy. The timing of the Sudanese outbreak may further be linked with the resignation of Gordon who, for all his faults of ignorance, caprice and misjudgement, was a dynamic and masterful personality; Muhammad Ra'uf was the mild and gentle ruler who reaped the whirlwind sown by his energetic predecessor.

The Mahdia takes its name from its leader, Muhammad Ahmad b. 'Abdallah, a man of Dunqulawi origin, who in June 1881 despatched letters from the island of Aba in the White Nile, informing the notables of the Sudan that he was the Expected Mahdi, the divine leader chosen by God at the end of time to fill the earth with justice and equity, even as it had been filled with oppression and wrong. He was then about forty years of age. From childhood he had been deeply religious and, although he had never been outside the Sudan, he had studied at the feet of more than one Sudanese teacher and been initiated into the Sammaniyya order. For some years he had lived at Aba, gaining among the surrounding tribes an increasing reputation for asceticism, holiness and supernatural powers. He was attended by a small company of devout men like himself, and had been joined within the previous two or three years by a disciple who was to eclipse them all.

This was a certain 'Abdallahi b. Muhammad, the son of a soothsayer of the Ta'aisha, a Baqqara tribe in the south of Darfur. 'Abdallahi shared the expectation of the *mahdi* which was current in the Sudan, and had even on one occasion hailed Zubayr with this title. 'Abdallahi's coming to Muhammad Ahmad may well have been a decisive event. In these years Muhammad Ahmad made two visits to Kordofan, and stayed a while in El Obeid, where political intrigue and resentment against the local administration were rife.

What were Muhammad Ahmad's motives? To many modern Sudanese, he is *Abu'l-Istiqlal,* 'The Father of Independence', a national leader who united the tribes by an Islamic ideology, drove out the alien rulers, and laid the foundations of a nation-state. This is an interpretation of the consequences of his revolt, rather than an appreciation of his motives. Another modern Sudanese view of him is of a *mujaddid,* a renewer of the Muslim Faith, come to purge Islam of faults and accretions. Much in Muhammad Ahmad's own statements supports this opinion. A frequent theme in his pronouncements is that he was sent to establish the Faith and Custom of the Prophet – the normative ideals of Islam. Seen from this point of view, Muhammad Ahmad is comparable to reformers of the eighteenth and nineteenth centuries such as Muhammad ibn 'Abd al-Wahhab, founder of the Wahhabi movement in Arabia.

But Muhammad Ahmad went further. His mission developed eschatological overtones. He claimed for himself unique status, reflected in the titles he associated with his name – the *Imam,* the Successor of the Apostle of God and the Expected Mahdi. As *Imam* he asserted headship of the community of true Muslims. As Successor of the Apostle of God he envisaged re-enacting the role of the Prophet, by restoring the community Muhammad had established. As the Expected Mahdi he was an eschatological figure whose advent foreshadowed the end of the age.

At times of crisis, the appearance of a *mahdi,* claiming divine sanction to overthrow the old order and set up a new theocracy, is a not uncommon development. Two medieval *mahdis* had established durable political régimes, 'Ubaydallah, founder of the Fatimid dynasty in North Africa and Egypt in the tenth century, and Muhammad b. Tumart, whose followers, the Almohads, had conquered and ruled north-west Africa and Moorish Spain in the twelfth century. There had been others more recently, including one who assailed, and was defeated by, Bonaparte's troops in Egypt at the end of the eighteenth century.

To an established government, the appearance of a *mahdi* is therefore a dangerous symptom. Muhammad Ra'uf apprehended the danger, but did not act with sufficient force to suppress it. An expedition sent to Aba in August 1881, to seize Muhammad Ahmad, miscarried, and troops under Muhammad Abu'l-Su'ud, head of the firm of Agad and Company, were beaten off by the Mahdi's followers. This victory of spears and clubs over firearms was hailed as a miracle. As soon as the government steamers had withdrawn, the Mahdi and his little group of followers crossed the White Nile and made their way to Qadir, a remote hill in southern Kordofan. Here malcontents began to assemble. In this period three main groups may be distinguished among the *Ansar,*[1] as the Mahdi called his supporters.

There were, first, the genuinely pious disciples, some of whom had been with him for years, who accepted him as the Expected Mahdi. Pietists, they deplored the state of the Sudan and wished the conduct of its people to be governed by the Holy Law of Islam in its full rigour. The administration was odious, not so much because of oppression and corruption in the usual sense, but because any government not patterned on the original Islamic theocracy was inherently depraved. When the Mahdi and these men spoke of misgovernment and purification, they were thinking in theological rather than political terms.

A second group of the Ansar had more practical grievances. These were the Ja'aliyyin and Danaqla of the dispersion, who had settled on the southern fringe of the Arab Sudan and worked as boatmen, traders and soldiers of fortune in the great opening-up of the south. Their livelihood was connected with the slave trade, and Gordon's policy, culminating in the harrying of the *jallaba,* had struck at the roots of their prosperity. These men were neither theologians nor devotees, but they could cover political and economic interests with a veil of religion; the institution of slavery was not repugnant to Islam, and wholesale employment of Christians by a Muslim government derogated from the prestige of their religion.

The third group consisted of Baqqara nomads, who shared neither the religious ideals of the Mahdi's disciples nor the political grievances of the northerners of the dispersion. To them the Mahdia made its appeal in simple and elementary terms: 'Kill the Turks and cease to pay taxes.' To the nomad, control by any settled government is hateful, and the firmer its control, the more hateful it becomes. The nomads of the southern fringe had in the previous ten years become increasingly conscious of government. The Rizayqat had suffered from the superior armament and forces of Zubayr. Then came the conquest of Darfur and substitution of Egyptian administration for the easy yoke of Sultan Ibrahim. It was the fickle, light-hearted Baqqara who formed the army of this pious revolution, and their importance is reflected in the unique status of their kinsman, 'Abdallahi, in the Mahdi's councils.

Qadir was still more difficult of access than Aba. An attempt to intercept the Ansar crossing Kordofan failed, and an expedition organized by the governor of Fashoda against the orders of Ra'uf Pasha was annihilated in December 1881. Ra'uf was recalled, and the 'Urabist government in Egypt appointed as his successor an energetic soldier with long experience in the Sudan, 'Abd al-Qadir Hilmi. Meanwhile a much more serious attempt to crush the Mahdi had been organized by the acting governor-general, a German telegraph official named Giegler. In spite of superior forces, this expedition also was overwhelmed in May 1882 by the Ansar. Each of these victories raised the Mahdi's prestige, and the booty acquired augmented his meagre resources.

Hitherto the Mahdi, in his refuge at Qadir, had been on the defensive. He now led his followers in a holy war against Kordofan where, in the provincial capital, El Obeid, he could count on a fifth column of sympathizers. Operations in Kordofan followed a pattern characteristic of the Mahdi's wars. Sporadic local risings first occurred, and were dealt with, usually effectively, by the forces of the administration, but as soon as one was suppressed, another broke out. The immense distances and difficult circumstances of these petty engagements laid a heavy burden on provincial troops. The second phase began with the arrival of a Mahdist army in the province. This, combined with more general tribal risings, tried the Turco-Egyptian provincial forces to the utmost. In pitched battles they were still usually victorious, but they were unable to consolidate their successes and had to withdraw to fortified bases, which, in the third phase, were gradually reduced by the Ansar. In Kordofan, by the autumn of 1882, only two garrisons still held out, at Bara and El Obeid.

The governor at El Obeid, Muhammad Sa'id, had taken early precautions by fortifying the administrative cantonment, which was separate from the commercial town. At the beginning of September 1882, the Mahdi with the main body of his supporters, augmented by large tribal levies, encamped near El Obeid. A general assault, delivered in the Friday Battle of 8 September, was a failure: as so often in history, a tribal army found itself checked by a fortified garrison. In the Mahdi's camp there were divided counsels. 'Abdallahi advised retreat to Qadir. Instead the Mahdi moved his camp closer to El Obeid and the Ansar settled down to besiege the town. At the same time a new Mahdist force was organized, of what were in effect regular soldiers, neither fanatical devotees nor tribal warriors. These were mainly Sudanese originating from the south who had served in the Turco-Egyptian forces and been captured in battle. Commanded by Hamdan Abu 'Anja, who belonged to a servile tribe, clients of the Ta'aisha, they were known not as Ansar, but by their former designation *Jihadiyya*; and they alone, it seems, were officially equipped with firearms.

As the year moved to its close, the situation of both Bara and El Obeid deteriorated. A relieving force sent from Khartoum was intercepted in October. After negotiations, the garrison of Bara surrendered on terms in January 1883, and swore allegiance to the Mahdi. A few days later, the determination of Muhammad Sa'id to resist was overborne by a council of his officers. On 19 January El Obeid capitulated and the Mahdi led the prayer of victory in the mosque. This was the first considerable town to fall into the hands of the Ansar, and its capture was followed by a ruthless search for treasure. The governor and chief officers had been granted their lives, but the Mahdi learnt that they were attempting to communicate with Khartoum. They were handed over to tribal chiefs, who made away with them.

While these events were taking place in Kordofan, there were sporadic risings in the Gezira and riverain districts south of Khartoum. But these areas were easily accessible by land or steamer, and the vigorous actions of Giegler and 'Abd al-Qadir Hilmi succeeded in holding in check the rebels on the Blue and White Nile. 'Abd al-Qadir indeed planned a vigorous counter-offensive against the Mahdists. He concentrated troops in Khartoum, organized three additional battalions of black *Jihadiyya*, and strengthened the chief administrative centres. He tried to counter the Mahdi's propaganda, and dealt harshly with officials whose loyalty he suspected. He appealed to Cairo for reinforcements, but the 'Urabist government was preoccupied with the threat of British intervention. 'Abd al-Qadir continued to hold office for a few months after the occupation of Egypt in September 1882 but, as a nominee of the 'Urabists, he was not in good standing with the new régime. He was recalled in February 1883, after a successful campaign against forces threatening Sennar.

Turco-Egyptian rule in the Sudan during its last two years, from the fall of El Obeid to that of Khartoum, was dominated by British policy towards Egypt. The British occupation of Egypt was at first regarded by Gladstone's government as temporary, to be ended as soon as Khedive Muhammad Tawfiq had been firmly re-established on his throne. The revolt in the Sudan was regarded as something outside the sphere of British responsibilities. The serious financial state of Egypt argued against large-scale measures to suppress the rebels or to regain lost territory. Gladstone anyway expressed the view that the Sudanese were rightly struggling to be free; military operations against them would be morally unjustifiable. Thus an illogical assemblage of political, financial and moral considerations led the British government, not only to evade involvement, but also to check attempts of the khedivial government to promote resolute action in the threatened provinces.

A success in the Sudan was, however, badly needed by Muhammad Tawfiq's ministers to restore the prestige of the khedivate and give it at least some semblance of autonomy *vis-à-vis* the occupying power. Britain permitted the Egyptian government to raise an expeditionary force. Many of the troops were demoralized survivors of 'Urabi's armies. A former British officer of the Indian Army, William Hicks, was appointed to command, but on his advance into Kordofan was accompanied by the governor-general, 'Ala' al-Din Siddiq Pasha.

The expedition that marched out from Dueim on the White Nile on 27 September 1883 was doomed from the start. Hicks and his Egyptian colleagues disagreed, his men lacked hope and the route in its later stages ran through waterless scrub. Advancing into Kordofan, the column was harassed by Ansar; proclamations from the Mahdi, scattered on the line of march, warned that it was hopeless to fight against the soldiers of God. On 5 November, the expeditionary force was surrounded at Shaykan, south of El Obeid, and cut to pieces by the Ansar and *Jihadiyya*. Hicks and 'Ala' al-Din perished with all their chief officers.

The victory of Shaykan convinced waverers all over the Sudan. The provinces neighbouring Kordofan were the first to fall. In Darfur an Austrian officer, Rudolf Slatin, had been governor since 1881, and had struggled to repress the rebel Rizayqat in the south. After the fall of El Obeid his position became precarious, and he publicly professed Islam in an attempt to secure the loyalty of his troops. A subordinate, Muhammad Khalid, generally called Zuqal, a kinsman of the Mahdi, was after Shaykan appointed by the Mahdi as governor of Darfur, and on 23 December 1883 Slatin submitted to him.

In the Bahr al-Ghazal Egypt's authority was upheld, to the limit of his feeble resources, by a young Englishman, F.M. Lupton, formerly an officer in the mercantile marine. Like his colleagues in Kordofan and Darfur, he succeeded at first in suppressing local revolts in which both Dinka and north-erners of the dispersion took part. But the victory at Shaykan doomed him, and he was cut off from Khartoum. A force sent by the Mahdi to invade the province reached the capital, Daym al-Zubayr, in April 1884, and Lupton had no choice but to surrender.

The fall of El Obeid was followed by the revolt to a region hitherto untouched, one moreover of vital strategic importance, the hinterland of Suakin. The Beja tribes, isolated by their language and way of life, were unaf-fected at first by the Mahdia. Not until the summer of 1883 did the Mahdi's emissary, 'Uthman Diqna,[2] summon them to holy war. He was a Suakinese of partially Beja descent, who had suffered arrest and imprisonment for slave trading across the Red Sea. The Hadendowa, the leading Beja tribe, also had a grievance, since they had been bilked of dues promised for transport work in connection with the Hicks expedition. The decisive event in turning them was 'Uthman's alliance with Shaykh al-Tahir al-Tayyib al-Majdhub, local head of an important Sufi order. By swearing allegiance to the Mahdi and recognizing 'Uthman as his representative, al-Tahir called from the soil a fanatical and devoted tribal army. Within a few months, the vital line of communication between Suakin and Berber had been cut, and two Egyptian forces had been defeated on the coast near Tokar. Sinkat, the nodal point on the route across the Red Sea Hills, and Tokar both fell in February 1884.

The battle of Shaykan inescapably confronted both the Egyptian and British governments with the problem of the future of the Sudan. Although the British sent troops to Suakin, which was of strategic importance as a Red Sea port, they were determined to avoid involvement in the interior, and in January 1884 insisted that the Egyptians evacuate their troops and officials. Largely in consequence of a press-campaign in Britain, Gordon was sent out to fulfil a mission that was variously understood by the parties concerned. The British government tasked him to report on the best method of carrying out evacuation. Baring,[3] the British agent and consul-general in Cairo and effective ruler of Egypt, thought Gordon was authorized to execute the evacuation. On the way, and after arrival in the Sudan, Gordon added to the confusion and misunderstanding. He was commissioned by the khedive as governor-general, and provided with two sets of documents, one speaking of restoring good government, the other announcing evacuation. By a fatal error, Gordon published the second set while passing through Berber on the way to Khartoum. Shortly before this he had written to the Mahdi, offering to make him sultan of Kordofan – an offer the Mahdi indignantly rejected. These two actions indicated to the Sudanese that Egypt had abdicated its responsibilities. Gordon's authority was now effective only so long as he had the force to maintain it.

He arrived in Khartoum on 18 February 1884. Quickly realizing the impossibility of accommodation with the Mahdi and peaceful evacuation of the Egyptians, Gordon swung to the other extreme. He felt bound to establish a strong government to check the Mahdi, demanded appointment of Zubayr Pasha to succeed him and proposed that Indian troops be sent to the Sudan to 'smash the Mahdi'. He announced that British troops would in a few days be at Khartoum – a dangerous piece of bluff. When on 13 March London overruled these proposals, which went far beyond the scope of its instructions and intentions, Gordon determined to remain at Khartoum until help came or the city fell.

The evacuation of the riverain garrisons was already becoming impossible. The telegraph-line to Egypt was cut on 12 March. On 27 April a Mahdist emissary arrived to carry Holy War into the province of Berber. The provincial capital fell in the middle of May. Khartoum was thus cut off, both from the Egyptian frontier and from Suakin. Meanwhile the Mahdi prepared an advance on Khartoum. He had left El Obeid in April, and the Mahdist vanguard took up siege positions outside the capital in September. The Mahdi himself arrived on 23 October and established his headquarters on the western bank of the White Nile. Khartoum, now strictly besieged, was doomed unless help came.

Under the pressure of public opinion in Britain, Gladstone's government at last agreed to send a relief expedition, but its organization did not get under way until the autumn. News of its advance, in January 1885, placed the besiegers in a dilemma. They failed to gauge its very limited strength; some counselled retreat to Kordofan. The Mahdi decided to assault the city before the relief force could arrive. The attack was delivered on 26 January 1885. The exhausted garrison was overwhelmed, and Gordon was killed in the fighting. On 28 January the relieving steamers arrived at the junction of the Niles, to learn that they had come too late.

With the fall of Khartoum the Mahdi controlled a great part of the former Egyptian Sudan, although Suakin, the far north and the equatorial regions were still held for the khedive. The Mahdi disliked the former capital, and transferred his headquarters to Omdurman on the west bank. He and the Ansar had seen the taking of Khartoum as but one in a series of conquests throughout the Muslim world. Their expectations were to be disappointed, for after a sudden and short illness the Mahdi died on 22 June 1885.

He left to his successor a rudimentary administrative system, which reflected both the religious ideology of his movement and the wars that had brought it to power. The Mahdi and Ansar were dominated by the idea that they were re-enacting the drama of early Islam. Hence the Mahdi equated his chief disciples with the Companions of the Prophet. He linked three of them with the successors of the Prophet as heads of the Muslim community. 'Abdallahi was designated *Khalifat al-Siddiq*, Successor of the Caliph Abu Bakr. 'Ali b. Muhammad Hilu, a pious disciple of long standing, was entitled *Khalifat al-Faruq*, Successor of the Caliph 'Umar. The Successor of 'Uthman, the third Caliph, was to be Muhammad al-Mahdi al-Sanusi, head of the Sanusiyya order, but he ignored the proposal, and the place remained vacant. A young relative of the Mahdi, Muhammad Sharif b. Hamid, was appointed *Khalifat al-Karrar*, Successor of the Caliph 'Ali the cousin of the Prophet.[4]

These were not empty titles, since each of the three *khalifas*, as they are usually called, commanded a division of the Mahdist army. The Khalifa 'Abdallahi, being of Baqqari origin, commanded the great, if fluctuating, tribal levies of the Baqqara. This division was known from its standard as the Black Flag. The Khalifa 'Ali had a small tribal force, drawn from his kinsmen in the southern Gezira and called the Green Flag. The Khalifa Muhammad Sharif commanded the riverain tribes of the main Nile and of the dispersion. His division was probably entitled the Red Flag.

The position of 'Abdallahi was as superior to that of his colleagues as that of Bonaparte to the two other consuls in 1799. He was given the title Commander of the Armies of the Mahdia, and from the outset controlled the administration as vizier (although this title was not used) of the Mahdi. His paramountcy excited jealousy, and on various occasions the Mahdi affirmed their implicit mutual reliance. One lengthy proclamation of the Mahdi in effect conferred plenary powers on 'Abdallahi. There was deep significance in his nomination as *Khalifat al-Siddiq*, since his prototype, Abu Bakr, had been closest to the Prophet of all the Companions, and had succeeded him on his death.

Subordinate to the Khalifas were officers who, in the first place, had often been early adherents to the Mahdi and had raised their districts or tribes in his support. They had thus a dual role as propagandists and, later, as military commanders. These officers have usually been called by European (and even by Sudanese) writers the Mahdi's 'emirs', although the title *amir* (commander) was officially superseded in 1883 by that of *'amil* (agent). Such officers, commissioned in writing by the Mahdi, might be anything from petty local leaders to military governors of extensive areas, such as 'Uthman Diqna in the east or Muhammad Khalid in Darfur. The rank and file, called by the outside world 'dervishes', a term usually applied to sufis, were from a very early date designated by the Mahdi *Ansar*, 'Helpers'.

Two other great officers of state were appointed during the time of the Mahdi: the treasurer and chief judge. The Mahdist treasury, again following early Islamic precedent, was entitled *Bayt al-mal*, 'The house of wealth', and was intended to hold all the material resources of the movement, in both cash and kind. The lighter taxes authorized by the Holy Law of Islam replaced the elaborate Egyptian system. But throughout the period of revolutionary war, the treasury was augmented chiefly from booty acquired in battle. It was no easy task to induce the warriors to hand this over to the common treasury, as repeated proclamations by the Mahdi and the Khalifa 'Abdallahi make clear. The treasury was put under Ahmad Sulayman, a man of Nubian origin and a friend of the Mahdi.

The chief judge, entitled *qadi al-Islam*, 'the judge of Islam', was Ahmad 'Ali, who had been a judge under the Turco-Egyptian régime in Darfur. In theory the law of the Mahdist community was the Holy Law of Islam, but the Mahdi in practice exercised extensive powers of legislation. This he did by proclamation and by decisions on points of law submitted to him. Although Ahmad 'Ali was the special delegate of the Mahdi's judicial functions, cases were also heard by the Mahdi himself, the khalifas and other chief officers. The Mahdist theocracy was in form a state in which supreme power was held directly from God by the Mahdi, and exercised by other officials only by delegation from him. Yet before the Mahdi's death a large part of the substance of power was already wielded by 'Abdallahi.

The Mahdi was the first Sudanese sovereign to exercise one of the traditional prerogatives of a Muslim ruler: that of striking money. After the sack of Khartoum, gold and silver acquired as booty were minted by his orders. The gold pounds of the Mahdi were of an unusually high standard of fineness and, in accordance with Gresham's Law, rapidly vanished from circulation. Dollars, at first of silver, later (in the Khalifa's reign) of increasingly debased metal, continued to be struck throughout the Mahdist period. The coins were modelled on Ottoman currency circulating in Egypt, but with

Omdurman as the mintmark. At no time, however, did foreign specie cease to circulate. The Mahdi ordained that the various types of currency should all pass at their face value, an edict confirmed by the Khalifa, early in his reign, that gave rise to frauds by the treasury's own officials. Foreign coins were preferred to the local *maqbul* (i.e. 'acceptable') currency, which was further held in low esteem owing to the prevalence of counterfeiting.

CHAPTER SEVEN

The Reign of the Khalifa 'Abdallahi: 1885–98

The death of the Mahdi brought to a head the tensions underlying the revolutionary movement. Although the ideology and organization of the Mahdia reflected the outlook and aims of pious devotees, and although its victories would have been impossible without the Baqqara, the fruits of conquest fell largely to the riverain tribesmen, especially to the Danaqla and Ja'aliyyin of the dispersion. At the centre of this last group, called in Mahdist documents *Awlad al-balad*, (i.e. villagers, sedentaries) were the Mahdi's own kinsmen, the *Ashraf*. Although many were late adherents to the movement, they claimed a privileged position, and their actions had been disavowed by the Mahdi himself in the last few weeks of his life.

Each group, whom victory was turning from allies into rivals, was represented in the Mahdist hierarchy. The leader of the devotees was the Khalifa 'Ali, a religious man without ambition, who played the part of mediator and conciliator in the crises following the Mahdi's death. The *Awlad al-balad* had as a figurehead the Mahdi's young kinsman, the Khalifa Muhammad Sharif. In so far as the Baqqara were prepared to recognize any authority, it was embodied in neither of these, but in the Khalifa 'Abdallahi, himself of Baqqari origin.

At the time of the Mahdi's death, 'Abdallahi headed a strong concentration of military power in Omdurman. A body of *Jihadiyya* under one of his clients was garrisoned there, as were Baqqari tribal levies of the Black Flag. The forces of the *Awlad al-balad*, belonging to the Red Flag division, were scattered in various parts of the Sudan. The Green Flag troops, few in number, could play no effective military role by themselves. At a council of notables, held immediately after the Mahdi's burial, the intention of the *Ashraf* to designate the Khalifa Muhammad Sharif as the new ruler was frustrated by the rest of the company. While the dispute raged, the Khalifa 'Abdallahi sat silent. His restraint was rewarded. One of the notables at last took his hand and swore allegiance. The others followed suit, last of all Muhammad Sharif himself. A public oath-taking followed in the open mosque outside the room where the Mahdi had died. Proclamations were despatched to inform the provincial governors and empower them to administer the oath of allegiance to their troops.

'Abdallahi now added to his style the new and unique title of *Khalifat al-Mahdi*, 'the successor of the Mahdi': he was now 'the Khalifa' *par excellence*. He bolstered his position by skilful propaganda, claiming the sanction of visions for his sovereignty. The *Ashraf* were not, however, prepared to abandon the struggle for power. Most of the great provincial commands and chief offices of state were held by them or their sympathizers. A conspiracy was hatched, in accordance with which the governor of Darfur, Muhammad Khalid, was to march on Omdurman with his very considerable forces. The Khalifa's handling of this crisis is typical of his astute and resourceful policy. He first removed the danger in the capital, by sending a Baqqari officer, Yunus al-Dikaym, to occupy the fertile Gezira, the granary of the capital, which the *Ashraf* intended to allot to the troops of Muhammad Khalid. Next he instructed his representative at Dueim to intercept the mails between Omdurman and the west. In April or May 1886 'Abdallahi, supported by the Khalifa 'Ali, proposed that the two junior khalifas relinquish their bodyguards and armouries to the control of Ya'qub, 'Abdallahi's brother and successor as commander of the Black Flag.

Meanwhile the army of Darfur had begun a slow advance towards the Nile. 'Abdallahi possessed two advantages. A large part of the army consisted of Baqqari levies, who could not be relied on to support Muhammad Khalid. Secondly, in Kordofan was stationed a powerful Black Flag Army under Hamdan Abu 'Anja, whose loyalty to the Khalifa was beyond question. Acting on instructions, which became steadily more uncompromising as 'Abdallahi's position improved in Omdurman, Hamdan intercepted the Darfurian army in April 1886 at Bara. Muhammad Khalid was arrested and deprived of his command without resistance. His forces were incorporated in those loyal to the Khalifa.

For six years the *Ashraf* and *Awlad al-balad* relapsed into impotence. Chance or policy removed their sympathizers from the chief commands, which 'Abdallahi bestowed on his kinsmen and clients. A year after the Mahdi's death, only two of the great provincial governors whom he had appointed remained in office. One of these, in the Bahr al-Ghazal, was to fall in 1887; the other, 'Uthman Diqna, an indispensable instrument for control of the Beja, remained until the overthrow of the Mahdist state. Elsewhere the military governors and high executive officers were clansmen or clients of 'Abdallahi. In subordinate offices, especially in the bureaucracy, the *Awlad al-balad* could not be superseded by the mostly illiterate and unsophisticated nomads, whom they wryly styled 'Our Lords the Ta'aisha'.

After ending the internal threat to his rule, the Khalifa took up an aspect of the Mahdi's work left incomplete at his death – promotion of the Holy War to extend the Mahdia (equated by the Ansar with true Islam) through-out the world. There had already been fighting on the frontiers. In December 1885 the Ansar of Dongola had been defeated by Anglo-Egyptian forces, and although 'Abdallahi believed an invasion of his territories to be imminent, the battle preceded a withdrawal of Egyptian troops from all posts south of

Wadi Halfa. The garrisons of Kasala and Sennar, which had held out with great fortitude and endurance even after the fall of Khartoum, surrendered in July and August 1885 respectively. An Egyptian officer, Sa'd Rif'at, evacuated the garrison of Gallabat and brought the refugees through Ethiopia to safety at Massawa. The intrepidity and resource of this man passed unnoticed by a generation whose deepest emotions had been roused by the failure of Gordon's mission.

Holy War was fought in three particular areas: in the west, on the Ethiopian marches and on the Egyptian frontier. The war in the west was essentially a pacification of Darfur. Muhammad Khalid had appointed as its governor a member of the old royal family, Yusuf Ibrahim, who at first acted as a loyal vassal of the Khalifa but by the summer of 1887 was obviously aiming to restore the Fur sultanate. Operations against him were entrusted to a kinsman of the Khalifa, 'Uthman Adam, called Janu, the governor of Kordofan. 'Uthman advanced into Darfur, defeated the rebels and re-established Mahdist administration.

The very success of the Mahdist movement led to the appearance of other messianic figures, aiming to subvert the rule of the Khalifa. One such, commonly known by his nickname Abu Jummayza, gained a large number of adherents on the western frontiers of Darfur, where he sought legitimacy by claiming to be the rightful third khalifa, Successor of 'Uthman. Abu Jummayza advanced into Darfur, gathering supporters as he went. Two of 'Uthman Adam's subordinates were heavily defeated. Faced with revolt throughout the province, he concentrated his forces in El Fasher. But the danger passed away as suddenly as it had arisen; Abu Jummayza died of smallpox, and the heart went out of his followers, who were defeated in a pitched battle outside El Fasher in February 1889. 'Uthman Adam had saved Darfur for the Khalifa, but after his premature death in 1891, his successor, Mahmud Ahmad, was to have considerable difficulty holding the province.

On the Ethiopian frontier, Holy War was simply a further phase of hostilities that had recurred throughout the Turco-Egyptian period, as indeed in earlier times. The absence of a defined frontier; opportunities for raiding which local war-lords found irresistible; and the coincidence of bellicose rulers in both Ethiopia and the Mahdist Sudan, made a clash inevitable. Fighting began in 1887 between the Mahdist commander at Gallabat and Ras 'Adar, the Ethiopian governor of the contiguous territory. The Ansar were worsted, and their chief killed. The Khalifa sent to Gallabat an expeditionary force, which was soon augmented by troops under Hamdan Abu 'Anja, who was given the chief command. He had difficulty in asserting authority over the troops, many of whom were on the verge of mutiny under a leader claiming to be the Prophet Jesus, whose Second Coming is expected, according to some traditions, after the appearance of the Mahdi. The conspiracy was suppressed, and in January 1888 Abu 'Anja made a large-scale raid into Ethiopia. Ras 'Adar was defeated, and the Mahdist army penetrated as far as Gondar, the ancient capital. Much booty fell into the hands of the Ansar, but the campaign as such was indecisive.

King John of Ethiopia sent offers of peace, which were rejected. He prepared for war, and was favoured by conditions in the Mahdist camp. Abu 'Anja had died in January 1889, and a dispute ensued over the command. In March the Ethiopian army drew near to Gallabat. At the first onset, the Ethiopians were victorious, but a chance bullet fatally wounded King John. That night the Ethiopians began to withdraw, pursued by the exultant Ansar. Among the booty taken was the crown of the dead king, which was sent with his head to Omdurman. Ethiopia fell into anarchy, from which Italy, which had occupied Massawa in 1885, profited by establishing control over Eritrea and thereby becoming a neighbour to the Mahdist state.

In Darfur and on the Ethiopian frontier, the Khalifa grappled with problems such as had faced Gordon and the Turco-Egyptian administrators before him. Holy War on the southern frontier of Egypt was something new, a legacy of the dream of universal conquest that had been frustrated by the Mahdi's death. A campaign against Egypt had been planned by the Mahdi, under the command of 'Abd al-Rahman al-Nujumi, a general of Ja'ali origin who had served with distinction in Kordofan and at Khartoum.

The Khalifa resumed the Mahdi's scheme, but the campaign was slow to get under way. Not until Anglo-Egyptian forces had withdrawn from Dongola, and 'Abdallahi had secured his position against domestic rivals, did an expedition really become feasible. Even then, inordinate delays occurred. These arose in part from the difficulties of constituting and keeping together a force, mainly of tribal warriors, and provisioning it for an advance through the arid districts of Nubia. And although al-Nujumi, the last of the great commanders originating from the *Awlad al-balad*, appears to have been completely loyal, the Khalifa appointed a Baqqari officer as his lieutenant in order to check his authority and actions.

While the expeditionary force remained in Dongola from November 1886 to May 1889, its morale decayed, its predatory activities antagonized the local people and its high command was paralysed by the Khalifa's mistrust. In April 1887 the Khalifa had sent messages inviting the Khedive, the Ottoman sultan and Queen Victoria to submit to the Mahdia. Now further messages of the same kind were sent, and the Ansar began their march northwards.

Unprovisioned and ill-armed, they struggled desperately down the western bank of the Nile. Once across the border they hoped to receive assistance from the Egyptians, whom they were coming to liberate. These hopes were disappointed; the Nubians were well aware of the Anglo-Egyptian military power concentrated around Wadi Halfa. In July the British commander sent al-Nujumi a demand for surrender. Al-Nujumi replied as arrogantly, asserting loyalty to the Khalifa and trust in the help of God. On 3 August 1889 the two armies met near the village of Tushki. The Mahdist expeditionary force was crushingly defeated, and al-Nujumi himself was killed. The threat to Egypt from the Mahdist state had passed.

The year 1889 was critical for the Khalifa. Although the Anglo-Egyptian victory at Tushki was not, as he had feared, followed by an immediate invasion of his territories, on the northern frontier was a vigilant enemy, whose material resources he affected to despise, but whose strength he dimly yet forebodingly apprehended. Elsewhere also the Mahdist state had attained its limits. Victories of 'Uthman Adam and al-Zaki Tamal had resulted in no acquisitions of territory, but merely established a precarious Mahdist supremacy in disputed border regions. The deaths of Abu 'Anja and al-Nujumi, both in 1889 (to be followed in 1891 by that of 'Uthman Adam) deprived him of his ablest generals. 'Uthman Diqna was unable to capture Suakin, even though he remained master of the hinterland; in 1889 old tensions between Beja and Arabic-speaking Ansar on the Suakin front developed into a quarrel characterized by the rivalry of their commanders, and the Khalifa had to intervene. The *élan* that had carried the Mahdi's followers to victory in the revolutionary war had passed away.

Besides these military and political difficulties the Khalifa was confronted in 1889–90 with an age-old problem, a devastating sequence of bad harvest, famine and epidemic. Such calamities had always taxed the resources of rulers in the Nile Valley; for the Khalifa they were aggravated by his military dispositions. Great armies were stationed in Darfur, at Gallabat and, until the Tushki campaign, at Dongola, consuming unproductively the diminishing supplies of corn. Tales were told of famished beggars snatching bread in the marketplaces with the last remains of their strength, of silent villages whose people starved quietly to death behind shut doors. There was nothing new in such stories, which may be paralleled from the chronicles of Egypt in previous centuries, but European opinion laid upon the Khalifa blame for a catastrophe he was powerless to avert and could do little to alleviate.

By a fatal mischance, the great famine coincided with one of his major acts of policy, the enforced migration of his tribe, the Ta'aisha, and their Baqqara neighbours from their homelands in Darfur to Omdurman. This act has a dual aspect. It successfully consummated a policy the Mahdi and Khalifa had followed from the start, of attaching the nomads closely and permanently to the régime, and turning them from casual raiders into a standing army. The first year of his rule had shown the Khalifa the desirability of surrounding himself with warriors on whose loyalty he could rely. The summons to the Ta'aisha was also connected with 'Uthman Adam's pacification of Darfur.

The Baqqara did not respond willingly. They were attached to their tribal lands, and the Khalifa, after all, was not their hereditary chief but a parvenu. For long they resisted both threats and promises, until in March 1888 the Khalifa's anger flared out in a proclamation, which is a superb piece of Arabic invective, commanding the Ta'aisha, under pain of destruction and dispersion, to place themselves under the orders of 'Uthman Adam. This command, backed by 'Uthman's military power, was effective. The great tribal migration began, and in the early months of 1889 Ta'aisha contingents reached Omdurman.

The coming-in of the Ta'aisha profoundly affected the future of the Khalifa's rule. They must have depleted the corn-supplies of Kordofan as they made their way to the river. Once in Omdurman they were a privileged élite, who had to be fed at all costs. The effects of famine were thus aggravated by this great tribal displacement, which also had political consequences. The settled, sophisticated *Awlad al-balad* had as little liking for these nomads as the lowland Scots had for the Highland clans in the Forty-five. The Khalifa's reliance upon tribal kin deepened the rift between 'Abdallahi and his more advanced subjects. The Ta'aisha, moreover, proved an ineffective instrument of government. They tried to elude the Khalifa's vigilance and slip back to their homelands – the hereditary chief himself was pursued and killed. They were unproductive, overbearing, as intolerant of discipline as ever, and became a liability to the Khalifa when he sought to establish a strong monarchy.

After Tushki the Khalifa had sought to conciliate his Sudanese opponents. Muhammad Khalid, who had been released from prison, was sent to investigate the troubles in 'Uthman Diqna's command; then to inquire into conditions in Dongola and to promote trade there. In April 1890 he actually superseded the Baqqari, Yunus al-Dikaym, as governor of Dongola. Other appointments seemed to betoken renewed participation of the *Awlad al-balad* in the high offices of state. Commerce was encouraged, both with Upper Egypt and Suakin.

But there were other, less agreeable, indications. In April 1886 the Khalifa had replaced Ahmad Sulayman, whom the Mahdi had appointed as commissioner of the state treasury, with a certain Ibrahim Muhammad 'Adlan, formerly a merchant. 'Adlan was a first-class administrator, and introduced into the haphazard arrangements for the receipt, storage and disbursement of state resources, both in cash and kind, methods based on Turco-Egyptian practice which survived until the end of the régime. The coming of the Ta'aisha was 'Adlan's downfall. He clashed with Ya'qub, the Khalifa's half-brother who, as commander of the Black Flag, had special responsibility for the Ta'aisha. He toured the Gezira to find corn to provision the troops in Omdurman, but his methods were apparently too lenient to suit the Khalifa. Early in 1890 he was disgraced and executed.

Prospects of improvement in the political status of the *Awlad al-balad* were soon dashed. In Dongola Muhammad Khalid quarrelled with his Baqqara subordinates and, a year after taking office, was recalled to Omdurman; once again, Yunus al-Dikaym took command in the north. In Omdurman a new conspiracy against the Khalifa developed. As in 1886, its promoters were the *Ashraf*, and its principal supporters the Danaqla sailors of the Gezira. Their ostensible complaint was lack of respect shown towards the Khalifa Muhammad Sharif and the Mahdi's family, but they had also economic grievances of a kind which would affect the *Awlad al-balad* rather than the Baqqara.

Under Muhammad Sharif, the conspirators made their headquarters around the Mahdi's tomb. On 23 November 1891 the Khalifa assembled his own supporters to cordon off the *Ashraf.* If fighting broke out the Ta'aisha might get out of control, so he opted to negotiate. The Khalifa 'Ali strove for a settlement, and on the 25th the insurgents laid down their arms. They were promised a general pardon; Muhammad Sharif would be given the honours and authority due his position, and the Mahdi's family would get a pension. Having disarmed his opponents, the Khalifa turned on them. A few weeks later, seven notables including the former treasurer, Ahmad Sulayman, were seized and sent to Fashoda, where al-Zaki Tamal put them to death. The Danaqla in the Gezira were rounded up, and released only after confiscation of a third of their goods. In March 1892 the Khalifa Muhammad Sharif was arrested and tried by a special body of commissioners. He was deprived of his dignities and flung into prison, where he remained until the eve of 'Abdallahi's own overthrow.

The threat posed by the *Ashraf* and *Awlad al-balad* was thus finally and completely broken. The next four years display 'Abdallahi as an autocrat. Those who disliked his rule were increasingly prepared to acquiesce in it, even as transformation of the early Mahdist theocracy into a secular despotism was becoming obvious. One sign of change was a new armed force, the *Mulazimiyya* which, from a small corps of orderlies, expanded from 1892 into a bodyguard of nine thousand, commanded by the Khalifa's son, 'Uthman. Composed half of slave-troops, half free Sudanese, but excluding Danaqla and Egyptians, and with its own treasury, to which the Gezira contributed corn and cash, the *Mulazimiyya* superseded the Ta'aisha, as the Ta'aisha had the *Jihadiyya,* as the principal military support of the régime.

In the tradition of oriental autocracy, the Khalifa began to withdraw from his people. In the past he had attended the parade of the Ansar, held each Friday outside Omdurman; now he appeared, surrounded by his bodyguard, only on the principal festivals. A great wall was raised around the part of Omdurman where he and his bodyguard were housed – a district until today known as the *Mulazimiyya* quarter. In his councils Ya'qub, who from the first had acted as vizier, and later his eldest son 'Uthman, were prominent. Although the two junior khalifas were perhaps regarded as having a claim to succession – on the analogy of the caliphs, whose 'successors' they were – 'Uthman was groomed in state affairs and, apparently in 1891, when he married Ya'qub's daughter, received the honorific title *Shaykh al-Din,* indicating his seniority in the Mahdist hierarchy. As 'Abdallahi cultivated the manner of a despot, his suspicions of those around him showed themselves. In 1893 the victor of Gallabat, al-Zaki Tamal, was arrested and starved to death. The two following years saw the destitution and death in prison of two successive chief judges, the first of whom, Ahmad 'Ali, had held office since the time of the Mahdi.

The Khalifa's temper in these years was no doubt affected by awareness that the Mahdist state was no longer immune from attack by its external enemies. This was the heyday of the European scramble for Africa. The Khalifa's military strength, which a century earlier would have been adequate to repulse any likely invader, was set against the superior might and organization of the European powers, at the very time when his rule was least questioned by his subjects, and had been established internally on elaborate administrative foundations. In 1891 an Anglo-Egyptian force from Suakin routed 'Uthman Diqna and captured his headquarters. In 1893 the Italians defeated a Mahdist expedition at Agordat in Eritrea, opening the way to their offensive against Kasala, which fell in July 1894. Yet the Khalifa rejected overtures from Menelik ii of Ethiopia, who was also threatened by the Italians.

Further threats appeared in the Southern Sudan, which was not effectively part of the Mahdist state. The Bahr al-Ghazal had not had a Mahdist governor since 1886. Emin Pasha, the last khedivial governor of Equatoria, had maintained a shadow of Egyptian authority on the Upper Nile until evacuating the province in 1889. There was a Mahdist garrison at Rejaf, but the river from Fashoda southwards was not permanently held, and away from the river Mahdism was but a name. In 1893 the Khalifa sent an expedition to strengthen his hold over the far south, but steamer connections with Omdurman remained infrequent and hazardous. Meanwhile the Belgians had established Leopold ii in the Congo, and were pushing across the Nile–Congo divide towards the former Egyptian provinces. They clashed with the Mahdists in 1894 when, moreover, a Franco-Congolese agreement opened the door to French advance to the Bahr al-Ghazal and the Upper Nile. In consequence of this, an expedition under Marchand was approved in November 1895 by the French foreign minister.

In March 1896 the British government suddenly and unexpectedly authorized an advance by Egyptian forces into Dongola. The reason for this is to be sought in the relations of the European great powers: it had no particular relevance to the situation in the Mahdist state, nor was it undertaken primarily for any advantages that might accrue to Egypt from a reconquest of the Sudan, which indeed was not contemplated at this stage. Neither was the advance intended to forestall Marchand's appearance on the Upper Nile, which was regarded as a remote contingency that in any case could not be affected by military action in Nubia. The event precipitating the British decision was Menelik's defeat of the Italians at Adowa on 1 March 1896. The British gesture of distracting the Mahdists from the vulnerable Italian flank at Kasala, was further intended to conciliate Germany and guard against dissolution of the Triple Alliance, two objectives of Lord Salisbury's foreign policy.[1]

The 'reconquest'[2] took place in two stages. A railway from Wadi Halfa was pushed up the Nile to support an expeditionary force under Kitchener. The Mahdist forces in Dongola were defeated in a series of actions, and by September 1896 the whole province had been occupied. Kitchener now began construction of a new railway across the Nubian Desert, from Wadi Halfa to Abu Hamad on the Nile. Abu Hamad fell in July 1897, and the Anglo-Egyptian forces prepared to penetrate to the heart of the Mahdist state.

In this crisis the Khalifa was ill-served by the general to whom he committed the defence of his dominions, Mahmud Ahmad. Mahmud made his head-quarters at Metemma, whose Ja'aliyyin inhabitants, having refused the Khalifa's order to evacuate and vainly appealed to Kitchener for help, resisted and were massacred. There Mahmud remained, unwilling or unable to move, badgering the Khalifa with despatches, seeking advice on every contingency, and failing to act on the instructions he received. He found great difficulty in provisioning his army, which began to melt away as the weeks passed.

Meanwhile the enemy was advancing. Berber fell without resistance in August 1897. In February 1898 'Uthman Diqna with his forces arrived to support Mahmud, but the old fighter and young general worked badly together. Soon afterwards the Mahdist army advanced from Metemma to the River Atbara, where it encamped. The Ansar were starving but, in the hour of defeat, their old heroic courage returned. Kitchener attacked on Good Friday, 8 April 1898. At the end of the day 3,000 Sudanese were dead and 4,000 wounded. 'Uthman Diqna escaped, while Mahmud Ahmad was taken prisoner, humil-iated by his captor. On the Anglo-Egyptian side the casualties were 81 killed and 487 wounded.

The advance on Omdurman began four months later. On 1 September the Egyptian and British forces were encamped near an abrupt hill, Jabal Surkab (Surgam), on the left bank of the Nile six miles north of Omdurman, a vicinity known as Karari. Against them the Khalifa threw his considerable reserves. Once again, but not without difficulty, Kitchener was victorious. Some 11,000 Sudanese were killed; Anglo-Egyptian losses were 49 killed and 382 wounded. Ya'qub died on the field. The Khalifa rode back to his deserted capital and led the remnant of his forces into Kordofan. The battle marked the end of the Mahdist state.

The significance of the Khalifa's reign has not always been appreciated. A legend grew up, fostered by foreign propaganda and current even today, depicting him as a barbarous despot, from whose tyranny the Sudanese were rescued by Anglo-Egyptian invasion. The reality is different. When he came to power, the initial drive of the Mahdia was at an end, and the objects of the revolutionary war had largely been attained. His primary problem was to restore order and make administration effective over a vast area in which four years of warfare against the established government had broken down the habits of obedience. His task was complicated by the uncertain loyalty of the *Awlad al-balad* and the insubordination and backwardness of the Baqqara.

He sought to establish his authority by developing an increasingly elab-orate and centralized administration. The forms of Mahdist theocracy were retained, but without the spirit. The other two khalifas were in no real sense his colleagues; his closest associate was his brother, Ya'qub. The great military commands were held almost exclusively by Baqqara. The Mahdi's simple fiscal system was abandoned, and new taxes, dues and confiscations, closely resembling the Turco-Egyptian taxes the Mahdi had come to destroy, were introduced; specialized treasuries, notably the Khalifa's own, siphoned off revenue from the original *Bayt al-mal.* The judiciary similarly acquired an increasingly complex organization, although no greater independence of the ruler in performance of its functions. The reign of the Khalifa is indeed characterized by the creation of a personal rule, exercised through a bureaucracy largely composed of Sudanese civil servants inherited from the Turco-Egyptian régime.

'Abdallahi prevented the Northern Sudan from relapsing into anarchy after the Mahdi's death. His success in establishing control so firmly that it was broken ultimately only by a foreign invader with superior military resources is a measure of his strength of personality and administrative talent. Yet the price was high. While 'Abdallahi, permanently resident in Omdurman, was never fully in control of provincial officials, his constant communication with them destroyed their initiative in emergencies. His reliance on the Baqqara opened a rift with the *Awlad al-balad* that weakened the state. Finally, the régime's sustained military character, which derived from the revolutionary period and continued in the policy of Holy War, prevented genuine resettlement of the country. The lurid image, still retailed today, of 'Abdallahi as a bloodthirsty despot is the creation of contemporary European writers and subsequent glossographers rather than of historians appreciative of the circumstances he confronted.

PART FOUR

The Anglo-Egyptian Condominium: 1899–1955

The cannon which swept away the Dervish hordes at Omdurman proclaimed to the world that on England – or, to be more strictly correct, on Egypt under British guidance – had devolved the solemn and responsible duty of introducing the light of Western civilization amongst the sorely tried people of the Soudan.

Lord Cromer, *Modern Egypt*, 1908

At the end of time the English will come to you, whose soldiers are called police: they will measure the earth even to the blades of the sedge grass. There will be no deliverance except through the coming of Jesus.

Attributed to Shaykh Farah wad Taktuk
(17th century), translated by S. Hillelson

CHAPTER EIGHT

Pacification and Consolidation: 1899–1913

The overthrow of the Mahdist state posed the immediate question of the future status and administration of the Sudan. Despite the fact that the Anglo-Egyptian conquest had been undertaken with the stated aim of recovering the khedive's lost Sudanese provinces, the British were unwilling to accede to the incorporation of those provinces with Egypt. Opinion in Britain was convinced that the Mahdia had been a reaction to oppressive Egyptian rule; to re-impose that rule would belie the moral arguments justifying British intervention. And Lord Cromer, since the British occupation of 1882 virtual ruler of Egypt, sought to avoid in the Sudan the status that had dogged his conduct of affairs. Administration under the khedivate would, he feared, open the way for the Capitulations and other international machinery.[1]

An obvious alternative was administration of the Sudan as a British colony. Yet this too was problematic. Egyptian claims had formed the basis for the conquest and provided a legal cover in the upper Nile Valley that France, Italy and Belgium could not match. To abrogate those claims was therefore impossible. This was borne out at the time of the Fashoda Crisis. Marchand had occupied Fashoda on 10 July 1898. When word reached Kitchener he immediately went there, telling Marchand that 'the presence of a French force at Fashoda and in the valley of the Nile was regarded as a direct infringement of the rights of the Egyptian government and of Great Britain'. It was only after a period of great tension that on 4 November the French government gave way and ordered Marchand to withdraw.

With neither British annexation nor incorporation under the khedivate a suitable solution, Cromer devised a 'hybrid form of government',[2] which appeared to honour Egyptian claims and safeguard British interests. This was embodied in two Anglo-Egyptian conventions of 1899, which came to be known as the Condominium Agreement since they created a theoretically joint sovereignty. British claims were openly based on conquest, while Egypt's were defined by reference to 'certain provinces in the Sudan which were in rebellion against the authority of His Highness the Khedive'. The Egyptian and British flags would be flown together in the Sudan, and appointment of the governor-general would be by khedivial decree but at the instance of the British government. The direct authority of the Egyptian government and its laws, application of the Capitulations and Mixed Tribunals[3] and any remaining Ottoman rights were rejected specifically or by omission.

The agreement reserved almost complete autonomy to the governor-general, ratification of whose appointment was assured by the British occupation of Egypt. Supreme military and civil authority in the Sudan was vested in him. Every governor-general from 1899 until independence was a British subject presiding over 'the Sudan Government'. Although condominium status temporarily placated Egyptian opinion, it became increasingly a bone of contention with Britain, especially after the First World War. British officials of the Sudan Government itself soon came to view 'condominium' as a lever by which Britain could put pressure on Egypt, sometimes to the detriment of the Sudanese.

The first governor-general appointed under the agreement was Lord Kitchener in 1899. His brief tenure was unsuccessful: a soldier rather than an administrator, Kitchener alienated his subordinates and neglected the plight of the exhausted civilian population. His departure left the tasks of pacification and rebuilding to his successor, Reginald Wingate, who had been in charge of the Egyptian Army's military intelligence department since 1887, and was to remain governor-general until 1917.

The first priority of the new régime was to eliminate popular resistance. The battle of Karari had destroyed the Mahdist state, but the Khalifa 'Abdallahi remained at large with a sizeable force. In November 1899 Wingate, not yet governor-general, defeated the Mahdists in battle at Umm Diwaykarat in southern Kordofan. 'Abdallahi and the Khalifa 'Ali were killed, and 'Uthman Shaykh al-Din was taken prisoner; 'Uthman Diqna escaped but was captured later and died a prisoner at Wadi Halfa in 1926.

The final defeat of organized resistance did not destroy the cult of the Mahdi. Despite the deaths of the Khalifa Muhammad Sharif and the two eldest sons of the Mahdi at Shukkaba in 1899,[4] religious pretenders arose from time to time. Some eschatological traditions anticipated the appearance, after the Mahdi, of al-Dajjal, the Anti-Christ, who would herald the second coming of the Prophet Jesus. In an atmosphere of expectancy and social upheaval there were many claimants to the title, but none won much support and all were dealt with harshly. Despite their insignificance, as viewed today, such risings influenced government policy.

Pacification of the southern provinces was hampered by poor communications and lack of staff and funds. The *sudd*, accumulated vegetation rendering the rivers impassable, had to be cleared. The Bahr al-Jabal was opened up in 1904; the Bahr al-Ghazal required regular expeditions that were facilitated after the First World War by mechanical dredgers. Despite improved navigation, the government was able only slowly to bring the vast region and its heterogeneous population under control. Posts were established, but military patrols as a means of bringing the hinterland under control were abandoned only when it was realized that these alienated as well as subdued, and were in any case expensive and without lasting results.

Indicative of the comprehensive task facing the government was the need to delimit the Sudan's international boundaries. Cromer in 1899 was careful not to define the Condominium as encompassing all the territory formerly belonging to Egypt. The Nile–Congo watershed was accepted in March 1899 as the line of demarcation between French and British control. North of this lay the sultanate of Darfur, autonomous once again, but tributary to Khartoum. The boundary with Eritrea was fixed between 1898 and 1902. An Anglo-Abyssinian Treaty in 1902 determined a frontier where, as in the past, there would still be constant trouble. The boundary with the Congo Free State was set in 1906; the Lado Enclave, leased for life to King Leopold II, reverted on his death in 1910 to the Sudan. The Uganda border was established in 1913; in 1914 the Sudan exchanged land on the Upper Nile for part of the former Enclave.

Under Wingate the administrative structure of the Condominium was erected on a basis of Turco-Egyptian and Mahdist precedents, British experience in Egypt and India and methods adopted through trial and error for the circumstances of the Sudan.

Dominating the administration was the governor-general who, as commander-in-chief of the Egyptian Army (until 1924 when the positions were separated) combined absolute civil and military authority. In theory responsible to the co-domini, he reported through the British representative in Cairo to the Foreign Office in London. Combined with the powers granted in the Condominium Agreement, this arrangement gave him more freedom than a colonial governor. Policy had a trilateral aspect, however, when officials in Khartoum, Cairo and London had different interests, but occupation of Egypt rendered debate intra-mural; British imperial interests and relations between the governor-general and British officials in Cairo trumped the technicalities of condominium. In practice, control by Cromer and his successors was limited to questions affecting Anglo-Egyptian relations, and decreased over time.

The Sudan Government was not therefore independent. It was bound by *Regulations for the Financial Administration of the Sudan* appended to the Condominium Agreement, by which the annual budget had to be approved by the Egyptian Council of Ministers, and by subsequent financial arrangements. The political necessity of low taxation required that funds be obtained to offset deficits. These funds came from the Egyptian Treasury until 1913, when the budget balanced, but the Sudan continued to depend on Egypt in two important ways: capital already invested, on which no interest was paid; and maintenance of an Egyptian army in the Sudan. To Egyptian objections that financial support should entail political control, the British replied that subsidies were long-term investments, and that the quiescence of her southern border more than adequately compensated Egypt for maintaining the army.

The Sudan Government's structure superficially resembled that of a British colony. Its Financial Secretary had great latitude, and a Legal Secretary framed the laws and ordinances and supervised the courts: in the early days both officials were superintended from Cairo. Eventually the most important official was the Civil Secretary, who headed the civil service and liaised with the provinces. In 1909 a Governor-General's Council of high officials was established, but during Wingate's term it had no independent influence.

Rudolf Slatin held a unique position. After escaping from Omdurman in 1895 he had helped to plan the Anglo-Egyptian invasion. Wingate created for him the office of Inspector-General; an Austrian, he resigned at the outbreak of the First World War. His nebulous bailiwick encompassed tribal and religious affairs; intimacy with Wingate made him important. His highly personal methods survived his departure, to the detriment of the Intelligence Department during episodes of revolt in the 1920s.

The country was divided into provinces, the number and boundaries of which were altered through the years. Each had a governor (*mudir*) responsible to the governor-general through the departments. Each provincial district (*markaz*) had a British inspector (*mufattish*), who from 1922 was called district commissioner. Each sub-district had a *mamur*, a post usually held by an Egyptian, though educated Sudanese were gradually introduced as sub-*mamurs* (from 1915) and *mamurs* shortly thereafter. Thus the administration was British in the higher ranks, and Egyptian and Sudanese in the lower.

The first three governors-general were all soldiers, and the first generation of British officials was drawn mainly from officers of the Egyptian army. The case for soldier-administrators was strongest in the South, where they were often employed on a contract basis. In the North, however, it was early felt by Cromer that a separate service was needed. Civilians were recruited as early as 1901, and in 1905 a system was established by which British university graduates with, in Cromer's words, 'good health, high character and fair abilities' were brought out. These became known as the Sudan Political Service.

The Political Service was an élite both isolated from the practice of administration elsewhere and largely immune to outside criticism. Independence of action, local authority and a paternal attitude created an image of 'father of the people', especially in the South, that was balanced by incorruptibility. Paternalism was more amenable to petitions than to demands, to tribal instincts than to individualism. A government, in the words of a British newspaper, of 'athletic public school boys accustomed to hard work rather than to hard thinking', embodied what Cromer had envisaged. After the First World War, however, the Service was ill-equipped to deal with changing political circumstances and the need for social and economic development.

That paternalism was so soon questioned was the result in part of limited educational advance. In the words of James Currie, the first Director of Education, a system was required to enable the masses 'to understand the elements of the system of government', to train 'a small class of competent artisans' and 'to produce a small administrative class for entry to the government service'. Thus to some officials 'over-education' posed a greater threat than no education. The opening in 1902 of the Gordon Memorial College, for which subscriptions had been raised in Britain, provided the venue for the first intermediate and secondary schools. The overall system was highly selective, biased in favour of notable families, and reflected the needs of government departments and the prevailing administrative policy.

Religious policy was determined largely by considerations of political security. Mahdism was suppressed: the Mahdi's *Ratib*, a devotional work, was proscribed; surviving members of the Mahdist hierarchy remained in prison or under watch, a policy justified by petty religious risings. The *tariqas*, long expressive of Sudanese Islam, were denied official recognition; the Khatmiyya's hereditary leaders, the Mirghani family, were an exception in consequence of a long record of loyalty. To combat heterodoxy, Wingate created in 1901 a Board of Ulema from the re-established hierarchy of orthodox-cult officials, the *mufti*, grand *qadi* and other notables. The government supported mosque construction, facilitated the pilgrimage and encouraged *kuttabs* in which the Qur'an was taught. Risking controversy in Britain, it strongly opposed Christian missionary activity in the Northern Sudan.

Concern for Muslim opinion also informed judicial policy. The *Sudan Penal Code* and *Code of Criminal Procedure* were based on Indian models. But matters of personal status came under the jurisdiction of the Sharī'a, administered by Muslim courts supervised by the grand *qadi*. *The Mohammedan Law Courts Ordinance and Procedure Regulations* of 1915 interestingly allowed him discretion to depart from Hanafi practice, and resulted in a reform of family law, pre-dating that in Egypt, in accordance with the modernizing views of 'Abduh and Qasim Amin.[5] The force of tribal law was also recognized as necessary and expedient, especially with reference to the lightly administered and far-flung nomad population.

Obsessed with the danger posed by 'fanatical' Islam, the régime sought to exclude Muslim influence from the southern provinces. Christian missionary organizations, frustrated in the north, were allotted spheres for proselytization, and education, in English, was entrusted to them. Efforts were made to discourage the use of Arabic and even 'Arab' dress. An Equatorial Corps was recruited in Mongalla province, and other territorial companies were soon added, while regular army units were removed. British officials tried to keep out the Muslim *jallaba* merchants. Some have discerned in these steps a policy to separate the south from the Sudan. In these early years, however, there was no such coordinated policy; local expediency rather than imperialist design is the recurring theme.

Wingate's governor-generalship witnessed steady growth of the Sudan's economy (from an admittedly poor baseline). A cardinal principal of economic policy was light taxation. Familiar systems were largely retained. A land tax and '*ushur* (a percentage of crop value), date tax and herd tax were levied on the settled population, and were frequently paid in kind. A herd tax levied on nomads was replaced in 1901 with communal 'tribute'. Assessment and collection were difficult; recognition of government authority was often the goal. Property taxes, market dues and tolls were also introduced. The major burden of taxation fell inevitably on the settled agricultural population. Revenue and expenditure increased respectively from about £E157,000 and £E332,000 in 1900 to £E1.65m and £E1.61m in 1913, when the Egyptian subvention ended.

By then Egypt had advanced some £E5.35m to cover the Sudan's budget deficits, and loaned, without interest, about £E5.365m for development projects. The railway built to facilitate the Anglo-Egyptian conquest was adapted for civilian use and extended to the Blue Nile, opposite Khartoum, in 1899. A spur from the Nile to the Red Sea was opened in 1906, terminating at Port Sudan, which replaced the bottlenecked port of Suakin. Railhead reached Sennar in 1909 and El Obeid in 1911. These extensions resulted in establishment of such important towns as Khartoum North, Atbara and Kosti, whence steamer service connected the North with the Southern Sudan. Road construction lagged far behind.

Development of agriculture was hindered by a chronic labour shortage. The government's policy towards the emotive issue of slavery came to reflect the potential consequences of this shortage. The Condominium Agreement explicitly prohibited the slave trade. In one respect the new government was more fortunately placed than Khedive Isma'il and Gordon had been in the 1870s: contrary to assertions still sometimes uncritically retailed, the trade seems to have declined sharply during the Mahdia. Its previous expansion had been, as we have seen, a corollary of the penetration of the Upper Nile and Bahr al-Ghazal, but these areas which, with the Nuba Mountains, had been principal hunting-grounds for slaves in the Turco-Egyptian period, had been virtually outside the range of Mahdist control during the reign of the Khalifa. The closing of slave markets in areas under Ottoman or British control was another factor in decline of the slave trade.

Domestic slavery, however, was subject to different considerations during the early years of the Condominium. Agricultural production was adversely affected by high wages paid to casual labourers at government construction sites, since cultivators left the land. Various recruitment schemes and wage controls had little success. West African pilgrims and other immigrants were encouraged to settle. Fearing the political and economic effects of sudden emancipation, the government acted only gradually to eradicate domestic slavery; even the trading of slaves, especially along the Ethiopian border, continued well into the 1920s.

Of the development projects undertaken during the Wingate era, the most ambitious and significant was the scheme to irrigate the Gezira for production of cotton. Experimental planting began as early as 1900. But the Gezira's potential could be realized only by a vast irrigation project, which received initial funding when Britain guaranteed a loan of £3m in 1913. The Gezira Scheme had to be postponed until the conclusion of the First World War, when it, like many aspects of Sudan Government policy, became embroiled in the increasingly hostile relationship of the co-domini.

CHAPTER NINE

Revolt and Reaction: 1914–36

The Sudan played no direct part in the First World War, yet the effects of the war were considerable in economic and political terms, and were felt also in the evolution of administrative policy. A campaign in 1916 against the autonomous sultanate of Darfur had its origins in deteriorating relations prior to the war, and in Anglo-French rivalry. 'Ali Dinar had ruled his ancestral kingdom since the overthrow of the Mahdist state, but increasingly felt the pressure of French expansion to the west. In 1909 the French conquered Wadai, and in 1911 seized part of Dar Masalit. These annexations worried Khartoum; there had been no delimitation between French and British controlled territories. With the Anglo-French alliance in the First World War, and Ottoman entry on the side of the Central Powers, 'Ali Dinar's posture towards the British became more belligerent. Although Wingate had decided as early as August 1915 to move against him, a pretext was manufactured only in February 1916.[1]

A force of between two and three thousand troops, supported by three aeroplanes, was concentrated in Kordofan and advanced with difficulty, owing to the heat and shortage of water, to within twelve miles of El Fasher, which was occupied on 23 May 1916 after a battle. 'Ali Dinar escaped, but on 6 November was ambushed and killed. An agreement with the French was reached in 1919 whereby Dar Masalit remained part of Darfur, and the sultanates of Tama and Sila came under French control. The frontier was finally delimited in 1924.

Of more concern to Britain at the outbreak of the First World War had been Muslim reaction to the Ottoman alliance with her enemies. The Sudan Government abandoned its hostile policy towards the Ansar and *tariqas*, and an attempt was made to influence the population through their leaders. The restrictions on 'Abd al-Rahman, the Mahdi's son, were relieved, and he toured areas of traditional Mahdist strength urging loyalty to the government. The apparent success of this collaboration indicated also Ansar acquiescence in the sayyid's leadership, and marked the beginning of 'Abd al-Rahman's rise to prominence. The ensuing sectarian rivalry had unforeseen political consequences. A more significant factor in ensuring loyalty was the war's positive economic effect. The demands of the British military in Egypt fuelled an increase in the value of external trade from about £E3m in 1914 to some £E6.9m in 1919; government revenue increased from £E1.86m in 1916 to £E4.4m in 1920. Inflation was offset by a rapid rise in wages, and demand for luxury goods evidenced a general prosperity.

The conquest of Darfur was the last major event of Wingate's long and important governor-generalship. In December 1916 he became British high commissioner for Egypt. He was succeeded by the Civil Secretary, Lee Stack, whose term witnessed increasing tension between the co-domini and the first stirrings of a Sudanese nationalist movement.

Flaws in the Sudan's improvisational condominium status became increasingly evident after the war, when the full force of Egyptian nationalism erupted. Egyptian sympathy for the Allies had been dissipated by material hardships during the war, and British declaration of a protectorate over Egypt in 1914 had been explained as a step towards independence at the war's conclusion. Expectancy was heightened by the announced Anglo-French intentions towards the Ottoman Empire's Arab possessions and by President Wilson's Fourteen Points. When it became clear that Britain planned no substantial alteration of Egypt's status, violent disturbances in 1919 brought matters to a head. Order was restored, but the British object of maintaining control and the nationalists' demand for independence were incompatible, and a series of abortive negotiations only hardened positions. In February 1922 the British government issued a declaration of Egypt's independence that reserved for settlement in future negotiations four fundamental issues, one of which was the Sudan.

The Egyptian revolution and subsequent negotiations reinforced Britain's strategic interest in the Sudan. Lest nationalism infect the Sudanese it was considered imperative to remove as many as possible of the Egyptians serving there. This would require creation of an all-Sudanese army, involving costs the Sudan Government was unable to incur and Britain refused to assume. In 1920 the British foreign secretary suggested that Egypt should bear the cost, as payment 'for the water she enjoys': 'the ulterior motive which British interests demand' was 'complete political and military independence' of the Sudan from Egypt. To replace Egyptian civilians, 'a system like that prevailing in Northern Nigeria' was adumbrated rather than one depending on 'an effendi class'[2] of educated Sudanese susceptible to influences dissonant with British interests. The 'system' referred to was Indirect Rule, under which administrative and judicial functions would be extended to traditional tribal authorities. The appeal of Indirect Rule was enhanced by the appearance of vague but real indications of Sudanese 'national' feelings.

There was little overt Sudanese sympathy for the Egyptian revolution. Indeed Stack argued that a 'spirit of national consciousness' might be expected to express itself as desirous of ending Egyptian participation in Sudanese affairs. But the first of a series of political organizations to appear after the war, the League of Sudan Union, in 1920, was decidedly anti-British. In 1922 an ex-army officer of Dinka origin, 'Ali 'Abd al-Latif, was imprisoned for submitting to the *Hadara* newspaper an article calling for 'self-determination for the Sudanese'. By the time of his release in 1923 he had become a celebrity. With several associates, drawn, significantly, from the ranks of government employees, he founded the White Flag League, apparently with Egyptian encouragement and financial backing. Its ostensible aim was the political 'unity of the Nile Valley'. British authorities characterized 'Ali 'Abd al-Latif and his ilk as dupes of Egyptian politicians; to legitimize discordant political views would weaken the British position *vis-à-vis* Egypt. It was easier, though unrealistic, to tar with one brush any critics of the régime.

Yet a distinction could have been drawn. The shadowy 'leagues' and 'unions' had very limited appeal, and were composed mainly of ex-NCOs and clerks, and prominently of Muslim Southerners. They had no tribal basis and lacked mass support. Less obtrusive but far more important were government officials, officers and merchants, of higher social origins, who were unwilling to place their future unrestrictedly in British hands. Although supporting continuation of the Condominium, they wanted a definite plan for eventual independence of the Sudan. Their concern had grown with the government's efforts to regulate and extend the authority of tribal shaykhs in 1922. They feared that precipitate British reaction to Egyptian intrigues and the White Flag League would thwart the aspirations of educated, law-abiding Sudanese in the government service. The moderates, however, were soon isolated by events.

British authorities were not alone in fearing secular opposition. The outbreak of the Egyptian revolution enhanced the potential role of religious leaders. A delegation of Sudanese notables, led by 'Ali al-Mirghani of the Khatmiyya, sent to London in 1919 ostensibly to congratulate King George v for winning the war, associated the traditional Sudanese leadership with the British as against Egyptian 'pretensions'. The delegation included 'Abd al-Rahman al-Mahdi, whose influence continued to grow thereafter, especially among the tribes of the western Sudan. Acrimonious debate over how to deal with this 'recrudescence' of Mahdism produced no definite policy, and the consequent 'drift' embittered relations. In 1921 an attack by disgruntled tribesmen on the government post at Nyala in Darfur was blamed on his agents. To reimpose restrictions risked alienating 'Abd al-Rahman's large and volatile following; to do nothing risked making him irresistible. The government's dilemma was clarified in 1924, when the White Flag League agitators threatened not only British dominance, but also the established religious and tribal order, which took the opportunity to strengthen its position, to dispose of discordant upstarts, and to place the government in its debt. By rallying to the British, the tribal and religious leaders, including 'Abd al-Rahman, precluded the possibility of mass support in defence of the Egyptian co-dominus.

Anglo-Egyptian relations had meanwhile been deteriorating. The framing of Egypt's constitution in 1923 occasioned a crisis when Britain prohibited reference to the king of Egypt[3] as 'sovereign of the Sudan'. In January 1924 the first parliamentary elections were swept by the nationalist Wafd under Sa'd

Zaghlul. In September he went to London for negotiations, in which the Sudan Government played a decisive part. Stack and the financial secretary, George Schuster, argued forcefully against any outcome involving a continued Egyptian role in the Sudan's administration.

Events in the Sudan added weight to their manoeuvres. Throughout the spring and summer anti-British demonstrations occurred with alarming frequency and increasing seriousness. In July 'Ali 'Abd al-Latif was arrested again and imprisoned. In August a revolt by an Egyptian battalion at Atbara was put down by British troops. Simultaneously cadets of the Military School in Khartoum marched through the streets; their leaders were jailed. The Sudan Government, fearful of being 'sold out' in London, insisted that any compromise would be fatal to British authority in Khartoum. As negotiations with Zaghlul deadlocked, the British government came to agree. What was needed, in Stack's words, was an 'excuse for drastic action'.

The excuse was provided on 19 November when Stack was assassinated in Cairo. Allenby, the high commissioner, without London's approval issued an ultimatum, requiring immediate evacuation of Egyptian army units from the Sudan and announcing an increase in the area to be irrigated in the Gezira to 'an unlimited figure as need may arise'. Although London later disavowed this second provision, it made clear how far the British might go to maintain their position in the Sudan, and made painfully obvious the vulnerability of Egypt's vital Nile waters. Zaghlul resigned, and evacuation of the Egyptian troops, meticulously planned well in advance, went ahead.

The evacuation was not carried out without incident. Egyptian units stationed in Khartoum North refused to entrain without direct orders from Cairo, and these were arranged. Meanwhile elements of the XIth Sudanese battalion marched through the streets of Khartoum, determined to join the Egyptians as, in their view, their oath of allegiance to the Egyptian king demanded. A British force opposed them, and after twice refusing orders the Sudanese were fired upon. They took refuge in the military hospital, where they were bombarded by British artillery, and fought to the last man. The remaining Egyptian troops were evacuated, and three Sudanese officers were later executed for their part in the revolt.

The tension building up since 1919 was at last relieved. Egyptian troops were forcibly removed, and Egyptian civilian officials would follow soon. The form of the Condominium was retained as an inducement to Egyptian co-operation; a Sudan Defence Force, consisting solely of Sudanese troops and financed by an Egyptian subvention, was established under a British commander, and the sirdarship and governor-generalship were finally separated. Complex political alignments of recent years were clarified: the few radicals all but disappeared, the traditional élite emerged triumphant, and educated moderates, tainted by association and made irrelevant by inability to influence events, were increasingly isolated.

The statutory beginnings of Indirect Rule, in the form of the *Powers of Nomad Sheikhs Ordinance* (1922), had within a year regularized the traditional judicial functions of about three hundred tribal shaykhs. But Stack had considered this only one aspect of a comprehensive devolution, necessitated as much by financial circumstances as administrative policy, another part of which was promotion of educated Sudanese to ever more responsible posts. *The Khartoum, Khartoum North and Omdurman Council Proclamation* of 1921 had established a 'consultative and advisory' body to discuss urban affairs, and Stack had envisaged similar councils at the district, provincial and central levels. This balanced policy died with him, as evidenced by a statement by John Maffey when he became governor-general in 1927:

> Advisory Councils cropped up as a possible means to our end. . . . Later on in certain intelligentsia areas, when we have made the Sudan safe for autocracy, such Councils would be in keeping with the broad principle. Otherwise Advisory Councils contain the seeds of grave danger and eventually present a free platform for capture by a pushful intelligensia.[4]

Indirect Rule required tribal cohesion and strong leadership. The centralizing impact of the Turco-Egyptian and Mahdist régimes, and of the direct methods employed since the Anglo-Egyptian conquest had, however, been antithetical to both prerequisites. The government was undeterred. Currie, the former director of education, after a visit to the Sudan, described the 'spectacle' of administrators searching for 'lost tribes and vanished chiefs', a criticism he later put more bluntly:

> The time has long passed when it was possible to gull the Native demanding equality of economic opportunity with patter about indirect rule, or fob him off with a social scheme in which a subsidized ruler – too frequently an obsolete antiquity – dances to the pipes of young gentlemen whose sole idea is that things shall 'stay put'. They cannot, by a hard fate, be squires in England, but to ape the part in Africa is fascinating.[5]

The principal architects of Indirect Rule were Maffey, whose views were based on Indian experience, and Harold MacMichael who, by dominating the civil secretary's department from 1919 to 1934, was the resident dean of administrative policy. In 1927 the *Powers of Sheikhs Ordinance* extended the authority, previously recognized in nomadic tribes, to the sedentary population, thus impinging on the jurisdiction of territorially based officials.

Fear of *effendiyya* was also reflected in education policy, which was radically altered by dogmatic subservience to Indirect Rule. Education had created a discontented class of de-tribalized individuals who, in 1924, had bitten the hand that fed them. In 1927 the governor of Darfur put the case this way:

> It may be argued that the progress of education and general enlightenment is merely bringing about natural evolution, and that the present individualism is but a step or phase in the process. Such an argument is . . . not only fallacious but dangerous. Tribal customs and organizations have been evolved through the ages; they have enabled tribes to survive as entities the stress of war and civil

commotion; these customs and traditions are . . . cherished and obeyed to a degree which is almost incredible by such tribes as remain today uncontaminated by modern progress.[6]

Native *khalwas* were increasingly substituted for government *kuttabs*.[7] There were six subsidized *khalwas* in 1918, and seven hundred and sixty-eight in 1930. In 1920 there had been eighty elementary schools; not another was opened in the North before 1929. Expenditure on education fell from a high of 3.9 per cent of the budget in 1915 to 1.9 per cent in 1926. The Military School in Khartoum was closed, as was the small school for training Sudanese sub-*mamurs*.

Adoption of Indirect Rule had an even greater significance in the Southern Sudan. We have seen that the régime had from the start sought to limit the spread of Islam there. After the war this objective, reinvigorated with the dogmatic dictates of Indirect Rule, was pursued with greater urgency. A Southern governors' meeting in 1922 proposed leaving administration 'in the hands of native authorities . . . under British supervision'; where tribal organization no longer existed, it might 'still be possible to re-create it'. Under provisions of the *Passports and Permits Ordinance* (1922), the South was classified as 'closed districts', in order to keep *jallaba* ('peddlers') out and keep Southerners in. Beginning in 1922, chiefs' courts (*lukikos*) were established under the guidance of British officials. Exclusion of Northerners and the requirements of Indirect Rule were administrative aspects of what would later be 'Southern Policy'; an equally important element was education, which had been left to missionary societies. From 1926 grants-in-aid were made to their schools. A conference at Rejaf in 1928 led to selection of six languages of instruction, and textbooks were as a result prepared. English was promoted as a lingua franca and necessary for advancement in government service; Arabic, and even common Arabic terms, were to be discouraged. Whereas in 1926 only four elementary boys' schools employed vernacular instruction, by 1930 there were thirty-two, and intermediate schools using English increased from one, with thirty-five students, to three, with one hundred and seventy-seven.

The combination of 'closed districts', Indirect Rule and education policy broadened the differences between North and South, and entailed both separate development and particularism. As in the North, the aim of policy was cessation or reversal of trends towards homogeneity. Critics have discerned in British policy as early as 1919 a design for eventual political independence of the South. A document prepared for the Milner mission in 1920 suggested that 'the possibility of the Southern (black) portion of the Soudan being . . . linked up with some central African system' was 'borne in mind'. But this and subsequent similar remarks were flippant and were neither reflected in, nor influential on, the development of administrative policy.

The mid-1920s were years of prosperity for the Sudan. The Gezira Scheme, which opened in 1926, had been postponed by the war and jeopardized by huge cost overruns, but the British government had rescued it by guaranteeing loans of almost £15m. In 1920 Allenby, to ease Egyptian fears, had agreed to limit the project to irrigation of 300,000 *feddans*, a figure that, by 1924, would have entailed recurrent loss; it was to this problem that the Gezira clause of his 1924 ultimatum to Egypt was addressed. In the aftermath of that crisis the Anglo-Egyptian Nile Waters Agreement (1929) imposed a system by which consumption rather than acreage to be irrigated determined Egypt's and the Sudan's shares.

The Gezira Scheme, a massive experiment in co-operative farming, essentially had three partners: the government, which would get 40 per cent of profits, the Sudan Plantations Syndicate (20 per cent) and the tenant farmers who worked the land (40 per cent). Of a forty-*feddan* tenancy, ten *feddans* were devoted to cotton, five each to millet and fodder and twenty left fallow. Marketing the cotton crop was the responsibility of the syndicate. As a result of the 1929 agreement with Egypt, the irrigated area was increased to over 500,000 *feddans*. The scheme served as a model for agricultural developments.

Other cotton-growing schemes begun before the First World War in the Gash and Baraka deltas of the eastern Sudan were developed after the war. The Gash Scheme (organized on a tripartite basis similar to that in the Gezira) was conceded to the Kassala Cotton Company, which was linked financially with the Sudan Plantations Syndicate. Cotton production in the Gash region led to construction of a railway between Kasala and Port Sudan. This was later extended to Sennar, so that by 1929 the Gezira was directly linked to the Red Sea coast.

The years of the Great Depression were particularly difficult for the Sudan. The danger of over-reliance on a single cash crop, cotton, was made obvious when simultaneously world demand slumped and local production collapsed owing to a series of crop diseases and locust invasions. Government revenue fell from about £E7m in 1929 to £E3.65m in 1932; a substantial percentage of revenue was committed to servicing the Gezira debt. Retrenchment was inevitable, as were complaints from those upon whom this seemed to fall with greatest severity. In 1931 the starting salaries of 'graduates'[8] in government employ were cut by 30 per cent. Those affected saw in this a further deliberate blow to their class, and a strike by Gordon College students ended in compromise.

Despite tensions during the Depression, the decade following the troubles of 1924 was politically quiet. The shock of 1924 and the consequent rush towards Indirect Rule isolated the politically active educated class. British settlement of the crisis had removed the Egyptian factor from Sudan politics, further obviating the necessity to the government of the educated class's allegiance. Although nominal condominium remained, there seemed little possibility that Egypt would again have an active role in the Sudan. The new mood was exhibited in study groups and literary societies stressing education and political sophistication as requisites for progress. Newspapers, usually short-lived, ventilated views and buoyed the confidence of the educated class; the most influential was *al-Fajr* (*The Dawn*), published between 1934 and 1937. Easing of government censorship in 1935 allowed more open expression of opinion, and educational and administrative policies, especially Indirect Rule, were attacked. The Sudanese attitude towards Egypt remained uncertain. Apparent surrender to the British in 1924, and its consequences, coupled with the Nile Waters Agreement of 1929, which took no notice of Sudanese opinion and awarded the lion's share of water to Egypt, caused great disillusionment. Yet Egypt was the only potential ally of a beleaguered nationalist cause that saw in the idea of 'the Sudan for the Sudanese' a free pass for British hegemony.

A rapidly changing international situation, culminating in the Italian invasion of Abyssinia in 1935, created a coincidence of Anglo-Egyptian interests with far-reaching consequences for the Sudan. In 1936 a treaty of alliance between the two countries secured British strategic aims in Egypt. The status of the Sudan remained unchanged. Egyptian troops, barred since 1924, would again be 'placed at the disposal' of the governor-general, and Egyptian immigration would be unlimited 'except for reasons of public order and health'. The two governments pledged that 'the primary aim of their administration in the Sudan must be the welfare of the Sudanese', who had again, however, not been consulted in the negotiations.

The treaty was poorly received in the Sudan. British officials feared that revived Egyptian influence might lead to another crisis like that of 1924. Intellectuals felt betrayed by Egyptian eagerness to participate more fully in the existing administration. Retention of condominium status seemed regressively to allow a future assertion of Egyptian sovereignty. The result of these misgivings was determination, on the part of the educated class, to make self-reliance the rule; and, on the government's part, actively to compete again for their allegiance.

CHAPTER TEN

The Development of Sudanese Nationalism: 1937–52

The appointment of Stewart Symes to the governor-generalship in 1934 heralded a change in attitude towards the educated class and administrative policy generally. Symes had served under Wingate, and was a man of definite views. While praising benefits of Indirect Rule, he executed reforms to develop 'an administration working first and foremost in collaboration not with tribal authorities but with the Sudanese intelligentsia'. As the reaction in the post-1924 era had been felt primarily in educational and administrative policy, so in the mid-1930s those areas witnessed the most wide-ranging reforms.

A committee to inquire into the Gordon College strike of 1931 extended its terms of reference to the lower levels of education. One recommendation was to transfer the Training College for elementary teachers from Khartoum to a rural area. The new principal, V.L. Griffiths, hoped that a fresh start, in surroundings similar to those where teachers would work, would develop initiative and a sense of professionalism. The college at Bakht er Ruda, in open country near Dueim, became the Institute of Education; it took on a major reform of teaching methods and produced a large number of textbooks. General reform of intermediate education, undertaken in 1939, was hampered by staff shortages and other exigencies of the Second World War; teachers tended to see greater opportunity in other levels of education and indeed other branches of government service.

To the law school established in Khartoum in 1931 were added, in 1936, schools of engineering, veterinary science and agriculture, so that positions in the government's technical departments might increasingly be filled by Sudanese. These were merged into a single institution, to which the name of the Gordon Memorial College was transferred in 1945. The new college combined with the Kitchener School of Medicine in 1951 to form the University College of Khartoum, affiliated with the University of London, and became, shortly after independence, Khartoum University.

Important administrative reforms reflected an underlying change in attitude. Indirect Rule (by the 1930s called 'Native Administration') would give way to 'local government', the basis of which in all but the most remote nomadic areas would be territorial, not tribal: a return in theory to the position of 1922. The three *Local Government Ordinances* of 1937 reformed the administration of municipalities, townships and rural areas; in the cities and towns, existing laws were consolidated. The process of reform led eventually to a comprehensive *Local Government Ordinance* in 1951.

Abandonment of dogmatic adherence to Indirect Rule, while born of a recognition of its defects, was accelerated by domestic political consequences of the 1936 Anglo-Egyptian Treaty. Whereas the educated class – nearly identical to the class of minor Sudanese officials – had been left in the wilderness after 1924, revived condominium reopened the rivalry of the co-domini for Sudanese allegiance. Past disappointments with Egypt, and ignominious conclusion of the treaty without reference to Sudanese opinion, were factors in the founding in 1938, notably with British encouragement, of the Graduates' General Congress. Most of its members were former pupils in post-elementary schools, and the government saw in them the successors of the moderates of 1924, not of pro-Egyptian radicals, and thus a potential bulwark against the influence of both Egypt and 'Abd al-Rahman al-Mahdi. The first general secretary was Isma'il al-Azhari, a descendant of a family of religious notables and a mathematics teacher at the Gordon College, who had studied at the American University of Beirut. In a letter to the government, Azhari included among the Congress's concerns 'matters of public interest involving the Government or lying within the scope of its policy', admitted that 'most of us are Government officials and are fully conscious of our obligations as such', but claimed also 'duties' as 'the only educated element in this country'.

That the government misjudged both the Congress's willingness to stay out of politics and its ability to forge a strong secular movement from the educated class became clear after the outbreak of the Second World War, in which the Sudan was directly involved. Kasala was occupied by the Italians for a few months in 1940, and afterwards an army of British, Indian and Sudanese troops, under General Platt, invaded Eritrea and won the decisive battle of Keren on 15 March 1941. This ended the danger on the Sudanese border, but a greater danger remained in the North, until Montgomery's victory at El Alamein in November 1942 destroyed the prospect of a German occupation of the Nile Valley.

During the war there was less concern over the loyalties of the Sudanese than in 1914–18, but British prejudices and fears were revived by the Congress's attempt to exploit for political gain the government's preoccupation. In April 1942, opponents of Abd al-Rahman al-Mahdi, led by Azhari, pressured the Congress executive to issue to the government a memorandum of demands obviously and provocatively beyond the limits to the Congress's activities that had been tacitly agreed. The primary demand was for

> the issue, on the first possible opportunity, by the British and Egyptian governments, of a joint declaration granting the Sudan, in its geographical boundaries, the right of self-determination, directly after this war; this right to be safeguarded by guarantees assuring full liberty of expression in connection

therewith; as well as guarantees assuring the Sudanese the right of determining their natural rights with Egypt in a special agreement between the Egyptian and Sudanese nations.

The government's response was harsh and unyielding. By submission of the memorandum and its wording, the Civil Secretary wrote, the Congress had 'forfeited the confidence of Government', which the Congress could restore only by confining itself 'to the internal and domestic affairs of the Sudanese and [renouncing] any claim, real or implied, to be the mouthpiece of the whole country'. That the government should consider domestic politics of secondary concern, and expect the Congress to do the same, was only natural while the outcome of the war in North Africa was still in doubt, and the episode is more revealing of the Congress's factionalization than of a determined course of action. Following this confrontation, its constitution was amended at the instigation of Azhari's group, the Ashigga [*Ashiqqa*] (literally 'brothers by the same father and mother'), to expand its membership, and the Ashigga won the ensuing executive elections. Thus the potential value to the government of the Congress as a moderating force was lost, and further co-operation was eschewed.

In 1943 the Ashigga under Azhari emerged as the first genuine political party in the Sudan, favouring union with Egypt. In 1944 it gained the tacit support of 'Ali al-Mirghani, the head of the Khatmiyya, whose dynastic history was so closely bound up with that of Egyptian influence in the Sudan. Perturbed at the rapid rise of 'Abd al-Rahman al-Mahdi, whose family had in the past triumphed at the expense of his own, he feared establishment, with British support, of a Mahdist monarchy in the Sudan. Although Sayyid 'Ali stood ostentatiously aloof from politics he exerted great influence behind the scenes, and his followers were less restrained. Only in alliance with Egypt, however tactical, could they see a safeguard against revival of the Mahdist state. And only with the support of the Khatmiyya could Azhari, for his part, see any hope for the future of the narrowly based Ashigga.

As a response to this development, moderate supporters of 'Abd al-Rahman established in 1945 the *Umma*[1] under his patronage, a political party favouring complete independence of the Sudan. It might seem that a party claiming total independence would have more appeal than one advocating union with Egypt, but two considerations militated against the general acceptance of nationalism of the Umma type. First, its leaders were known to be prepared, as the Ashigga were not, to co-operate with the existing administration in the progressive realization of independence: hence it was easy to represent them as tools of British imperialism. Secondly, the patronage of Sayyid 'Abd al-Rahman made it difficult for non-Ansari moderates to separate the cause of complete independence from the personal ambitions of the Mahdi's son. Thus, as in 1924, the two wings of the politically minded class were broadly identified as favouring either an independent Sudan achieved with British co-operation ('the Sudan for the Sudanese'), or union with Egypt ('the unity of the Nile valley'). Events surrounding the factionalization of the Congress, which had shown promise as a secular body, illustrated the fundamental if much-deprecated fact that the sectarian leaders retained the keys to political strength.

The timing of the Congress memorandum of 1942 was unfortunate not only for the reasons already given, but because the government was then more than ever before amenable to suggestions of further associating the Sudanese in the administration of the country. The idea of provincial and central advisory councils, first mooted in the early twenties but lost in the flood-tide of Indirect Rule, had been revived by Newbold. The falling-out with the Congress after April 1942 hastened this development, as the government sought to create a body more broadly based than the Congress and thus able, it was hoped, to siphon its support. But the organ created by *The Advisory Council for the Northern Sudan Order* of 1943 was inevitably seen as a response to public pressure. The Advisory Council's president was the governor-general, its vice-president and effective leader the civil secretary. Twenty-eight ordinary members were provided for, eighteen from provincial councils (also established in 1943), and ten selected by the governor-general to represent social and economic interests. The Council met eight times between 1945 and 1948, when it ceased to exist.

While establishment of the Advisory Council was an attempt by the government to come to terms with Sudanese nationalism, it was severely criticized on several grounds. The Council was purely advisory. Its agenda and the length of its sessions and debates rested with the government. The provincial members were almost all tribal leaders, and the ten appointed by the governor-general were almost all government officials. Council debates, while focusing at times on important subjects, were denounced, against a background of rising political tension, as trivial and meaningless: the Council created an impression of government accountability but was really just a powerless debating society of yes-men and ignorant provincials. Moreover the Council encompassed only the Northern Sudan, which the government justified by the politically undeveloped state of the South and its lack of qualified representatives, but which Northerners suspected as foreshadowing separation. The Congress boycotted the Council, the representative quality of which was thus further dissipated.

With the end of the war the Sudan's status again became a serious irritant to Anglo-Egyptian relations. In November 1945 the governor-general, Hubert Huddleston, told the Advisory Council that its views and those of 'other representative bodies' would be solicited if the co-domini discussed the Sudan. In December Egypt formally requested renegotiation of the 1936 treaty, and the British agreed. For the first time it seemed that the Sudanese might influence the outcome of negotiations, provided the political parties could agree on a line of approach. Independent members of the Congress worked out a formula to reconcile the two nationalist groups, and in March 1946 an all-party Sudanese delegation went to Cairo. There the delegation broke up when the Egyptians insisted on recognition of the union of Egypt and the Sudan. The Umma and their allies went home, while the unionists, under Azhari, remained to receive from the Egyptians sole recognition as spokesmen of the Sudanese.

Negotiations between Isma'il Sidqi, the Egyptian prime minister, and Ernest Bevin, the British foreign secretary, went ahead in London. A draft treated the Sudan question in a separate protocol, which stated:

> The policy which the High Contracting Parties undertake to follow in the Sudan within the framework of unity between the Sudan and Egypt under the common Crown of Egypt, will have for its essential objective to secure the well-being of the Sudan . . . the development of self-government, and consequently the right to choose the future status of the Sudan. Until the High Contracting Parties, in full common agreement, realize the latter objective, after consultation with the Sudanese, the Agreement of 1899 will continue and Article 11 of the Treaty of 1936 . . . will remain in force.

This formula pleased no one. The governor-general threatened to quit, and after the British prime minister stated that 'no change in the existing administration of the Sudan is contemplated', Sidqi resigned. In January 1947 the British and Egyptians announced that negotiations had been broken off, and in July Egypt brought its case to the United Nations. In prolonged debate Egypt appeared to be arguing against a Sudanese right to self-determination, and the question was shelved. But the wording of the protocol had embarrassed the Sudan Government by exposing British willingness to 'sell out' the Sudan. The Umma threatened non-cooperation, and riots occurred involving supporters of the rival parties.

Anticipating events, the government had announced in April 1946 that it was 'aiming at a free independent Sudan which will be able as soon as independence has been achieved to define for itself its relations with Great Britain and Egypt'. A committee would plot ways to speed Sudanization, and a conference was called to recommend the 'next steps in associating the Sudanese more closely with the administration of their country'. Conferees were drawn from the government, the Advisory Council and pro-independence parties; the Graduates' Congress and other parties refused to take part. A first report, in March 1947, called for establishment of a legislative assembly, representing the whole country, to replace the Advisory Council, and an executive council, at least half of whose members should be Sudanese, to supplant the governor-general's council.

The unanimous recommendation that a legislative assembly should represent the whole country necessitated reconsideration of policy towards the South. We have seen that the Southern provinces had been dealt with separately since the Anglo-Egyptian conquest. The basis for a broad cultural unity, provided throughout the North by Islam and Arabic, was lacking in the South. Pacification and establishment of administration had been much more slowly accomplished than in the North, where the Sudan Government was heir to a well-rooted tradition of centralized government derived from its Turco-Egyptian and Mahdist predecessors. The backwardness of Southerners, as compared with riverain and urban Sudanese, impeded rapid integration of the two regions. Economic stringency had beset the government until the end of the First World War, and finance had been concentrated in the Gezira Scheme afterwards.

The post-1918 period saw continuation and refinement of this distinction, largely in response to Indirect Rule which, as in the North, appealed to British officials for practical, political and philosophical reasons. Indirect Rule should be inexpensive and require few trained personnel; would isolate the South from the dangerous nationalist currents appearing in the North; and would allow development of the South along its own lines, influenced by British and Christian ideals and safe from Muslim penetration. British administrators and Christian missionaries shared an interest in success, but the proprietary instincts of the British in administration, and of the missionaries with regard to education and to culture generally, were allowed too free a rein. Allotment of missionary 'spheres' transferred to Africa the anachronistic sectarian rivalries of Europe. Elimination of Northern administrative personnel and traders, and of the use of Arabic, artificially insulated the Southern peoples from forces with which, in a unified Sudanese state, they would eventually have to contend. If this period had been used to prepare the South for integration, criticism by Northern Sudanese and others would have been blunted and the future faced with more equanimity. But when, in the late 1940s, integration was in fact adopted hastily as government policy, it was far too late for a period of thoughtful transition. 'Southern Policy', which was but the most notable example of Indirect Rule, had succeeded in subsidiary aims but failed in its ultimate political application.

In June 1947, in response to recommendations of the administrative conference, James Robertson, who upon Newbold's death in 1944 had become civil secretary, held a conference at Juba to discuss the status of the South and its role in the proposed legislative assembly. The South, he stated, was 'inextricably bound for future development to the Middle East and Arabia and Northern Sudan', and its peoples should therefore 'be equipped to take their places in the future as socially and economically the equals of their partners of the Northern Sudan'. Ironically, the region's own leaders now argued for the newly abandoned 'Southern Policy', and for the slow and cautious advance of people who, they said, were not yet 'grown up'. Northern representatives responded that the best way to learn the art of government was to participate in it, while British provincial officials sought safeguards for the Southerners. A telling exchange concerned the slave trade, which the British had ended but memorialized, and Northerners unconvincingly condemned.

In July 1947 the recommendations of the administrative conference were accepted by the governor-general's council, which agreed that the consequent legislation should 'ensure the healthy and steady development of the Southern people'. No such 'safeguards' were explicit, however, in the draft ordinance submitted to the British and Egyptian governments. London accepted the draft which, despite Egyptian objections, was promulgated as the *Executive Council and Legislative Assembly Ordinance*. The governor-general's council was replaced by an executive council of twelve to eighteen members, at least half to be Sudanese. The assembly, which would choose its own leader, would consist of up to ten nominated members, thirteen Southerners and fifty-two Northerners, ten elected directly and forty-two indirectly. The executive council was responsible for initiating and proposing legislation. Private members' bills had to be submitted first to the executive council if they concerned defence, currency or 'the status of religious or racial minorities'. The governor-general retained a veto over all legislation. The assembly was barred from legislating on matters dealing with the ordinance itself, relations with the co-domini and with other foreign governments and the question of Sudanese nationality. Elections, boycotted by the unionists, took place on 15 November 1948. The Umma and its allies gained control of the assembly, which elected that party's secretary-general, 'Abdallah Khalil, its leader at the first session which opened on 15 December.

The impasse in Anglo-Egyptian relations ironically sped political developments in the Sudan. Pressure from the United States for an agreement that would safeguard Western interests in the Suez Canal stoked Umma fears that the British might 'sell' the Sudan in order to keep the Canal. The Umma therefore increased their demands for immediate self-government with a view towards early independence. Meanwhile a new political party, the National Front, which while unionist like the Ashigga favoured dominion status under the Egyptian crown, won support of Sayyid 'Ali and many of his followers. The British tried to persuade them to participate in the Legislative Assembly as a counter to the Umma, while the Umma itself sought Khatmiyya participation as a way of checking the extreme unionists. These attempts at conciliation failed. On 16 November 1950 Egypt declared its intention to abrogate the 1899 and 1936 Anglo-Egyptian Agreements. The Umma-dominated assembly in Khartoum thereupon passed a resolution requesting self-government in 1951. The close vote (thirty-nine to thirty-eight) allowed the governor-general instead to adopt a motion passed earlier to create a Constitutional Amendment Commission. Boycotted by the Ashigga and Khatmiyya but supported by the Umma, the commission of thirteen Sudanese chaired by a British expert convened on 29 March 1951.

On 8 October Egypt abrogated the 1899 agreement and the 1936 treaty and announced a constitution for the Sudan. Although this unilateral act was rejected by the British and all Sudanese parties except the Ashigga, it nonetheless threw open the long-standing sovereignty question. Arguing that the Sudan was now without a legal government, six members of the Constitutional Amendment Commission voted to replace the governor-general with an international body. The government thereupon dissolved the commission, but its British chairman issued a report based on the recommendations previously discussed. These formed the basis of the *Self-Government*

Statute which was enacted by the Legislative Assembly on 23 April 1952. This provided for an all-Sudanese cabinet responsible to a bicameral parliament: a chamber of deputies of eighty-one elected members, and a senate of fifty, twenty appointed by the governor-general and thirty elected by provincial colleges. The governor-general kept responsibility for the public service and external affairs, and a veto over legislation affecting the South. The sovereignty question was fudged by reference to the governor-general as the 'Supreme Constitutional Authority' in the Sudan. London approved the statute in October. Meanwhile the Egyptian government, which, having unilaterally dissolved the Condominium, could hardly approve or reject a proposal dealing with it, had attempted to reconcile Sudanese opinion by withdrawing its proposed constitution. This manoeuvre was rejected by the Umma and became irrelevant with the overthrow of King Faruq in July 1952.

Before turning to the final stage of the movement towards self-determination, we may summarize the main economic developments of this period. The economy continued to be firmly based upon agriculture, and depended on cotton as its major cash crop. In 1944 the government decided not to renew the Plantations Syndicate's concession to operate the Gezira Scheme when it expired in 1950. In 1949 an ordinance provided for a Gezira Board to assume management, with the share of profits previously allotted the syndicate to be channelled into research and social development in the Gezira. Sudanization of the inspecting and engineering staff, hitherto British, proceeded rapidly. Agricultural projects were undertaken in other areas. Experimental work on mechanized grain production began in 1945 on the Ghadambaliyya plains near Gedaref.

Cotton had been grown on a small scale since 1931 in the Zande district of Equatoria province. An ambitious project was conceived during the war by the director of agriculture and forests, J.D. Tothill, who had held a similar post in Uganda. 'An Experiment in the Social Emergence of Indigenous Races in Remote Regions', for which he chose Zande district, aimed at 'the complete social emergence and social and economic stability of the Zande people'. Financed by the central government and administered by an Equatoria Projects Board, the Zande Scheme improved communications and transport, and established a power station and oil, soap and cloth mills. By 1954, 175,000 acres were under cotton, with a yield of 6.37m pounds. Tothill's proposals were gradually and fundamentally altered, however, and the scheme never achieved his aims. Poor wages at first necessitated forced labour. Social dislocation resulted from implementation of the scheme; deterioration in relations between chiefs and people contributed to dissatisfaction. British administrators' paternalism, and local distrust of their Northern Sudanese successors, resulted in only modest success for a scheme that might have mitigated Southern fears at independence.[2]

The Second World War, like the First, was a boom period for the Sudan economy generally. The value of imports rose from £E8m in 1941 to £E42m in 1951, and exports from £E8.9m to £E62m, largely owing to the profitability of cotton. Budget surpluses allowed greater attention to development, and a special budget of £E13.75m was adopted for the period 1946–51; for 1951–56 a second development budget of £E34m was adopted, concentrating on improved communications, production schemes, social services and public utilities. Serious difficulties attended these plans. While the agricultural population benefited from the increased value of their products, the small but important urban working class suffered as wages failed to keep pace with the increased cost of living. From 1938 to 1947 this had risen by over 100 per cent. Dura, the staple food grain, doubled in price from 1939 to 1945, and the 1948 price was triple that of 1946.

This imbalance produced tensions which, combined with political developments, contributed to the growth of a militant labour movement after the war. Labour relations in the period 1946–53 were characterized by workers' mistrust of the government, the country's largest employer, by frequent strikes, and by increasing politicization of the movement and its association with the drive towards self-determination. The labour movement had its origins in Atbara, where 90 per cent of the inhabitants were Sudan Railways employees and their dependents. In June 1946 a Workers' Affairs Association (WAA) of railway artisans was formed, but government recognition was withheld pending consideration of the whole question of trade unions. A government plan to establish works committees was seen as an attempt to control the embryonic movement, just as its plans in the political sphere were seen as tactics of delay and disruption of the nationalist cause. A demonstration was held in July, and leaders of the WAA were arrested. A strike followed which, after the mediation of Sudanese politicians, resulted in government recognition of the WAA. A pattern was thus established by which the strike became not the ultimate recourse but the first weapon to enforce workers' demands.

Between 1948 and 1952 a body of labour legislation was enacted, based on British and colonial precedents. The most important instrument, the *Trade Union Ordinance* of 1948, provided for registration and legal operation of unions. By 1952 nearly one hundred unions had registered, many insignificant and short-lived. The most important remained the Sudan Railway Workers' Union (SRWU), which in 1951 had 17,000 members. By 1953 it was estimated that some 100,000 Sudanese were unionized. Steps were taken early to associate the various unions under an umbrella organization, which came into being as the Workers' Congress in 1949 and was superseded in 1950 by the Sudan Workers' Trade Union Federation (SWTUF). The SWTUF adopted overt political aims when in 1951 it proclaimed its intention of defeating British imperialism and achieving self-determination for the Sudan. With the Ashigga and other groups the SWTUF formed the United Front for the Liberation of the Sudan, generally seen as a communist front organization.[3] The SWTUF played an important part in the final phase of the nationalist movement, but its position was weakened by inability to mobilize member unions in general strikes. Thus in 1952 a general strike was called off when some unions refused to co-operate, and a severe rebuff was suffered when the SWTUF called a three-day general strike to protest the Anglo-Egyptian Agreement of 1953. The early connection between the labour and nationalist movements was unfortunate in that the former became prey to the same party and sectarian influences that had bedevilled the Graduates' Congress and subsequent attempts to achieve associations of Sudanese free from tribal and religious bonds.[4]

CHAPTER ELEVEN

The Achievement of Independence, 1953–56

The period between the Egyptian Revolution in July 1952 and independence of the Sudan on 1 January 1956 was clouded by an issue inherent in condominium: ultimate sovereignty in the Sudan. British control of Egypt had rendered the question moot until after the First World War, when Egyptian nationalists began to concentrate attention on the Sudan and Suez Canal. The disturbances of 1924 might have ended the Condominium, but the British in London (and Cairo) wanted the Sudan as leverage over Egypt; the moment passed. The Anglo-Egyptian agreement of 1936 and Sudanese nationalism revived the sovereignty issue, at a time when Britain's independence of action was limited. Forced to compete with Egypt for Sudanese support, the Khartoum régime entered that phase of colonial history wherein official reforms only increase nationalists' pressure. The tempo was at times slowed by divisions in the nationalist movement, and at other times increased by the Anglo-Egyptian struggle. The insistence of successive Egyptian governments on the 'unity of the Nile Valley' ensured a large measure of Sudanese acquiescence in Britain's continuing role in the Sudan. The Egyptian revolution finally broke the impasse.

Before the overthrow of King Faruq, the Egyptian government's expressed willingness to accede to Sudanese self-determination was dismissed as trickery. The revolutionary government headed by General Neguib, who had been educated in the Sudan and was popular there, decided to call the British bluff. He opened negotiations with the Umma party, which had never recovered from the shock of the Sidqi–Bevin protocol, and in October 1952 agreement was reached. This called for Sudanese self-determination, to be preceded by a transitional period of self-government during which the governor-general would act in concert with an international commission while a similar commission would prepare for elections. Another agreement, signed in January 1953 by the leading Sudanese parties, endorsed the Egyptian proposals. Faced with an unprecedented unanimity of Sudanese political parties and the Egyptian government, the British had run out of room to manoeuvre, and a new Anglo-Egyptian Agreement was consequently reached in short order.[1]

The new Agreement, signed on 12 February 1953, adopted most of the terms reached by Egypt and the political parties. A transitional period, during which sovereignty would be 'kept in reserve', was not to exceed three years. The governor-general, as 'supreme constitutional authority', would exercise his powers with the assistance of a five-member commission of two Sudanese, an Egyptian, a Briton and a Pakistani. He retained responsibility to the co-domini for foreign affairs and the *Self-Government Statute,* which would be amended to accord with the agreement. An international commission was to prepare for parliamentary elections. The transitional period would end, and foreign troops would be evacuated, within three months of the parliament's resolution that arrangements for self-determination should be set in motion. Provision was made for a Constituent Assembly to draw up a constitution and thus propose whether the Sudan would be linked to Egypt or completely independent.

The electoral commission, comprising an Egyptian, a Briton, an American and three Sudanese representing the Umma, the unionists and the South, made important modifications in the election rules. Whereas the *Self-Government Statute* had provided for direct elections in at least thirty-five constituencies, the commission, in accordance with a principle enunciated in the agreement between the political parties and the Egyptians, raised the number to sixty-eight (of a total of ninety-seven seats). Qualifications for voting were determined, and a special graduates' constituency, with an added qualification, completion of an educational course of secondary standard, had its representation increased from three to five. Elections, delayed until after the rainy season, were held in November and December 1953.

The unionists, as we have seen, had boycotted previous representative assemblies. Their participation in the 1953 election thus marked the first direct test of the major political views. The Ashigga, after a period of internal division and decline, had re-emerged as the leading element in a National Unionist Party (NUP) led by Isma'il al-Azhari. Its main rival, under the patronage of 'Abd al-Rahman al-Mahdi and led by his son, al-Siddiq, was the Umma. The Socialist Republican Party, established in 1951 with secret British support was, despite its name, a group of conservative tribal chiefs who favoured complete independence but feared and resented 'Abd al-Rahman's alleged personal ambitions. A Southern Party, established formally in 1953, contested the twenty-two Southern constituencies. A number of independent candidates, of various motivations and sympathies, also stood for election.

The election resulted in a decisive NUP majority. Of the ninety-seven seats at stake in the lower house, the NUP took fifty, and the Umma a disappointing twenty-three. The Socialist Republicans won a mere three seats and soon disintegrated. Independent candidates, including a communist returned in the graduates' constituency, won twelve seats, and the Southern Party won nine. The NUP also dominated the Senate, where its twenty-one elected and ten nominated members gave the party a clear majority. The voting showed that the NUP drew most of its support from the towns, settled riverain areas and areas of Khatmiyya strength. The Umma won all but one of its seats in Darfur, Kordofan and Blue Nile Provinces, where Mahdism was strong. Subsequent events suggested that rather than rejecting 'complete independence' as advocated by the Umma and British, the electorate was voicing mistrust of their long collaboration, and a desire to have done with the existing régime. The NUP victory was similarly less a mandate for union than for change, which the NUP, by a policy of non-cooperation and the role of its leaders in the nationalist cause, now represented. Advocacy of union had itself by 1953 been seen as an avenue towards an independence which would also circumscribe potential Mahdist supremacy. Even had the NUP followed up its election victory with steps towards effecting union with Egypt – and it did not – events both inside and outside the country presented impediments to such a course.

The Sudanese parliament opened in January 1954 with Azhari, the country's first prime minister, naming an all-NUP cabinet. The Umma, bristling in the unaccustomed role of opposition, showed the full force of its hostility to union on the occasion of the parliament's ceremonial opening on 1 March. Some 40,000 Ansar, many of whom had come in from the countryside, gathered in Khartoum to demonstrate at the arrival of General Neguib, who was to attend the inaugural ceremony. Riots broke out, resulting in several fatalities (including the British commandant of police), and the opening had to be postponed. Disaffection with extreme unionism was increased by subsequent events in Egypt. Colonel Nasser ousted the personally popular Neguib in November 1954, and suppressed both the Egyptian communists and Muslim Brotherhood, organizations to which young Sudanese especially were attracted.

Further evidence of limitations on the new government in Khartoum was given by developments in the South. There disenchantment was increased by the rapid progress of sudanization. This had been government policy for years, but its pace was quickened after the conclusion of the Anglo-Egyptian Agreement in 1953. Under its terms Azhari's government established a Sudanization Committee in February 1954 with the aim of completing the transfer of administration to Sudanese hands as soon as possible, 'to provide the free and neutral atmosphere requisite for Self-Determination'. British administrative officials were dismissed, a process eased by generous compensation. But of some eight hundred posts sudanized, a mere six went to Southerners. Thus the political decision taken at the time of the Juba Conference, that the South was 'inextricably bound' to the north, seemed, with sudanization, to be confirmed as the British abandonment feared by Southern leaders. Following months of unrest during which, in July 1955, striking Southern workers on the Zande Scheme were shot down by Northern troops attempting to disperse them, the Equatoria Corps refused orders in August. Hopes that the British would intervene on their behalf were dashed when the new governor-general, Alexander Knox Helm, ordered the mutineers to lay down their arms. With this most complied, but disorder had by then spread throughout the South, with great loss of life, especially among resident Northerners. Although order was eventually restored, these events were an ominous advent to independence.[2]

Whereas the Umma Party's determination and strength in the wake of electoral defeat had been amply demonstrated in March 1954, it was ironic that the victory of the NUP did nothing to unify its various factions. While the ostensible goal of the Umma had been and remained complete independence of the Sudan, supporters of the NUP were divided as to the extent of the relationship with Egypt they envisioned. Further, while the Umma was the political arm of the Ansar, the more amorphous NUP had never been assured the support of the Khatmiyya. As NUP leader, Azhari had therefore to rely for influence on his personal reputation as an opponent of the British, and to manage party affairs by a series of political manoeuvres. Irreconcilable opposition in the country to union, and Azhari's own more subtle view, probably shared by 'Ali al-Mirghani, that unionism had always been essentially a tactic employed to exploit the Anglo-Egyptian rivalry – subsidiary to a grand strategy for independence – led him gradually to abandon the pro-Egyptian stance. Whether or not this about-face was occasioned more by opportunism than by principle, it robbed the NUP of its ideological content and brought about a degeneration of the party into personal factions. In December 1954 three members of the NUP cabinet were dismissed by Azhari; within days they formed, with the approval of Sayyid 'Ali, the Republican Independence Party, with the professed aim of independence in close co-operation with Egypt. In June 1955 Muhammad Nur al-Din, vice-president of the NUP, was dismissed from the cabinet, and charges were exchanged between him and the prime minister as to whose faction constituted the official party. Union with Egypt having by now been largely abandoned, these intra-party disputes were essentially little more than personal conflicts on the eve of independence.

With the major political leaders agreed on the fundamental question of the country's future status, Azhari sought to bypass the procedures requisite for self-determination that had been laid down in the 1953 Anglo-Egyptian Agreement. In August 1955 the parliament passed a resolution demanding evacuation of British and Egyptian forces, and by mid-November the troops had been withdrawn. On 8 October the Umma Party proposed a coalition government, a suggestion rejected by Azhari, whose control of events was, however, perceptibly weakening as his moment of glory approached. On 10 November he lost a vote of confidence by four votes and resigned, only to be reinstated on the 15th by a two-vote margin. On 3 December Sayyid 'Abd al-Rahman and Sayyid 'Ali, meeting publicly for the first time in almost a decade, united in calling for a coalition government immediately after independence, a call to which Azhari felt compelled to agree. On 19 December the lower house resolved unanimously to declare the independence of the Sudan, a motion adopted by the senate on the 22nd. A Transitional Constitution, under which the parliamentary régime would continue to govern a 'Sovereign, Democratic Republic', and the powers of the governor-general would be vested in a five-man Supreme Commission, was enacted by the parliament on 31 December. The last governor-general had departed on leave two weeks earlier, and did not return. On 1 January 1956 the rush to independence, which only a decade before had seemed a legacy for some future generation, was completed when the flags of the co-domini, the last symbols of Cromer's 'hybrid form of government', were lowered in Khartoum.

PART FIVE

The Independent Sudan

We, under democracy, are placing the people's powers in the hands of the people by every means. Additional elections . . . are not the only means. There are other means. I believe that the most successful way to place the people's powers in the hands of the people is revolution.

Babikr 'Awadallah in a radio address
following the May 1969 *coup*

The Sudanese People's Forces have decided unanimously – in order to save the country and its independence, to avoid bloodshed and support the people and their choice – to yield to the wishes of the people and assume power.

General 'Abd al-Rahman Muhammad
Hassan Siwar al-Dahab in a
radio address on 6 April 1985

At the end of the six (6) year interim period there shall be an internationally monitored referendum, organized jointly by the GOS and the SPLM/A, for the people of South Sudan to: confirm the unity of the Sudan by voting to adopt the system of government established under the Peace Agreement; or to vote for secession.

Agreed Text on the Right to Self-Determination
for the People of South Sudan, Machakos
Protocol, 20 July 2002

CHAPTER TWELVE

Parliamentary and Military Government: 1956–69

The inception of the Republic could not fail to remind Sudanese of the foundation, over seventy years before, of the Mahdist state. Yet there was little real similarity between the two. The ideology of the Mahdia was purely religious: compromise between it and the khedivial administration in the Sudan was out of the question. The Mahdist state was born out of the devastation of a revolutionary war, in which the established administrative system had been subverted, and the precarious economic development of the Turco-Egyptian period arrested. The nationalist founders of the Republic, on the other hand, were deeply affected by Western culture and political ideas. They sought not to destroy, but to control the administration built up under the Condominium, and professed, with varying degrees of sincerity and understanding, attachment to parliamentary democracy. Hence the Republic was essentially the successor of the Condominium government, and New Year's Day 1956 marks only in a formal and conventional sense a new era in Sudanese history. The real line of demarcation must be placed either earlier, on 9 January 1954, when the essential transfer of power from British to Sudanese hands took place or, less aptly, on 17 November 1958, when the army *coup d'état* ended the first phase of parliamentary government.

The sense of anti-climax that attended formal independence of the Sudan[1] reflected continuity also in the tenor of politics. Azhari had great difficulty in maintaining his position as prime minister. His government lost a vote in parliament in January 1956, but survived with a confidence motion. At the end of the month the resignation of three ministers forced Azhari to form a coalition government. The new cabinet included Mirghani Hamza and Muhammad Nur al-Din, and the Umma politicians 'Abdallah Khalil and Ibrahim Ahmad. In June twenty-one members of the parliamentary NUP formed, with the support of Sayyid 'Ali, the People's Democratic Party (PDP); on 5 July 'Abdallah Khalil was elected prime minister. A new coalition cabinet, including members of the PDP but excluding Azhari, was sworn in.

The new government, by bringing together supporters of the rival religious leaders, appeared to reflect a priority of national over sectarian loyalties. The opposite was true: the trappings of power had been handed to those who actually held it. This paper alliance of the rival sects was reminiscent of their efforts, over thirty years before, to crush nascent secular nationalism. The alliance of 1956 was if anything more artificial and tactical: the coalition partners held fundamentally divergent views, and had united only to defeat Azhari. The brief history of the first parliamentary period was thus characterized from the start by petty rivalries and crippling suspicions. The Umma was seen to be manoeuvring for appointment of Sayyid 'Abd al-Rahman as life-president of the Sudan; the PDP, much of which looked for inspiration to revolutionary Egypt, was vigilant of the interests of Sayyid 'Ali.

During the 1956–58 parliamentary period the characteristics of sovereignty were assumed. The new republic was recognized by foreign governments, and became a member of the Arab League and United Nations. Membership of international financial bodies followed. A diplomatic corps was established under Mohamed Ahmed Mahgoub, the Umma foreign minister. In 1957 steps were taken to initiate a Sudanese currency,[2] the first since the days of the Mahdist state, and results of the Sudan's first scientific census were announced, putting the population at 10,200,000. On this basis parliamentary constituencies were redrawn and their number was increased from 97 to 173 in preparation for elections which, after a postponement, were scheduled for 1958.

Economic policy during this period concentrated on enlarging the country's agricultural capacity and improving communications. The Managil Extension to the Gezira Scheme, to increase the area under cotton to almost 500,000 acres, was well under way in 1956, with completion planned for 1961–62. A new five-year plan beginning in 1957 was estimated to cost £S137 million. Continuing concentration of capital resources in cotton-growing schemes, a cause for anxiety since the 1920s, proved disastrous in the late 1950s. The 1957–58 crops were poor, and falling world demand combined with the government's insistent maintenance of a fixed minimum price resulted in a huge stock of unsold cotton and serious depletion in the country's currency reserves.

The coalition government's conduct of foreign affairs was similarly vexed, not least in relations with Egypt. Although the Suez crisis in 1956 produced strong Sudanese support for Egypt, serious tensions arose. The Sudan had ignored provisions of the 1929 Nile Waters Agreement when implementing its new irrigation projects, and Egyptian plans for the High Dam at Aswan made settlement more urgent. The dam would have serious repercussions in Nubia, and the Sudanese demanded revision of the Agreement before construction began. Another irritant was the sudden Egyptian claim, in February 1958, to two areas, one on the Nile, the other on the Red Sea coast, on the grounds that these lay north of the border specified by the Condominium Agreement. Egypt sent troops to occupy the areas, which had long been administered by Khartoum and participated in the 1953 elections. The resulting crisis was resolved without formal agreement when Egypt withdrew her troops.

The *Sudd*. Until cut through laborious (and continuous) effort during the colonial era, the masses of floating vegetation called *Sudd* (Ar. barrier) barred the way to outsiders trying to reach the upper reaches of the Nile.

The tomb of Mahdi. Destroyed by the British in 1898, the tomb is shown here as it was rebuilt by the Mahdi's son, Sayyid Abd al-Rahman.

The Fashoda Incident, 1898. After the battle of Omdurman, the British commander, Kitchener, hurried south to stake Anglo-Egyptian claims. At Fashoda he met Major Marchard, whose expedition across Africa had planted the French flag on the upper Nile. Marchard is shown here approaching the *Dal* to meet Kitchener (on deck, rear).

Khartoun 1898. After the fall of Khartoun to the forces of the Mahdi in 1885 the town was abandoned and a new capital established at Omdurman, across the Nile. When Anglo-Egyptian forces defeated the Mahdists at Karari in September 1898 they found Khartoun in ruins.

The founding of Juba, 1928. Juba is now the capital of Southern Sudan.

The Gezira Scheme. At its inception in the 1920s, this was Africa's largest agricultural development and produced the Sudan's major cash crop, cotton. Today international interest is again being shown in the country's potential as a food producer.

Al-Sadiq al-Mahdi, prime minister 1966–7, 1986–9. Great-grandson of the Mahdi and still a leading figure in the country's politics, Sayyid al-Sadiq personifies continuity and change in the history of the modern Sudan.

Independence Day, January 1, 1956. The Sudan was one of the first African dependencies to win its independence from European (and in its case, Egyptian) rule.

A second important area of foreign relations concerned acceptance of aid from the United States. Conversations began in mid-1957. The deteriorating economic position and ambitious development plans gave force to the government's readiness to accept American aid. But a political backdrop of growing Arab hostility to the West, and the United States' moves to counter this, created tension within the governing coalition. The pro-Egyptian PDP saw the aid agreement as necessarily strengthening US (and anti-Egyptian) influence in the Sudan. Resolution awaited a new parliament after the 1958 elections.

The Umma–PDP alliance nonetheless continued during the 1958 election campaign. Their agreement not to oppose each other in the constituencies, the consequent conservation of financial resources, a redistribution of seats and naturalization of large numbers of pro-Umma Fallata resulted in victory at the polls.[3] The new parliament consisted of 63 Umma, 26 PDP, 40 Southern Liberal and 44 NUP members. The Umma and PDP entered into a new coalition government, with 'Abdallah Khalil retaining the premiership.

The Southern Liberal Party had been founded shortly after the 1953 elections. Educated Southerners' grave suspicions of Northern politicians, exacerbated by events since 1954, had found expression in their support for federal status for the South.[4] Unity on this issue could not, however, overcome tribal and personal differences or the cynical opportunism of their own leaders. The mask of Southern solidarity was torn away after the 1958 elections, when the votes of individual Liberal MPs' tended to go to the highest bidder. Following ratification of the US Aid Agreement in July 1958 parliament was adjourned to avoid a government defeat on a confidence motion.

By mid-1958 a political crisis was brewing. Deteriorating economic conditions were underlined by the incapacity of the government. Political machinations reached a finale in the late summer when Umma leaders began actively to explore a coalition with Azhari's NUP. This was complicated by rumours of a NUP–PDP rapprochement that, if consummated, would remove the Umma from power. Before any of these plans could be fulfilled, however, the army stepped in and swept away parties, politicians and the parliamentary régime itself.

On 17 November 1958, a few hours before parliament was to reconvene, the army took control of key installations in the capital. The commander-in-chief, General Ibrahim Abboud, claimed in a radio address that the army had acted to save the country from the chaotic régime of the politicians. A state of emergency was declared. The Supreme Commission, which since independence had replaced the governor-general, was dismissed. The transitional constitution was suspended, ministers were arrested, political parties dissolved, and unions abolished. The Sudan was proclaimed a 'democratic republic' with popular sovereignty. Power was invested in a thirteen-member Supreme Council of the Armed Forces, which delegated 'full legislative, executive and judicial powers' to Abboud. A council of ministers (seven officers and five civilians) was named, with Abboud as prime minister and minister of defence.

An intriguing aspect of the *coup* has been the extent of 'Abdallah Khalil's involvement. It is now clear that he (who before entering politics had a long and distinguished military career) had discussed with Abboud a temporary army takeover, to be followed by a government in which they and Azhari would play leading parts, supported by the army. The possibility of a new parliamentary coalition, excluding him, may therefore have figured prominently in the prime minister's thinking. Events would show that Abboud and his colleagues had ideas of their own. As former prime ministers, 'Abdallah Khalil and Azhari were pensioned off and receded from view.

The *coup* triggered feelings neither of euphoria nor of great regret, at home or abroad. It was but the latest in a series in the Muslim world, beginning in Egypt in 1952 and continuing in Iraq and Pakistan in 1958. Sudanese opinion was more relieved than jubilant, less excited than exhausted after years of cynical and sterile party politics. Support was forthcoming from the still pre-eminent religious leaders: Sayyid 'Ali welcomed the *coup*, among the leaders of which were prominent members of the Khatmiyya; Sayyid 'Abd al-Rahman's response was more guarded, foreshadowing eventual Umma hostility towards the military régime.

The view that the takeover had been planned as a temporary measure gained force from events of the régime's first year in power. The *coup* had gone smoothly, but struggles within the army ensued, as factions and personalities competed for dominance. Abboud himself was a benevolent figure, seemingly removed from and indifferent to these disputes, and to this may be laid the fact that he survived. In March 1959 two regional commanders, Brigadier Muhy al-Din Ahmad 'Abdallah and Brigadier 'Abd al-Rahim Shannan, moved troops into the capital. 'Abdallah Khalil and the two sayyids intervened, and the troops withdrew, but two days later they were back in greater strength. The disgruntled commanders demanded and got the resignation of the Supreme Council, and Abboud, the army commander-in-chief, appointed a new one including them.

In May another crisis occurred when supporters of Shannan again led troops into Khartoum. Now General Hasan Beshir Nasr, who had been chief planner of the *coup* and was the real strongman of the régime, acted forcefully. The plotters were arrested at Shendi, and the troops returned to headquarters. Muhy al-Din and Shannan were brought before a court martial, and sentenced to death on a charge of incitement to mutiny. The sentences were commuted, but both were imprisoned until after the revolution of October 1964. In 1959, after young officers of the Infantry School at Omdurman mutinied, they were arrested, tried and executed. The régime thus gave notice that it would tolerate no further dissension in the ranks.

The death in March 1959 of Sayyid 'Abd al-Rahman al-Mahdi was a notable event. The great sectarian and nationalist leader had dominated politics in the Sudan since the re-emergence of the Ansar during the First World War. The modern Mahdist sect is largely his creation, while the independence of the Sudan in 1956 was seen as the culmination of his life's work. He was succeeded as head of the Ansar by his son, Sayyid al-Siddiq.

Contributing to the impression of a military régime's ability to get things done was a new Nile Waters Agreement with Egypt. In 1955 the Sudan, while opposing the Aswan Dam project, had put forward three principles as a basis for a deal: the Sudan's share must be determined before work began on a dam; the Sudan must be free in future to build any works deemed necessary for the use of her share of the Nile waters; and Egypt must pay for the reset-tlement and 'adequate alternate livelihood' of the people of Wadi Halfa, whose removal the new dam would necessitate.[5] Negotiations resumed in October 1959 and a new Nile Waters Agreement was quickly concluded. The Sudan was to receive £E15 million to cover losses at Wadi Halfa (a figure far short of what would be required for compensation and resettlement); and upon completion of the High Dam the Sudan would be allocated 18.5 billion cubic metres of water per year as against 55.5 bcm for Egypt, with a margin of 10 bcm for evaporation losses. Work on the dam began in 1960.

The foreign policy pursued by the military régime featured non-alignment and support for African independence movements. The Nile Waters Agree-ment opened a new period of Sudanese–Egyptian relations, sealed by the visit of President Nasser in 1960. Abboud made state visits to the USA and USSR; President Brezhnev, Premier Chou En Lai and President Tito of Yugoslavia came to the Sudan. Military equipment was accepted from Britain, and Food for Peace from the USA. Diplomatic and economic boycotts of South Africa and Portugal were instituted in 1963. In the same year the establishment of the first African Development Bank was agreed to in a meeting of finance ministers in Khartoum.

Resettlement of the people of Wadi Halfa developed into a serious political issue with long-term repercussions.[6] Despite their near-unanimous opposition, the government decided to move them to a site near Khashm al-Qirba on the Atbara. Demonstrations began at once in the Halfa area, followed by others in Khartoum and elsewhere. The grievances of the Nubians formed a rallying-point for opposition to the régime; students, schoolboys and trade unionists played a prominent part. Coming in the wake of the 1959 *coup* attempt, these demonstrations took on a distinct political character, and the govern-ment dealt harshly with them.

The opposition thus sparked mounted steadily in 1960–61. The régime was dominated by members of the Shayqiyya tribe with strong Khatmiyya connections. Further evidence of this orientation lay in the retirement of General 'Abd al-Wahhab, an Umma supporter, and the positive attitude towards the régime of the PDP. In November 1960 leaders of the outlawed political parties (except the PDP) petitioned for a return to civilian rule. In 1961 the newly reconstituted railway workers' union was dissolved after it called a strike; the university was shut down after student demonstrations; and another petition, by Azhari and 'Abdallah Khalil, resulted in their detention at Juba, along with leaders of the other parties except the PDP. A further blow was the death, in September 1961, of Sayyid al-Siddiq, who was succeeded as leader of the Ansar by his brother, al-Hadi, and in his political role by his son, al-Sadiq.

Suppression of the parties was related to the development of two extremist groups, the Sudanese Communist Party (SCP) and the Muslim Brotherhood. The SCP originated in Egypt, where in 1944 its predecessor was launched by Sudanese students who, two years later, founded the Sudanese Movement for National Liberation. Between 1946 and 1951 the party was riven by internal disputes. Proscribed by the Condominium régime and its parliamentary and military successors, the party organized behind a number of fronts and found its chief support among three sections of the population: Western-educated students and members of the intelligentsia, trade unionists and tenant farmers' associations. Leadership of the railway union, the WAA, was in communist hands from 1947, as was that of the umbrella organization of unions, the SWTUF, from 1952. The party's fortunes declined when it condemned the Anglo-Egyptian Agreement of 1953, and subsequent calls for strikes were unsuccessful. The party contested the 1953 elections as the Anti-Imperialist Front, winning one seat in the lower house. In 1957 it joined the National Front against the Umma-dominated coalition government. When the military régime banned political parties in 1958, the communists, under 'Abd al-Khaliq Mahjub, therefore had considerable experience in underground organization. From 1962, through fronts, they were active in kindling opposition to the régime.[7]

Parallel to development of communism was the increasing attraction of the Muslim Brothers. Founded in Egypt in 1928, the brotherhood remains, in its several national expressions, a militant organization with a fundamentalist Islamic ideology. Like the communists, it was suppressed in Egypt after the 1952 revolution. During the closing days of the Abboud régime the brotherhood was already led by Hasan al-Turabi, then a lecturer in the university, whose personal resiliency has since matched that of the movement in the political history of the Sudan.

In its administrative policy the military régime bore a resemblance to its Condominium predecessor. Following recommendations of a commission appointed in August 1959 to consider the association of the people in the governing of the country, the régime promulgated three ordinances, the *Province Administration Act*, the *Central Council Act* and the *Local Government Act*, establishing local, provincial and central advisory councils. Thus the régime sought, as the British had in the 1940s, to circumvent political parties and rely for legitimacy on innocuous consultative bodies. The Central Council, resembling a parliament, was without independent authority and had little impact.

In the economic field the military régime achieved mixed results. In 1959 the reserve price that had combined with falling demand to create a huge supply of unsold cotton, was abandoned. Annual budgets were regularly in surplus. In 1960 a Central Bank was inaugurated. An Agricultural Bank was established to provide credit for farmers; in 1962 the Industrial Bank of the Sudan began to promote and expand private industry. In 1960 the International Bank for Reconstruction and Development (IBRD) granted a loan for completion of the Managil Extension; arrangements were made in 1961 with the IBRD and West Germany to finance construction of the Roseires Dam. In March 1962 a railway line was extended from southern Kordofan to Wau in the Bahr al-Ghazal. Trade agreements were concluded with the USSR, other eastern European states, Britain and the USA. Bilateral economic relations with Yugoslavia and West Germany were particularly active.

In 1962 a 'Ten-Year Plan for economic and social development' was announced. Investment over the period was to total £S512m, of which £S285m would come from special development budgets for major projects. The plan concentrated on agriculture and irrigation schemes, transport and communications and lessening dependence on the agricultural sector, especially cotton. The plan proved over-ambitious as the government, like its predecessors, failed to take account of the Sudan's essential dependence for surplus revenue on agriculture, which remained prey to world-market and local conditions. As surpluses failed to reach the level needed to fund special development budgets, projects were trimmed and confidence eroded, while the country's indebtedness rose alarmingly.

A problem more serious than economic difficulties had been developing in the Southern Sudan. In the wake of the 1955 disturbances the Southern provinces had been quiet, and the wrangling of Southern politicians in Khartoum had few repercussions for constituents. The policies of the military régime, however, escalated tensions beyond political debate, and eventually, or so it seemed to the government, beyond political solution. A large body of Southern opinion became convinced that no Khartoum régime could be trusted.

In its Southern administrative policy the military, free from the restrictions of parliamentary government, was tactless to the point of provocation. Northerners were appointed to provincial and district positions while Southerners were bypassed or transferred to the North. But it was in the related areas of education and religion that the Abboud government was most inept. We have seen that Southern education, under the Condominium, had been in the hands of foreign missionaries whose schools were, after 1927, subsidized and, after the Second World War, supplemented by government institutions. In 1954 the International Commission on Secondary Education recommended that missionary schools be nationalized, with Arabic, not English, the universal language of instruction. These nation-building suggestions, taken in hand by the government of 'Abdallah Khalil in 1957, betrayed ignorance of Southern sensitivities. The Abboud régime took stronger steps. The gradual progress of arabicization and islamization, to which the policies of the Condominium had served as a partial barrier, was to be hastened through aggressive action. Six intermediate Islamic Institutes were opened, mosques were constructed and subsidized, missions were prohibited from opening new schools and the day of rest was changed from Sunday to Friday. Missionaries going on leave were denied re-entry to the Sudan. Religious activities of missionaries outside church were prohibited.

Thus a policy which, had it been instituted gradually in the early days of Condominium rule, would have served to produce a broader national character, appeared under the heavy hand of the military to be aimed at suppressing an emerging though still unclearly articulated Southern identity. As missionary activities had been seen, in Condominium days, as part of a policy to bring about a separate evolution of Southern society, their curtailment was viewed, especially by Southern intellectuals, as a thinly veiled political provocation. The government in turn blamed the missionaries for inciting Southern hostility towards the régime. In 1962 the *Missionary Societies Act*, an attempt 'to regulate, by means of a system of licenses, the activities of Missionary Societies in the Sudan', was a crude device to allow unlimited interference with missionaries. The intention foreshadowed in this Act was clarified in 1964 when the government ordered the expulsion of all foreign missionaries in the South.

Rising discontent in the South was revealed by political developments. Leading Southern intellectuals and politicians fled the country. In 1962 Father Saturnino Lahure, Joseph Oduho and William Deng established in Leopoldville (Kinshasa) the Sudan Closed Districts National Union (SACDNU); in 1963 this became the Sudan African National Union (SANU) with headquarters in Kampala. SANU, like earlier Southern parties, was hampered by internal splits and personal differences within its leadership. It provided, however, evidence to the world at large of events in the South, and spoke for the growing number of refugees who, as security broke down, had fled to neighbouring countries; it was estimated in 1964 that 60,000 refugees were in Uganda. In response to SANU's appeals, the UN began to provide funds for the relief of refugees.

A more disturbing symptom of burgeoning crisis was the establishment in 1963 of the Anya Nya guerrilla army, which derived its name from a Madi poison. The Anya Nya had as its nucleus veterans of the 1955 mutiny who had eluded capture by taking to the bush. In January 1964 an Anya Nya force attacked Wau. Although repulsed, the attack, and efforts by the government to suppress the Anya Nya, publicized the movement and made it a rallying-point for Southern opposition. Emergence of the Anya Nya also signalled the spread of the conflict to the rural population. The increasing intractability of the 'Southern problem' and Khartoum's obvious inability to deal with it led indirectly to the fall of the Abboud régime.

That fall came swiftly and unexpectedly. In September 1964 the government appointed a commission to investigate causes of Southern unrest and propose solutions. The commission invited discussion, but when the Khartoum University students' union concluded that no solution was possible while the military remained in power, the ministry of education banned further meetings. This order was defied; police attempted to disperse a meeting, a student was shot and killed and a funeral procession of 30,000 people spawned demonstrations and riots. Teachers, students and lawyers established a Professionals' Front, soon joined by other associations and unions, which called for a general strike. This was taken up by workers and civil servants in the capital; demonstrations spread to provincial centres. Leaders of banned political parties formed a United Front. Dissension within the army itself precluded drastic action. On 26 October Abboud dissolved the Supreme Council and cabinet. The United and Professional Fronts agreed to form a Transitional Government under Abboud as president and Sirr al-Khatim al-Khalifa, a politically unaffiliated civil servant, as prime minister. The new cabinet had seven ministers from the Professionals' Front, two Southerners and one representing each of five political parties (Umma, NUP, PDP, Muslim Brothers and communists). Abboud was soon pensioned off and replaced as head of state by a five-man commission, as before the 1958 *coup*. Other members of the Supreme Council were arrested and imprisoned in Darfur.

The fall of the Abboud régime, in contrast to the overthrow of its civilian predecessor in 1958, occasioned public celebration. And although popular excitement could not mask the difficulties facing the improvised Transitional Government, early reforms erased vestiges of military rule. The provisional constitution was reinstated. The council system was dismantled. Political prisoners were released. Censorship was lifted. Political parties were legalized, the autonomy of the university was restored and steps were taken to check corruption.

Some difficulties of the Transitional Government were inherent in its composition. The Professionals' Front, formed in the revolutionary atmosphere of October and influenced by the strong communist element in the leadership of its member associations, favoured radical change. Most political parties, quiescent under the army and insignificant in bringing it down, wanted early national elections in order to re-establish legitimacy; the Professionals' Front, communists and PDP argued that conditions in the South precluded immediate elections. The deadlock was broken in February 1965 when thousands of Ansar demonstrated in Khartoum; the cabinet resigned, and attempts to reorganize it failed. Sirr al-Khatim al-Khalifa formed a new coalition dominated by the Umma, NUP and Muslim Brothers; the PDP and communists dithered, but when elections were called for the end of April the PDP boycotted them.

Under the Transitional Government steps were taken to solve the Southern problem. On 6 December 1964 – 'Black Sunday' – clashes between Southerners and Northerners in Khartoum left scores dead, and reinforced the necessity of a settlement. Representatives of SANU had already proposed negotiations, conditioned on an amnesty, repeal of the *Closed Districts Ordinance* and *Missionary Societies Act* and recognition of SANU for the purpose of contesting elections. On 10 December a general amnesty was granted all Sudanese who had left the country since January 1955, but SANU leaders refused to return without agreement on the future status of the South, and therefore insisted that any conference be held outside the Sudan, in the full light of world opinion. After further talks in Kampala, SANU agreed to attend a conference at Juba in February, and to appeal to all Southerners to cease fighting; the government promised to ensure the safety of SANU delegates and lift the state of emergency as soon as fighting abated. Plans changed after the cabinet crisis in Khartoum, fighting around Juba intensified, and a SANU faction under William Deng agreed that the conference could take place in Khartoum.

The Round Table Conference opened in Khartoum on 16 March 1965. Representatives of the major political parties, the Professionals' Front, SANU, leading Southerners, and foreign observers attended. In an opening address the prime minister blamed the Southern problem on 'natural geographical and sociological factors', Britain's 'evil colonial policies' and 'hypocritical European missionaries'. The Northern political parties, mindful of impending elections, eschewed both intransigent insistence on Northern supremacy and imaginative concessions to Southern demands: they rejected both unitary and federal systems, and proposed a regional government with devolved control of education, health, commerce, agriculture and internal security. SANU and the newly formed Southern Front called for a regional plebiscite to decide among alternatives of federation, union and independence. In its final report the conference agreed on principles to guide national policy in the South, but 'could not reach a unanimous resolution' on constitutional status. A committee appointed to consider plans for constitutional and administrative reform reported in late 1966, without appreciable effect. The Round Table Conference achieved landmark status in the lore of Southern politics; its failure, on the eve of national elections, had been predictable.

In preparation for those elections reforms were adopted. The upper house had been abolished, and the franchise extended to women and eighteen-year-olds. Some fifteen parties, mostly ephemeral vehicles for individuals, registered. Fundamental positions of the major parties were little different from those espoused in 1958. The Umma still depended largely on support from areas where the Ansar were numerous, while the NUP maintained its hold in the towns and settled regions along the main Nile. Polling took place in late April and early May. The Umma won seventy-six seats, the NUP fifty-four, the Islamic Charter Front (effectively the Muslim Brothers) five and the communists eight (all in the special graduates' constituency, which had been revived). Twenty-four independents were elected, including ten from the Beja Congress and seven from the Nuba Mountains. The PDP won three seats despite its boycott, and split because its leader, 'Ali 'Abd al-Rahman, had allied with the communists under the Transitional Government. Despite postponement of elections in the South, the region produced twenty new MPs, mostly Northern merchants who, the Supreme Court ruled, had fulfilled requirements for nomination and were thus elected unopposed.

The Umma and NUP formed a coalition government under Mohammed Ahmed Mahgoub, the former foreign minister, which commanded a vast majority in parliament. Strong leadership and unity of purpose could have provided unprecedented stability. But personal ambitions, especially of the vainglorious Mahgoub and cynical Azhari, the NUP's veteran leader, were too strong, and ideological differences too great. Tinkering with the still provisional constitution was by now habitual; an amendment allowed Azhari's election as permanent president of the Supreme Council of State, thereby politicizing it. Each coalition partner took six seats in the cabinet, with three ministerial appointments reserved as usual for Southerners. SANU's Andrew Wieu and Alfred Wol were named to the cabinet, but soon resigned over the appointment of Buth Diu of the revived but insignificant Liberal Party.

The history of the second parliamentary period is dominated by two problems: civil war in the South, and bitterness between (and within) the political parties. These combined with the resulting lack of direction in economic affairs to destroy it.

In its conduct of Southern affairs the civilian government seemed to have learned little from its military predecessor. In July 1965, two violent incidents sparked an exodus of Southerners to neighbouring states: on the 8th Northern troops at Juba went on a rampage that left hundreds dead and whole sections of the town in ashes; on the 11th at Wau a further mass killing of Southerners occurred. While the government stated that lawlessness must be crushed and order restored before constitutional reforms could be discussed, SANU in exile demanded the intervention of the United Nations. The Anya Nya responded with atrocities of their own. A pattern developed, in which civilians were caught up; villages spared by one side were burnt by the other. Government control was soon limited to major towns and fortified posts.

Rapid deterioration of conditions in the South was reflected in the evolution of political groupings both within and outside the Sudan. In Khartoum the Southern Front, a loosely knit group of intellectuals with ties to SANU in exile, became in June 1965 an official political party led by Clement Mboro. It supported self-determination for the South, and published an influential newspaper, *The Vigilant.* William Deng's SANU faction, which itself took on the trappings of a political party in 1965, remained committed to federalism. The influence of these parties was limited largely to Southerners in Khartoum and in government-held towns of the South: neither spoke for Southerners in exile or for the Anya Nya.

Southern political organizations outside the Sudan continued to suffer from internal rifts. Differences between Aggrey Jaden and Joseph Oduho, who led factions of SANU in exile, were briefly reconciled in December 1965 when the latter's new Azanian Liberation Front was joined by Jaden's faction of SANU. Espousing complete independence for the South, the Azanian Liberation Front (ALF) neither won Anya Nya support nor unified the exiles' leadership, but tried to coordinate their activities. It failed even to maintain the unity of his own executive; Aggrey Jaden was dismissed as vice-president, and in August 1967 he established a Southern Sudan Provisional Government. Thus intensification of the war and accession of the Mahgoub government in June 1965 had two important results: Southerners were convinced that the North was intent on a military solution, which increased the legitimacy of the Anya Nya; and Southern politicians in exile, while still incapable of uniting the political and military arms of the struggle, were increasingly determined to win independence for the South. Both developments weakened the positions of Southern parties in Khartoum. The deaths of two important Southern leaders complicated matters further. In January 1967 Father Saturnino Lahure was killed near the Ugandan border, and in May 1968 William Deng, president of SANU, was ambushed with six associates and killed, probably by a government patrol, in the Bahr al-Ghazal.

A subordination of national interest to personal ambition is evident as well in Northern political developments during this period. Although Mahgoub was prime minister, the leader of the Umma was al-Sadiq al-Mahdi, who in 1965 was too young to run for parliament. When he turned thirty, the Oxford-educated great-grandson of the Mahdi clashed inevitably with the pompous but ineffective Mahgoub. Al-Sadiq's desire to assume the premiership met also with the opposition of his uncle, the Imam al-Hadi, religious leader of the Ansar. The Umma rift was exploited by its old rival, Azhari, who tested his strength *vis-à-vis* Mahgoub by disputing which of them should represent the Sudan at summit meetings. The frailty of the ruling coalition was revealed when NUP ministers supported Azhari by resigning, only to rejoin when Mahgoub gave way.

A more serious indication of the coalition's disdain for principles was its attitude towards the Communist Party. In November 1965 the Muslim Brothers demanded that the SCP be banned. A resolution was passed by a huge majority in parliament, and the constitution was amended to outlaw communism. The SCP was summarily disbanded, its property confiscated and its members of parliament unseated. Arrests followed. The Supreme Court ruled the ban illegal, but its judgement was disregarded. Political expediency rather than popular demand was behind the government's action, a fact not lost on the public, especially after the Chief Justice resigned in protest. The communists responded with the simple device of establishing the Socialist Party, the executive of which included leading communists.

Al-Sadiq al-Mahdi's anomalous position was resolved after he turned thirty and won a by-election for parliament. Whether it had been agreed that this should precipitate Mahgoub's resignation is unclear, but he declined to step down. A motion of no confidence in the prime minister was duly introduced in July 1966. Azhari threw the support of the NUP behind the motion, which carried by one-hundred-and-twenty-six votes to thirty. Al-Sadiq al-Mahdi became prime minister and a new cabinet was formed.

The brief premiership of al-Sadiq al-Mahdi, from July 1966 to May 1967, witnessed an attempt to enact a permanent constitution. Parliament's right to act as constituent assembly was hampered so long as Southerners went unrepresented. In March 1967 the government therefore held elections in thirty-six Southern constituencies. Volatile conditions resulted in a small poll. The Umma emerged with fifteen seats, SANU with ten and the NUP with five, while the rest were won by the Unity and Liberal Parties and independents. But when a Constitutional Draft Committee was appointed, only seven of forty-two members were Southerners, and SANU and the Southern Front refused to participate. Al-Sadiq himself favoured an Islamic constitution, which perhaps his weakening position within the Umma demanded, but thereby undermined hopes that he would break with the bankrupt policies of his predecessors.

On taking office al-Sadiq had indeed attempted to transcend the sectarian basis of Sudanese politics. He advocated reforms in agrarian and social policy that were, however, unacceptable to his conservative uncle. Al-Sadiq's ability to attract popular support across traditional lines provoked an alliance in parliament between the Imam's supporters and the NUP, and in May 1967 Azhari, for the second time in less than a year, abandoned the leader of his nominal coalition partner and brought down the government. The Umma was now effectively split, and a ramshackle coalition of the NUP, the Imam's wing of the Umma, and various others was formed, with Mahgoub returning as prime minister. Al-Sadiq and his faction of the Umma went into opposition.

The 1968 elections were contested by a multiplicity of parties and fronts, few of which had organizations or programmes. In the new parliament the Democratic Unionist Party (DUP, a re-amalgamation of the NUP and PDP) emerged with 101 seats. The disastrous consequences of the Umma's internal split became evident when al-Sadiq's wing won thirty-six seats and the Imam's wing thirty; al-Sadiq lost his own seat. SANU and the Southern Front won fifteen and ten seats respectively. A coalition of the DUP and Imam's wing of the Umma was formed, Mahgoub retained the premiership and Azhari was re-elected president of the Supreme Council. Despite its huge majority, the coalition was too diverse and mutually suspicious, and its leader, Mahgoub, too weak, to provide much hope of stable government.

The Sudan's foreign relations during the second parliamentary period were dominated by Middle Eastern and African affairs. A pattern was established in which the Sudan, because of its location, Afro-Arab population and non-alignment, would be called to mediate regional disputes. This role was complicated by the war in the Southern Sudan. During a decade that witnessed the independence of most of Africa's remaining colonies, the founding of the Organization of African Unity, and establishment of a vocal Afro-Asian presence in the UN, the Sudanese government was embarrassed by the contradiction between its policy towards the South and its support for African secessionist movements. This support led inevitably to disputes with neighbouring states. In 1966 foreign mediation was needed to restore relations with Chad after border clashes. A dispute with Ethiopia was worsened by the passage of arms for the Anya Nya through that country, and by Sudanese support for Eritrean secessionists. Relations with the Central African Republic and Congo (Kinshasa), which sheltered large numbers of Southern refugees, were likewise strained, and revolutionaries in the Congo were openly aided by the Sudan.

In Arab affairs the Sudan played a more positive part, largely owing to the interest taken by Mahgoub. The Arab–Israeli war of 1967 evoked strong Sudanese support of Egypt and breaches with Britain and the US; relations with Britain were restored in 1968, but with the US only in 1972. Western support for Israel led to a new era of military and economic co-operation with the USSR, which would continue until the *coup* of 1971. The Sudan's position as honest broker was underscored by an Arab summit meeting in Khartoum in August 1967. The Sudan was also active in mediating the Egyptian–Saudi dispute over Yemen.

Mahgoub's preoccupation with external affairs, and the debilitating rifts between and within the political parties, were reflected in apparent inattention to the Sudanese economy. Although GDP increased in the 1960s by some 44.6 per cent, and the agricultural sector's share decreased from 47.7 per cent in 1965 to 35.6 per cent in 1969, agricultural production in 1969 still accounted for no less than 97.2 per cent of export earnings; while the economy was diversifying, reliance on agriculture, especially cotton, for foreign exchange actually increased. An Industrial Development Corporation was established in 1965 to manage public investment, and in 1967 the *Organization and Promotion of Industrial Investment Act* was designed to encourage private investment. In 1968 an Agricultural Reform Corporation was established to manage the private cotton schemes the government began to nationalize. The Sudan's balance of payments showed a surplus only in 1969; in no year did the value of exports exceed that of imports. While government revenue increased from £S74m in 1964–65 to £S92m in 1967–68, indebtedness increased alarmingly, to £S46m in 1969. Reliance on indirect taxes, always contingent on demand, continued, with direct taxation accounting in 1967–68 for only 4.4 per cent of government revenue.

Economic growth was prejudiced by the instability of successive coalition governments and volatile labour relations. Following the October revolution a rapid revival of unionism had occurred. Restraints imposed by the military régime were removed, only to be re-enacted ineptly by its parliamentary successor. The imbalance of this development may be seen in the number of new unions that appeared and in the increase in union membership. In 1964 some 74 unions had a total membership of about 125,000. By 1968 there were 357 unions, but membership had risen to only about 162,000: some 263 unions had fewer than 200 members each, while only one, the railway workers, had more than 25,000. Concerted industrial action thus became more difficult, but damaging local strikes, often with political overtones, increased. The government's inability to control labour disputes, like its maladroit handling of student unrest, was a symptom of underlying political malaise.

The crisis of the second parliamentary régime was not basically economic, but political. Strong action in Khartoum was needed not simply to deal with day-to-day affairs, but to restore public confidence in the parliamentary system. Such confidence, if it existed after the ousting of the Abboud régime, could not survive the personal and ideological disputes that had dominated political life since independence. Each new manoeuvre contributed to exasperation with politicians and contempt for parliamentary democracy itself. In April 1969 the Umma split was finally healed, leading quickly to the fall of Mahgoub's government. Mahgoub stayed on in a familiar caretaker role, while elections were planned. The revitalized Umma and DUP entered negotiations over a new constitution and announced agreement in early May. This was by now irrelevant, however, for the discredited politicians had, as in 1958, allowed for too long the subversion of the parliamentary system to personal advantage. When the army returned to power at the end of May 1969 the second parliamentary régime had as few defenders as the first.

CHAPTER THIRTEEN

The Era of Jaafar Nimeiri: 1969–85

The 1969 *coup* was led by a 'Free Officers' movement under Colonel Jaafar Muhammad Nimeiri, who had been implicated on two previous occasions, in 1957 and 1966, in plots against the government. Swift and bloodless, the takeover provoked no immediate overt resistance. The provisional constitution, Supreme Council, constituent assembly, public service commission and electoral commission were dissolved, public meetings banned and newspapers closed down until strict censorship could be imposed. Political parties were outlawed and their property confiscated; leading politicians, including Azhari and Mahgoub, were placed under arrest, and senior army officers were retired. The country was renamed the Democratic Republic of the Sudan.

A Revolutionary Command Council (RCC) of ten, nine of whom were young officers, was formed under Nimeiri's presidency; the sole civilian member, the ex-Chief Justice, Babikr 'Awadallah, was named prime minister. A cabinet of twenty-three was responsible to the RCC. Four RCC members and at least eight ministers were communists or leftists. Several members of the 1964–65 Transitional Government, two Southerners and figures drawn from the intelligentsia and business entered the cabinet; the prime minister said that the government would be 'leftist, socialist but not extremist or fanatic'. While the balance of power reposed in the RCC, and the strength of left-wing elements in the new establishment would soon prove misleading, the 'May Revolution' represented a shift to the left and away from the traditional style of Sudanese politics, contingent as that was on sectarian and personal loyalties.

The new régime considered itself the successor not to the previous military régime of Abboud, but to the combined forces of junior officers and the Professionals' Front that had toppled him in 1964. The fact that the Communist Party was not exempted from the order to disband was an omen of the struggle for control that was to dominate the first two years of the régime. The period witnessed elimination of challenges from right and left, and ended in consolidation of Nimeiri's personal position.

From the traditional parties the new order had little to fear. With their leaders under arrest and their main weapon, an appeal to parliamentary democracy, blunted by transparent self-interest, the parties were powerless to organize resistance. In August 1969 Isma'il al-Azhari died. The nationalist leader who had fought for, and in 1956 presided over, the demise of British rule, had since then been an unconstructive power-broker; Sudanese now recalled his earlier role. A threat to the new régime came in any case not from the NUP, some of whose members were amenable to its pronounced aims, but from the Mahdists. Discussions with al-Sadiq al-Mahdi broke down over his objection to communists in the government, and he was arrested. The Imam al-Hadi made no attempt even to appear conciliatory, but withdrew with his lieutenants to Aba Island, the cradle of Mahdism and stronghold of his family.

In March 1970 relations with the Ansar reached a climax. After riots in Omdurman, with heavy loss of life, the government launched an air attack on Aba, followed by an invasion of ground troops. Resistance was fierce, and subsequent estimates of fatalities among the Ansar were as high as 12,000. The Imam al-Hadi, grandson of the Mahdi, was killed during an apparent attempt to escape to Ethiopia. Aba was occupied, and the extensive holdings of the Mahdi's family were confiscated. Al-Sadiq al-Mahdi went into exile. This assertion of authority removed, for the foreseeable future, the danger of organized Ansar resistance, and served as a warning to disestablished political parties generally. But the violent nature of the assertion, unparalleled in the history of the independent Sudan, ensured permanent disaffection of a large and powerful element of the population.

Removal of this threat from the right paved the way for violent confrontation with the left. Directly after the 1969 *coup* it had seemed that the new régime would follow a course closely patterned on that of the communist programme. It extended relations with the socialist and Arab states, and took steps to form a one-party system and to develop national capital. Events soon showed that adoption of some communist positions was based on the officers' need for support from the left. Even before the impending showdown with the Ansar, Nimeiri moved gradually to dilute communist influence within the government. Relations deteriorated sharply from mid-1970. In November three members of the RCC were dismissed, the officer corps was purged and leading communist civilians were arrested. In early 1971 Nimeiri publicly accused the communists of subversion and, in a calculated appeal to an underlying Sudanese antipathy to communism, called for destruction of 'the communist movement'. In this he acted precipitately.

In July Major Hashim al-'Ata', with officers deposed from the RCC in the previous November, staged a *coup*. Nimeiri was arrested, and a 'democratic' system, involving 'industrial and agricultural revolution', was proclaimed. A new RCC was formed, and pro-communist demonstrations were staged in Khartoum. But the revolutionaries misjudged the response of the Sudanese, and of neighbouring states, to an openly communist régime. The Libyan leader, Colonel Gaddafi, ordered a British airliner bound for Khartoum to land in Libya, and arrested two leading conspirators. President Sadat ordered Egyptian troops stationed south of Khartoum to resist the *coup*. Troops loyal to Nimeiri moved on the capital from Shendi. Meanwhile he had escaped from detention and rallied his forces; the revolt was easily crushed. Hashim al-'Ata' and his colleagues were summarily executed. Al-Shafi' Ahmad al-Shaykh, the veteran labour leader, 'Abd al-Khaliq Mahjub, head of the communist party, and Joseph Garang, the leading Southern communist, were hanged, despite resolute denial of involvement in the *coup* and in defiance of international pleas for clemency.[1] A massive purge was initiated, and relations with the Eastern Bloc, accused by Nimeiri of complicity, deteriorated rapidly.

The abortive *coup* had important long-term effects. Suppression of the Ansar and communists undoubtedly increased Nimeiri's personal popularity but left the régime without the support of any major political or sectarian grouping. Nimeiri therefore acted quickly to strengthen his base and shore up his personal position. A referendum on his presidency in September reportedly resulted in a 98.6 per cent affirmative vote for Nimeiri, who was duly sworn in for a six-year term as president. Steps were taken to speed the establishment and organization of the Sudan Socialist Union (SSU).

Another consequence was recognition that foreign policy should be more closely aligned with domestic politics. Upon assuming power in 1969 the régime had asserted support for liberation movements in Africa, closer ties with Eastern Europe and total commitment to the Arab cause in the struggle with Israel. One of its first acts was to recognize the government of East Germany, and in 1970 Nimeiri embarked on tours of Eastern Europe, China and North Korea. Nimeiri also expounded views of Arab Socialism identified with those of Nasser and Gaddafi. In December 1969 Libya, Egypt and the Sudan agreed in the Tripoli Charter to co-ordinate foreign policies, a scheme that developed into a federation of Arab Republics which, despite domestic opposition and his own misgivings, Nimeiri publicly supported. Relations with the West deteriorated, owing to American support for Israel, Israeli support for Southern secessionists and the nationalization of foreign, mainly British, banks and companies.

The 1969 *coup* had raised hopes that a peaceful solution could be found for the Southern problem. Measures were announced to induce Southern co-operation, but rhetoric outpaced action, a failure blamed unconvincingly, after the 1971 *coup*, on the communist Joseph Garang. Nimeiri responded to continuing Anya Nya activity with a policy of suppression, which was, however, no more effective in 1969–70 than it had been under previous régimes.

Meanwhile divisions within the Southern leadership began to show signs of settlement. The Southern Sudan Provisional Government, established by Aggrey Jaden in 1967, had like previous attempts to place the Anya Nya under unified political command, failed. In 1969 Gordon Mayen founded the Nile Provisional Government, while General Emedio Taffeng established an organization called the Anyidi State Government, encompassing all factions except Mayen's. The sophistication of the Anya Nya campaign reached an unprecedented level under Taffeng, and attracted increasing international attention and support, but the problem of maintaining a unified command arose yet again. In July 1970 Colonel Joseph Lagu, commanding in Eastern Equatoria, successfully challenged Taffeng's authority. Leadership of the Anya Nya was concentrated, under Lagu, in a Southern Sudan Liberation Movement (SSLM).

By 1971 it was clear that Khartoum's attempts to reach a military solution were failing in the face of the Anya Nya's growing strength. After the July *coup* Nimeiri lacked the active collaboration of major political, sectarian or regional groupings, just as Lagu, having finally united the political and military leadership of Southern resistance, approached the régime, from a position of strength, to seek new negotiations. Nimeiri appointed Abel Alier to replace Joseph Garang as minister for Southern affairs. Secret meetings with Southern leaders in exile led to a conference in Addis Ababa in February 1972, at which representatives of the SSLM and the government reached agreement. In March the Addis Ababa accord became the *Regional Self-Government Act for the Southern Provinces*, and a ceasefire was declared.

The Addis Ababa Agreement grouped the three Southern provinces into a self-governing Region with its own assembly and High Executive Council (HEC) chaired by a presidential appointee. Khartoum would devolve powers over local government, education, public health, natural resources and police. Reserved to the sovereign national government were defence, foreign affairs, currency, inter-regional communications and the broad functions of economic, social and educational planning. Juba was designated the regional capital. The agreement was vague in important respects. Several annexes dealt with a future constitution, revenue, repatriation and resettlement of refugees and, most importantly, arrangements for a ceasefire. Indeed, it was probably these last that guaranteed respect of the agreement: a joint commission of the government, the SSLM and foreign entities would supervise the ceasefire. The national army in the South would consist of '12,000 officers and men of whom 6,000 shall be citizens of the Region and the other 6,000 from outside the Region'. Gradual integration of forces was to occur under a Joint Military Commission of senior officers from each side. Ratification and implementation of the agreement took place on 27 March 1972. Nimeiri later named Abel Alier president of the HEC, and the first Regional Assembly of sixty members was elected in November 1973.

The new regional government was at once beset by the ethnic and personal rivalries of its leaders. Integration of the Anya Nya into the national army was inevitably fraught, and although mutinous incidents at Wau and Akobo in 1976 and Juba in 1977 were exceptional, unemployed ex-guerrillas formed a disaffected interest group. Worse, Abel Alier gradually lost support as social and economic benefits expected from the peace settlement were slow to materialize, corruption was widely perceived and evident Dinka dominance was resented. Elections in 1978 led to Alier's resignation and brought into the Regional Assembly many of his most vociferous opponents, including Joseph Oduho, Benjamin Bol and Clement Mboro. Lagu became president of the HEC, with Samuel Aru Bol as vice-president. This set the stage for a power struggle in which Lagu, to retain his position, made important concessions to the allies of the ousted Alier. Corruption scandals further weakened the régime, and in February 1980 Nimeiri stepped in, dissolved the Regional Assembly and dismissed Lagu. Elections were held in April, and following a showdown between Alier and Aru Bol, Alier retained the presidency of the HEC.

Thus the inability or unwillingness of Southern politicians to put regional interests above their own was exploited in Nimeiri's constant juggling act. His clearly sinister proposal to 'redivide' the South into three 'regions' was supported by Lagu and other Equatorians chafed by overweening Dinkas. The Regional Assembly rejected this scheme in March 1981. Proponents pressed on, however, and in October Nimeiri dissolved the assembly, dismissed Alier and appointed an officer, Gismalla Abdalla Rassas, to head an interim government pending a referendum on redivision. Opponents of the plan were jailed, but in February 1982 Nimeiri cancelled the referendum, calling instead for new elections. These resulted in no clear majority, and after elaborate manoeuvres the divisionists triumphed and Joseph James Tombura, an Azande, was elected president of the HEC. In June 1983 Nimeiri unilaterally decreed division of the South into three regions corresponding to the old provinces.

The 'redivision' issue was one of several that divided Southerners and rekindled hostility to Khartoum. Some Anya Nya fighters, whether from principled opposition or disagreeable unemployment, had never accepted the Addis Ababa Agreement that, in any case, was now repeatedly and openly contravened. Dissatisfaction grew in inverse proportion to the pace of economic development. Prominent projects, such as the Jonglei Canal and the siting of an oil refinery at Kosti rather than in the South, where oil had been discovered, seemed to be of no benefit to the region. The new university at Juba did little to improve the lot of Southerners: there were but 4 among 158 students admitted to the scientific and technical faculties in 1984 when, moreover, a derisory 9 of 1,637 places at Khartoum University went to Southerners. In the period 1972–77 only 20 per cent of the money allocated to the South under Special Development Budgets was actually spent. Stagnation was ironically highlighted by rapid growth of a new bureaucracy, by corruption, inefficiency and an unfolding economic crisis. Southerners watched with suspicion and dismay as Nimeiri's commitment to secularism gave way – especially after a 1977 'reconciliation' with the religious right – and was abandoned in September 1983 when the Sharī'a was declared applicable to all Sudanese.

Armed resistance in the South was therefore rekindled not only by disregard of the Addis Ababa Agreement but also by thinly veiled recourse to failed policies of the past. The first such resistance, undertaken by a tribally based separatist group calling itself Anya Nya II, was soon superseded by the far more powerful and sophisticated Sudan People's Liberation Movement/Army (SPLM/SPLA), established in the summer of 1983 after the mutiny of an army battalion at Bor. Led by Colonel John Garang (unrelated to Joseph Garang), its unusually highly disciplined forces won a rapid series of victories against Khartoum's demoralized and poorly equipped forces, and by 1986 had taken control of most of the region. The SPLA received arms and other support from Ethiopia and, until the overthrow of Nimeiri in 1985, from Libya, but most of its materiel came from raids on, and defections from, government forces. The Nimeiri régime's slow initial response was followed by an inept carrot-and-stick approach that, however, lacked credibility in the light of history. Avowedly anti-separatist, but revolutionary and leftist, the SPLM/SPLA insisted on removal of Nimeiri himself, and to this end held secret talks with various Northern-based opposition groups.

That opposition had grown despite Nimeiri's attempts to broaden the base of his support through various demarches. One of these was in local government. The move away from Indirect Rule by the British in the 1930s and subsequent modification of the system had left considerable authority in the hands of tribal leaders in rural areas. These had proved to be a bulwark of conservatism. The Nimeiri régime was determined once and for all to deflate the shaykhs, and to integrate government into a new pyramidal structure closely linked with its Sudan Socialist Union. Councils had little revenue; many had no obvious function. Mainly advisory, they further bureaucratized a system already top-heavy. Thus while the principle was established of divorcing traditional authority from administrative responsibility, the principle of separating politics from administration was abandoned.[2]

Further steps towards decentralization were likewise taken to ensure central control. Establishment of the semi-autonomous Southern Region involved a degree of devolution unmatched by the 'regionalization' of the whole country in 1980. Then, five new 'regions' were established, and while certain powers of the central government were transferred to them, the staff and money needed to carry these out were not. 'Regionalization' thus added new layers of bureaucracy, administrators and assemblies, who had salaries but not autonomy.

A constituent assembly elected in October 1972 drafted a constitution that was promulgated in May 1973. A document of some 225 articles, it established a presidential system concentrating great authority in a head of state, elected by 'plebiscite', whose emergency powers included the right to suspend the constitution. The judiciary was directly responsible to the president. The thorny question of whether the state should be 'Islamic' was inanely sidestepped: while 'society should be guided by Islam', the state should 'endeavour to express' the values of both Islam and Christianity.

The 1973 constitution proclaimed the Sudan Socialist Union (SSU) the country's 'sole political organization'. Inaugurated in January 1972, the SSU was organized along lines both parallel to and intersecting the new administrative system's, at the local, district and provincial levels. Real control was vested in a central Political Bureau appointed by Nimeiri as chairman of the SSU. Despite periodic alterations of its nominal functions and scope, the

SSU remained until its liquidation in 1985 a vehicle for distributing patron-age. With an enormous bureaucracy and myriad formal responsibilities, it was never a real political party. Similarly the People's Assembly or parliament, while occasionally showing flashes of independence, was a rubber stamp. The old parties, officially defunct, retained a shadowy existence, and prominent ex-members formed cores of opposition or collaboration. But neither the SSU nor the Assembly ever threatened Nimeiri's personal dominance.

The numerous *coup* attempts that punctuated the Nimeiri years never-theless illustrate both the weakness of opposition and the insecurity of the régime. The most serious plot occurred in 1976, when al-Sadiq al-Mahdi, in Britain, master-minded a *coup* attempt with Libyan support. This was sup-pressed after several days of bloody street-fighting in the capital. Over one hundred executions ensued, and al-Sadiq and Sharif Husayn al-Hindi, scion of a notable religious family and a former NUP finance minister who with other politicians had established a National Front in exile, were tried *in absentia* and sentenced to death.

Although Nimeiri appeared to emerge from this violent confrontation with renewed strength, both domestic and international politics required reorientation of the régime and settlement with the National Front. The oppo-sition's surprising strength, and its support in Libya and Ethiopia, promised continuing instability and consequent disruption of the government's plans for foreign-financed economic development. For its part, the National Front had to recognize the likely survival of the régime as long as it retained the powerful support of the army and of Egypt, the Umma's historic enemy. Further, the differences between the Front and the régime were not of an immutable ideological character; since 1971 Nimeiri had jettisoned much of the revolu-tionary rhetoric that had so alarmed the religious right. In late 1976 mediation between Nimeiri and al-Sadiq al-Mahdi was undertaken, and the two met secretly at Port Sudan in July 1977. Agreement was reached on certain reforms, and an amnesty was declared. Al-Sadiq returned from exile in September. Sharif al-Hindi and others continued to demand more fundamental measures of reform, but al-Sadiq's return vitiated the strength and prestige of the opposi-tion in exile, while the vaunted 'process' of National Reconciliation benefited the régime more than it did its erstwhile opponents.

In elections to the People's Assembly in February 1978, candidates asso-ciated with the old Umma, DUP and Muslim Brothers won 80 of the 304 seats, while 'independents' took another 60. Al-Sadiq al-Mahdi, Hasan al-Turabi and other former opponents were appointed to the Political Bureau of the SSU. Al-Sadiq resigned after Nimeiri's outspoken support for the Camp David accords later in the year, but in 1979, as the régime tempered that support, relations warmed again. In 1980 the Ansar boycotted Assembly elections and, after further defeats in the now seemingly endless reconciliation process, in 1982 al-Sadiq al-Mahdi declared rapprochement a failure. His arrest and imprisonment in 1983 ironically clarified his opposition and helped to restore his prestige, while at the same time the increasingly close identification of the Muslim Brothers with the régime did much to dilute their appeals to principle.

Domestic politics after 1976 thus consisted of almost constant manoeuvring, tentative and temporary alliances, cabinet reshuffles and highly publicized new beginnings, all orchestrated by President Nimeiri who, against a background of theoretical 'reconciliation', stayed at least one step ahead of his opponents. Having failed to bring down the régime by force, they proved powerless to achieve basic reforms from within. Obviously opposed to the structure and leadership of the government, they yet found it impossible to break completely with it. The result was Nimeiri's continued personal dominance of a régime which, however, by the early 1980s, had clearly lost popular support.

Essential to neutralizing the opposition was Nimeiri's increasing attention to the role of Islam, which deprived the old parties of that argument against him that was most likely to attract mass support. Although initially this commitment was vague and brought no fundamental changes of policy, from the late 1970s a more substantive approach was adopted. The determination to bring Sudanese law into conformity with the precepts of Islam was underscored by the appointment of Hasan al-Turabi as attorney-general and, more dramatically, by comprehensive assertion of the Sharī'a in 1983. While this assured the support of the powerful Muslim Brothers, it further alienated secularists, Southerners and those Muslims to whom Nimeiri's version of the Sharī'a was unpalatable. Nimeiri's motives for turning towards Islam were deeply suspect, and his open association with minor *fakis* and obscure fanatics tainted the policy and the régime.

The 1970s witnessed a gradual shift in Sudanese foreign relations. Following the 1971 *coup* attempt, relations with the Socialist Bloc declined, while those with the West, China and most of the Arab states improved. Diplomatic relations with the US were resumed in 1972 but continued to be complicated by the Arab–Israeli dispute. In March 1973 the US ambassador was among three diplomats killed by Palestinians in Khartoum, and Nimeiri's decision to hand over the convicted murderers to the Palestine Liberation Organization necessarily strained relations with the US. The perceived threat of Soviet-backed régimes in Ethiopia and Libya, increasing dependence on Western and especially American aid, and Nimeiri's apparent belief in the domestic value of close American support, produced strong bilateral relations that lasted until the end of the régime. Relations with Egypt were similarly close, although these too were occasionally strained. A plan for 'economic and political integration' with Egypt was announced in February 1974, and in 1977 a mutual defence pact was signed. The Nimeiri régime stood out in support of President Sadat's peace treaty with Israel. In October 1982 Egypt and the Sudan signed an Integration Charter establishing various unified institutions and a Higher Council with its own budget. This was the furthest step yet taken towards the old Egyptian ideal of the Unity of the Nile Valley, and was predictably deprecated by the Ansar, Southerners and others, who saw the Charter as proof of the Sudan's subservience to Egypt and the US.

The disclosure in 1985 that the government had collaborated in transporting Ethiopian Jews to Israel produced similar embarrassment. But as relations with Libya and Ethiopia were soured by civil war in Chad, by Sudanese support for Eritrean separatists and by Ethiopian assistance to the SPLM/SPLA, alignment with Egypt and the US remained a central feature of Nimeiri's policy.

The Sudanese economy alternated after the 1969 revolution between periods of great optimism characterized by extravagant predictions and the launching of ambitious development projects, and periods of near bankruptcy, when foreign credit alone sustained the country. This inconsistency was caused partly by factors beyond Sudanese control: fluctuations in world market prices, slumps in demand for the Sudan's exports and exaggerated local effects of world recession and inflation. Problems were caused also by unbalanced investment policies, mismanagement, investors' uncertainty and difficulties of long-range planning when investment capital was closely tied to export performance. In the last years of the Nimeiri régime corruption became rampant, with deleterious effects on the economy, while the announced implementation of the Sharī'a in 1983 disrupted an already confused situation. By the mid-1980s an enormous foreign debt, inflation, shortages, devaluations and, ultimately, famine combined to bring the Sudan to a crisis of unprecedented proportions which, in part, led to the downfall of Nimeiri.

The 1971 *coup* attempt was a turning-point in economic policy as in domestic politics and foreign affairs. Prior to that the régime had instituted sweeping nationalization of both foreign and Sudanese companies and the banking and insurance industries. Some of these expropriations were reversed in early 1973. Bilateral trading arrangements with socialist states, especially with Eastern Europe, expanded rapidly, and foreign assistance came predominantly from the same sources. A Five-Year Industrial Development Plan was introduced in 1970 and later extended to seven years. But after the failed *coup* of 1971 and the Addis Ababa Agreement in 1972 the Sudan turned to the West and neighbouring Arab states. Emphasis shifted from state intervention to balanced co-operation between the government and its agencies on the one hand, and foreign companies and governments and the international aid agencies on the other. While efforts were made to increase manufacturing capacity, the government recognized that prosperity would depend, as in the past, on the success of agriculture. It was thus doubly unfortunate that ambitious schemes for rapid development came at a time of world recession and trade dislocation. While these were beyond the government's control, its strategy for dealing with them was not. Two fundamental errors proved costly: concentration on new schemes at the expense of those already in operation, and the financing of huge, long-term projects without the financial resources to meet short-term costs. Both of these errors were compounded by huge increases in the price of oil in the 1970s, leaving the Sudan severely exposed.

In the mid-1970s realization that the country's vast and largely untapped reserves of cultivable land were a major asset led to a number of ambitious proposals designed to make the Sudan the 'breadbasket' of the Middle East. In 1976 only 17 million of an estimated 200 million acres of cultivable land were under the plough. In 1973 the government and the Arab Fund for Economic and Social Development announced a twenty-five-year Basic Programme for Agricultural Development in the Sudan, calling for investment of some $6 billion during the first ten years. A number of projects were set in motion, but inattention to existing works, poor maintenance, shortages and other problems led to a decline in agricultural production, even as the cropped area was expanded by four million acres.

The tradition of huge development projects, begun with the Gezira Scheme and involving similar promises and risks, continued, with mixed results. Three innovative projects attracting special attention were the Rahad Scheme to cultivate cotton, groundnuts and other crops on 300,000 acres of irrigated land; the Kenana sugar project, designed to satisfy the enormous Sudanese demand and supply the Middle East; and the Jonglei Canal scheme in the South, a plan to by-pass the *sudd*, where much water is lost to evaporation, and thereby increase the Nile flow to the North and Egypt. The Jonglei project fell victim to the civil war (as did oil exploration). The Rahad and Kenana schemes were completed; at Kenana construction delays, cost overruns and mismanagement meant that sugar cost more to produce than to import. By the end of the 1970s the dream of the Sudan as breadbasket of the Middle East was over, to be replaced in subsequent years by the nightmare of drought and famine.

By the early 1980s the government had largely lost control of economic policy, and it lacked the will to take strong recovery measures. Weak world prices for the Sudan's dwindling exports, shortages that led to inflation, black-marketeering, the crippling of production and mismanagement and corruption on unprecedented levels all required drastic action. This was largely resisted for political reasons, but in May 1979 the government agreed to the International Monetary Fund's terms for continued support, which included cuts in public expenditure, reduction or elimination of subsidies and greater emphasis on exports, a programme blamed for urban riots that erupted in August. Yet in 1980–81 an explosion in the value of imports coincided with an actual decline in exports. With the country's external debt topping $3 billion, the World Bank halted aid and the IMF made emergency loans dependent on adoption of strict measures. In November 1981 Nimeiri therefore announced a recovery programme that included yet another devaluation, increased taxes on imports and the end of subsidies on basic foodstuffs, measures that temporarily satisfied foreign creditors and fell mainly on the poor.

The expectation of export-led recovery went unfulfilled. Devaluation increased the price of imports, while shortages, transport difficulties and lack of credit hindered production. Rampant black-marketeering resulted. A decline in exports led to a shortage of foreign exchange and thus reduced supplies of oil and other requirements for agriculture. Prospects for controlling corruption were poor when high officials themselves were its chief sponsors. When in September 1982 it had become clear that the government could not meet its obligations, which were far higher than had been revealed, the IMF cancelled a previously arranged 'standby credit'. By 1984–85 the Sudan's economic problems had become insoluble: the urban riots and rural famine that marked the final phase of the Nimeiri era were the inescapable evidence of political as well as economic collapse.

That collapse was reflected in the decline or breakdown of institutions in all areas of national life. The education system suffered from political interference and a lack of funds. The quality and distribution of medical care declined, as resources were increasingly channelled from public hospitals to private clinics. The press, radio and television became mouthpieces for the régime. Trade unions and professional associations were hamstrung, superseded by hollow official organs, or ignored altogether, their leaders either publicly espousing the official line or subjecting themselves to periodic arrest and imprisonment without trial. Government departments proliferated, but were often façades for political patronage and were immobilized by lack of finance and direction. Political appointments to meaningless posts devalued government service, as even distinguished officials of the old school gave way to Nimeiri's transparent blandishments. The law was disregarded, and courts were reduced to mere enforcers of the President's wishes. Islam itself was mocked, as Nimeiri assumed the title of Imam and described as Islamic a state in collapse. Apathy and cynicism resulted, and the conviction was widespread that nothing short of radical change in the political structure could reverse the trend.

By the mid-1980s Nimeiri's mastery of Sudanese politics was his last remaining asset. His deftness at dividing and ruling was legend; he had collaborated with almost every political group, from communists to Muslim Brothers, from ex-Anya Nya guerrillas to traditional tribal chiefs. But demoralized and without credibility, his opponents' energies were spent in irrelevant ideological debate and personal intrigue. When Nimeiri's personal rule collapsed in 1985 it was under the weight of an unprecedented combination of foreign pressure, economic disaster, famine, civil war, popular disgust and the overweening self-confidence of a ruler who had come to despise his own people.

Throughout 1984, as the régime lurched from one crisis to another, it seemed to many that the end was at last in sight. Yet still no clear focus of opposition, no party, interest group or individual emerged to challenge Nimeiri directly. Serious strikes by various professionals were followed in April by the declaration of a state of emergency. A virtual reign of terror ensued, during which specially constituted 'courts of decisive justice', presided over by Muslim Brothers, purported to render 'Islamic' justice for a wide range of novel offences. Floggings, amputations and executions were met with incredulity and despair at home and abroad. When even the docile People's Assembly hesitated to rubber-stamp drastic constitutional amendments, Nimeiri dissolved it. In January 1985 Mahmud Muhammad Taha, the seventy-six-year-old leader of the Republican Brothers, who objected to the régime's brand of Sharī'a, was arrested and, after a showtrial, was executed for 'heresy'. In March Nimeiri turned on the Muslim Brothers, his last civilian supporters, and imprisoned their leaders on a variety of charges, including plotting to overthrow the government. There remained the army, on which in his last resort Nimeiri had to rely. Apparently sure of its continued support he left Khartoum, amid anti-government riots, in late March for a visit to Washington.

Although in retrospect the overthrow of Nimeiri in April 1985 appears to have been inevitable, in fact the outcome was uncertain until the army publicly abandoned him. Demonstrations in the Three Towns were met by police and troops and suppressed with loss of life. A general strike was called and received an enthusiastic response. Nimeiri cut short his visit to the US and enplaned for Khartoum but, before he had reached Cairo the commander-in-chief, General 'Abd al-Rahman Muhammad Siwar al-Dahab, announced on national radio that the army would 'yield to the wishes of the people'. Nimeiri remained in exile in Egypt, and a Transitional Military Council was constituted to rule the country. Doubts about the intentions of these officers were drowned in the general rejoicing over the downfall of the man who had ruled the Sudan longer than any other in its modern history.

CHAPTER FOURTEEN

The Transitional Government and the Third Parliamentary Régime: 1985–89[1]

There were striking similarities between the overthrow of Nimeiri and the fall of the Abboud régime in 1964. Both occurred after periods of rising dissatisfaction with economic policies and in the context of civil war. In each case the end came as the result of popular fury, channelled and led by trade unions and professional associations rather than political parties. Initial attempts at suppression were met by determined resistance, casualties in the streets and divided counsels within the army. In neither 1964 nor 1985 was there a concerted conspiracy, and in the transitional periods that ensued new political forces tried and failed to prevent a return to party politics. In 1964 the army fled from power; in 1985 it appropriated it to protect its own position, and presided over a resumption of traditional politics.

That Nimeiri's overthrow resulted from a reluctant military *coup* was clear within hours. Reflecting the deep social divisions that he had so skilfully exploited, the army was itself riven by factions, and the generals' decision to topple the régime avoided a *coup* from below and revolution in the streets. United only in opposing Nimeiri, civilian leaders of the uprising accepted General Siwar al-Dahab's pledge of the army's transitional role, and deferred to his threat to treat as treason continuation of the general strike. In deciding, however suspiciously, to 'give the generals a chance', the strike leaders in effect called off the uprising, and forfeited an historic opportunity. Amid euphoria in Khartoum, a discordant note was struck when John Garang, the SPLM leader, in a clandestine radio address denounced 'Nimeiriism without Nimeiri', and demanded that the army hand over power to civilians. The situation was fluid, with no party or interest group having obvious mass support, and no certainty about what direction the generals would take. The essentially improvisational nature of the April *coup* was one reason for this; the continuing divisions of Sudanese politics were another.

In their first weeks in power, the officers reacted to events, but by the end of April, because of ineffective civilian opposition, they were safely in command. On 9 April a fifteen-man Transitional Military Council was announced, under Siwar al-Dahab, to act as head of state and source of legislation. The constitution was suspended, the moribund SSU dissolved. Political detainees were released after a mob stormed the notorious Kober Prison; Nimeiri's security police were disbanded only after a mass demonstration. All laws remained in effect, including the omnibus *State Security Act* and the infamous 'September Laws' establishing Nimeiri's Sharī'a. Some officials were arrested, but most were not, and the trials that followed were crowd-pleasing rather than purgative. Too many prominent individuals had held office under Nimeiri to make a clean sweep realistic.

Contributing to the upheaval of late March and early April was the Alliance of National Forces for National Salvation, a coalition of mass organizations. Its charter, signed originally by trade unions and vestigial political parties (the Umma, DUP and communists), called for a three-year transitional period during which the 1956 provisional constitution, as amended in 1964, would be reinstated, basic freedoms restored, self-government revived in the South and the country freed from 'dependence on world imperialism'. The force of these demands was dissipated by factionalization. The National Islamic Front rejected the charter, and signatories flouted its provisions. The Alliance continued to represent a major strand of opinion, but attention reverted from mass meetings to back rooms, and from 'new forces' to old politics.

Within weeks of the *coup* dozens of 'parties' had announced their otherwise unnoticed existence. The Alliance's call for a transitional period, during which new political formations might occur, failed in the face of traditional parties' opposition. They, having collaborated with Nimeiri and had no role in his downfall, were anxious to establish legitimacy through elections, as in 1965. After complicated manoeuvres the Transitional Military Council (TMC) appointed a cabinet led by Gazuli Dafalla, president of the doctors' union; a diplomat, Ibrahim Taha Ayub, was named foreign minister; the defence portfolio went to Brigadier Uthman Abdalla Muhammad of the TMC. Southern activists rejected tokenism, so three old-school politicians were appointed, one of them, Samuel Aru Bol, in the meaningless post of deputy prime minister. Obviously subordinate to the TMC, this caretaker cabinet's main duties were to carry on the day-to-day affairs of administration. The cabinet had no constituency and its influence declined as elections neared.

Agreement on an interim constitution occurred after long debate. Based on the provisional constitution of 1956 as amended in 1964, the document also incorporated subsequent provisions for Southern autonomy, and in- cluded arrangements for immediate legislation. Attempted compromises over Sharī'a and the 'September Laws', however leniently enforced, provoked dis- appointment or derision. Indeed the constitution exemplified the transitional government's tendency to postpone difficult decisions for consideration by its successor. Although a case could be made for this, the new parliamentary régime would have benefited from a few accomplished facts in difficult areas.

In promising to restore civilian rule within a year the TMC was as good as its word. Elections to a constituent assembly were held in April 1986. The graduates' constituency, now enlarged to encompass other 'modern forces', was revived. The war prevented polling in thirty-seven Southern constituencies. The Umma emerged as the largest party with one hundred seats and al-Sadiq al-Mahdi, having failed to construct a national government, formed a coalition with the DUP and smaller parties. The official opposition was the National Islamic Front (NIF), which emerged with fifty-one seats and the greatest increase in public support as measured against the last free elections of eighteen years earlier. A five-man Supreme Council would again act as collective head of state, under the presidency of Ahmed 'Uthman al-Mirghani. Thus the government was headed by a descendant of the Mahdi, and the council of state by a scion of the Mirghanis. The TMC was dissolved and Siwar al-Dahab went gracefully into retirement.

Three related issues dominated the period 1986–89: continuing war in the South, the nature of the national constitution and the economy. Despite twenty years in the political wilderness, al-Sadiq failed to take decisive action over the question of an Islamic constitution and the role in society of the Shari'a. In temporizing he squandered his inherited aura of national leadership, and resumed a sectarian role. In this he was no worse than his sometime coalition partners, the DUP and, towards the end, the NIF, whose participation in the endless debate was negative and unconstructive.

To Southerners, al-Sadiq's indecision appeared more sinister. The war intensified while the impression gained strength that Khartoum governments, whether military or civilian, were more interested in islamization than reconciliation. Revealing disregard for civilian lives and a view of Sudanese history at variance with its nationalist rhetoric, the government armed Baggara militias in the west. These *murahalin* reverted to the ways of their ancestors and raided into the Southern provinces, with devastating effect. Moreover the drought and famine that had contributed to Nimayri's downfall had spread and worsened, making refugees of millions in the eastern Sudan as well as the west, in the Bahr al-Ghazal and in neighbouring Ethiopia, even as the war continued. As many as 500,000 died, many under the horrific conditions prevailing in makeshift camps unacknowledged by their own government. Southerners pouring into Kordofan and Darfur were left to the mercy of the Missiriyya and Rizayqat. A massacre of Dinka refugees at al-Daaien in 1987 came to epitomize both the plight of defenceless Southerners and the fecklessness of the Khartoum régime.[2] When reports finally attracted foreign attention a massive international relief effort ensued, notably under the umbrella of Operation Lifeline Sudan.

Meanwhile contacts forged by the National Alliance and the SPLM were fitfully pursued, hampered by mutual suspicions of the army, Alliance, SPLM and Northern parties. The Koka Dam Agreement of the Alliance and SPLM in March 1986 formed a positive basis for negotiation, but posed a threat to Khartoum politicians and Southern factions. The very success of the SPLA in a fragmented and confused Southern military landscape caused constant recalibration of political positions; the optimal moment for one side to negotiate was the worst time for its opponents. When, for example, the SPLA made highly embarrassing forays into 'Northern' territory in 1987, outrage in Khartoum left little room for imaginative concessions.

An apparent breakthrough came in November 1988, when the SPLM and DUP (with Egyptian support behind the scenes) reached agreement on a plan to end the war. This called for a constitutional convention and freezing of the 'September Laws'. Anticipating reaction from the religious right, al-Sadiq, while expressing personal approval, refused to adopt this as government policy. The DUP thereupon withdrew from the coalition. In February 1989 al-Sadiq announced a coalition with the NIF making Hasan al-Turabi his deputy and foreign minister. This was more than the army would stand for; in a tense standoff lasting several weeks, the army insisted on a broader government with a stated commitment to end the war. Al-Sadiq's temporizing and backpedalling by now appeared a policy, and it was only at the end of March that a new government took office, excluding the NIF, which took to the streets. The government approved the terms of the SPLM-DUP Agreement (although still not adopting it as official policy), and in April sent a delegation to Ethiopia to open talks with the SPLM.

These developments had occurred against a backdrop of resurging SPLA success in the field. In March 1988 Gordon Kong brought most of the 'Anya-Nya 2' rebels into the SPLA fold, opening the way for major advances against the government in the Nuer areas of western Upper Nile. By late 1988 almost all of Equatoria had fallen to the rebels. As the political situation in Khartoum deteriorated and morale within the army plunged, the SPLA maintained a degree of unity and control historically unique among Southern guerrilla groups. But Garang's freedom of political movement was unmatched in Khartoum. When the SPLA proclaimed a unilateral ceasefire in May, al-Sadiq again prevaricated and delayed; the SPLM's irreducible terms for negotiating remained essentially those it had agreed to with the DUP, but these, if implemented, would array the full force of the NIF against the government and indeed the parliamentary régime. The secession of the South had by now become a talking point even in NIF circles, since it would at a stroke render the country that remained almost entirely Muslim and ready for Shari'a; concomitant gerrymandering would place all of the country's proven oil reserves to the North of the new international border. Al-Sadiq's hand-wringing was further highlighted when Garang made a successful foreign tour, offering in Washington and London the sort of concessions to the Khartoum régime that made him rather than it appear in control of affairs.

John Garang's reception on the world stage was one indication among many that the Sudan's foreign relations under the TMC and the third parliamentary period were inseparable from the looming chaos at home. Relations with the West especially were hampered by the treatment meted out to international aid and relief agencies. Immediately after the ousting of Nimeiri the TMC had admitted the food emergency in the western Sudan and appealed for aid, which was forthcoming. But the long-term emergency of war in the South was responsible for hundreds of thousands of casualties, both directly owing to the fighting and more insidiously through famine and disease; the SPLM set up its own relief arm to coordinate aid in the territories that came under its control. Al-Sadiq's government freely employed the 'food weapon'. Operation Lifeline Sudan was harassed by both the government and rebels, each side detecting in its activities assistance to the other; innocent civilians were caught in the middle, to the consternation of world opinion. That opinion was further turned against Khartoum by the TMC's rapprochement with Libya, long a pariah in Western eyes; under al-Sadiq rapprochement became Sudanese dependence because of economic collapse and the consequent need for aid that others were no longer willing to supply without the sort of harsh measures of retrenchment that historically heralded the end of a régime.

Relations with Egypt deteriorated throughout the third parliamentary period. A great-grandson of the Mahdi, al-Sadiq led a party whose founding reasons for existence included opposition to Egyptian pretensions in the Sudan. Nimeiri had enjoyed close Egyptian support, often at the expense of Ansar, Umma and al-Sadiq himself. In 1989 al-Sadiq abrogated the joint-defence agreement Nimeiri had reached in 1976 with President Sadat. Nor was Egypt's rôle in engineering the DUP-SPLM Agreement at the end of 1988 seen in Khartoum as entirely benign; Egyptian alignment with the DUP and its predecessor unionist groupings was to the Umma (and others) unwarranted interference in Sudanese affairs. When an Egyptian hand was occasionally discerned in the pronouncements and activities of the SPLM itself, even the old spectre of Egyptian machinations for control of the Upper Nile arose.

In its defence, the third parliamentary régime faced in 1986 Nimeiri's legacy of social and economic disaster, and with little means of combating it. Boxed in by party-politics and civil war, al-Sadiq's successive coalitions also had to deal with deferred expectations of a restless population whose living standards had long been in decline and whose improvisations alone had seemed to keep the country afloat. Nor did international agencies and their Western sponsors make special allowances. The proliferation of foreign aid agencies in the country, while embarrassing some Sudanese and providing opportunities for employment and fraud, did little to restore stability or engender growth. Attempts to come to terms with the IMF failed, and in February 1986 the Sudan was declared ineligible for further loans; the Sudanese pound was devalued and new austerity measures were announced. In October 1987 another devaluation took place, and further retrenchment was announced in line with IMF policy. When price controls were lifted at the end of 1988, a state of emergency had to be declared to control violent demonstrations; in the face of trade-union and other concerted opposition al-Sadiq withdrew some measures and offered to increase the salaries of civil servants. As in other spheres, the government appeared hopelessly weak in the face of opposition.

By the middle of 1989 al-Sadiq's régime had ironically come to resemble Nimeiri's in important ways. Although his authority was formally based in an elected parliament, the series of deals he had made with the DUP, NIF and army to stay in power discredited the parliamentary process. In economic affairs the régime appeared simply to have given up. By prosecuting the war through tribal militias al-Sadiq had abdicated a principal attribute of sovereignty. By vacillating between calls for abolishing the 'September Laws' and support for penal codes based on Sharī'a he had exasperated secularists and confirmed the suspicions of Southerners. When negotiations with the SPLM appeared in June 1989 at last to be bearing fruit, observers detected another manoeuvre to retain power in Khartoum.

To some elements in the army, and their allies in the NIF, al-Sadiq's deal with the SPLM to freeze implementation of Islamic law, continue a ceasefire and pull out of military pacts with Egypt and Libya, appeared more dangerous. On 30 June, the army overthrew the régime in a nearly bloodless *coup*. A fifteen-member Revolutionary Command Council for National Salvation was formed; General 'Umar Hasan Ahmed al-Bashir became commander-in-chief, prime minister and minister of defence. The constitution was suspended, parliament was dissolved, political parties and trade unions were banned and newspapers closed down. Leading politicians, including al-Sadiq al-Mahdi, were arrested, and the army officer corps was drastically purged. The political orientation of the new régime was somewhat obscure for several months. What was clear from the outset, however, was its opposition to the terms of al-Sadiq's deal with the SPLM. But while that deal was cited as a reason for the *coup*, and for its timing, failure to come to grips with the Sudan's political, economic and social problems should not be lost sight of. That failure was both personal and systemic, as events before and after clearly showed.

CHAPTER FIFTEEN

The National Islamic Front in Power, 1989–99

The initial Sudanese response to the overthrow of parliamentary democracy was predictably similar to that of 1958 and 1969. Opinion in 1989 was remarkably consistent that the new military régime, like its predecessors, would not last long because of its narrow base of popular support. In this most Sudanese and foreign observers misjudged the régime, which in some respects was unlike any the Sudan had experienced, underestimated its tenacity and placed unrealistic hope in its feckless opponents.[1]

In its first months the RCC gave only tantalizing hints of ideological orientation. This was the result of two factors: both the relative power within the régime of key individuals, and relations between the RCC and NIF, had not yet been determined. General Bashir denied such relations, and veterans of previous régimes joined secularists and Southerners in the new cabinet. Moreover the RCC's initial acts were in keeping with the new broom expected of the military: steps were taken to root out corruption; trials of a few notorious characters ended in long sentences and even executions. When protests erupted against austerity measures, harsh sentences were imposed on strike leaders; further arrests, detentions without trial and reports of torture were variously interpreted.

By early 1990 the fact that the NIF was the driving force behind the régime was reflected in public opposition and violent repression. The government repeatedly purported to discern plots against it; scores of officers and politicians were arrested in March 1990, and some 28 officers were court-martialled and executed. New military tribunals superseded civilian courts. International agencies documented instances of torture, deaths under suspicious circumstances in detention, 'disappearances' and executions without trial. 'Ghost houses' – secret places of interrogation and torture – dealt with suspected opponents. The army was purged, and mass recruitment of Muslim Brothers undertaken. Hundreds of civilians from across the political spectrum were arrested. Demonstrations and strikes were dealt with harshly. The teaching staff of the University of Khartoum was purged, and layoffs from government-controlled industries, notably the politicized railways, were widespread. Extra-legal organs of the régime were increasingly the agents of repression; new, armed entities were established to neutralize the state apparatus. Women were hounded out of public life, 'Islamic' punishments decreed and the judiciary, civil service and diplomatic corps were purged. In March 1991 the régime imposed the Sharī'a, in part excepting the South.

By 1991 civil servants recognized that their jobs depended on acquiescence in the NIF's evolving policies. The repeated need to purge the army, put down dissent, reshuffle the cabinet for ideological purity and align with NIF prescriptions even technical aspects of administration, revealed the character of a régime at odds with the traditional Sudanese political and institutional framework. An example was the People's Defence Force, which drafted young men, indoctrinated them in jihad and sent them to fight in the border regions and South. Imposition of the Sharī'a, and other steps towards an 'Islamic' state, conformed with the wishes of the only organized body of opinion on which the régime could depend.

Hasan al-Turabi, leader of the NIF, remained an *éminence grise*, occupying before 1996 no important post but in personal control of the party. With the passage of time he had become a world figure, admired by some as a puritanical visionary, denounced by others as an apostle of terror and exporter of violence; his long career shows remarkable adaptability. Born in Kassala in 1932, the son of a *qadi*, he took degrees in Khartoum, London and Paris and taught law at Khartoum until 1965, when he was elected to parliament from the special graduate constituency. Related by marriage to al-Sadiq al-Mahdi, he yet vied for the leadership of the religious right, and emerged as a champion of the Islamic state. When the Muslim Brothers were suppressed after the May Revolution, Turabi was imprisoned, but after the failed *coup* of 1976 he joined in 'national reconciliation' and became a member of the SSU. He was attorney general (1979–83) and an official adviser to Nimeiri until 1985 when, in the twilight of the régime, he was again jailed. Long association with Nimeiri gave Turabi the time and means to organize his movement, but also opened him (and it) to the charge of collaboration. Nevertheless, as we have seen, the NIF emerged from the 1986 elections as the third largest party and official opposition in parliament. After the 1989 *coup* Turabi was among those imprisoned, but his subsequent ascendancy led to speculation that detention masked connivance in or even direction of the *coup*, and he was undoubtedly the leading figure in the Sudan during the régime's first decade in power.

Whatever the extent of Turabi's personal role, from at least early 1990 the régime espoused NIF positions. This closeness (if not identity) of views ensured both the continued hostility of every other important Sudanese political grouping, at home and in exile, and the ability of the NIF to have its way with a junta dependent on its support. Thus purges of the army and cabinet shuffles continued, former politicians were arrested and re-arrested and urban violence recurred sporadically; assassination attempts were made on Bashir and Turabi himself in 1992. Establishment that year of a hand-picked Transitional National Assembly contrasted starkly with the activities abroad of the National Democratic Alliance (NDA), an umbrella group founded soon after the *coup* of almost all Sudanese political bodies and trade unions except the NIF but including, from early 1990, the SPLM. The effectiveness of the NDA was vitiated by its political heterogeneity and personal ambitions; members were irreconcilable over Sharī'a, and a façade of unity was permitted only by a programme of obfuscating platitudes. The so-called Legitimate Command of the Armed Forces, comprising exiled officers purged from the Sudanese army, allied formally with the SPLM/SPLA.

Attempts to broaden the popular base of the régime were transparently self-serving. In 1993 the RCC was formally dissolved and Bashir assumed the title of president; theoretically loosening central control, in 1994 the régime divided the Sudan into twenty-six provinces. But NIF dominance remained, and the continuing civil war and international isolation of the Sudan pro-voked renewed association of the régime with symbols of Islam. In 1996 the Transitional National Assembly that had rubber-stamped legislation was replaced by a body packed through restrictive electoral rules guaranteeing an NIF majority. It duly elected Hasan al-Turabi as Speaker, while a vote was staged to confirm Bashir as president. In 1998 a new constitution was adopted by rigged vote. Behind the enshrinement of Islam as sole source of national legislation observers detected a test of strength between Turabi and Bashir, who assumed sweeping new powers. When political associations, parties in all but name, were legalized, a plethora duly emerged, most notably Turabi's new vehicle, the National Congress Party.[2] In a series of political and legislative manoeuvres he and Bashir jockeyed for support, a process that briefly improved the prospects of the régime's opponents at home and in exile. On the eve of a vote by the assembly, however, engineered by Turabi to curb presidential powers, Bashir sent in the army, dissolved the assembly and declared a national emergency. New elections were called for 2000.

That Khartoum increasingly depicted the war in the South as jihad against infidels, domestic and foreign, is thus unsurprising. In its conduct of the war, however, from a confused and unimaginative start in 1989 the régime achieved some success. This was in part fortuitous, the result of two related factors: the splintering of the SPLM/SPLA, which allowed the régime to win the support – occasional, temporary and often of dubious value – of Southerners disaffected from John Garang and the movement he led; and the collapse of the *Dergue* in Ethiopia. But both the initial weakness of the junta and relative strength of the SPLA in the aftermath of the 1989 *coup* militated against early progress towards a settlement.

Although the timing of the 1989 *coup* had made obvious the opposition of its leaders to the deal al-Sadiq al-Mahdi had struck with the SPLM, the Bashir régime nevertheless purported to offer the olive branch. Lacking substance, its early proposals were rejected with scathing contempt by the SPLM, which then had the upper hand in the fighting and was anyway loath to renegotiate with a junta the agreements reached with an elected government. While a ceasefire was repeatedly extended, and the régime convened a Khartoum 'peace conference' (without the SPLM), both sides redoubled efforts to win foreign support. By mid-1990 most of the South was under SPLM/SPLA control, Juba and Wau were surrounded and inroads had been made into the Northern marches.

The tide turned abruptly in 1991. Khartoum's self-defeating support of Iraq's conquest of Kuwait had already confirmed its pariah status. An NIF conference in April called Muslims everywhere to holy war in the Southern Sudan: foreign jihadists poured in, while Westerners fled the country; the Sudan became a haven for revolutionaries and hangers-on from across the Muslim world, notably Usama b. Ladin but including many lesser lights. The collapse of the Mengistu régime in Ethiopia in May cost the SPLM/SPLA its main foreign backer and base, and created an exodus of hundreds of thousands of Southern refugees back to the Sudan, where many died, unfed, in squalid camps.

In August a disastrous split of the SPLM was revealed when three senior commanders, Riak Machar Teny, Gordon Kong Chol and Lam Akol Ajawin, tried to overthrow John Garang: suspicious, he had acted to forestall the plot, thus precipitating the *coup* before preparations were complete. It failed; the Nasir Group, as the movement was called after its base, was widely depicted as personal and tribal: two of the conspirators were Nuer, one Shilluk, while Garang and the bulk of his followers were Dinka.[3] Open warfare on several fronts, and the famine partly caused by it, led to enormous civilian casualties. In events sometimes conflated as the 'Bor Massacre', thousands of Dinka were killed in horrific circumstances, and tens of thousands made refugees; Bor was destroyed. Attempts to heal the rift failed, and years of highly charged but fruitless mediation ensued. Garang's faction (called successively SPLM/SPLA-Torit and SPLM/SPLA Mainstream) was always the stronger. But the Nasir Group (or SPLM/SPLA-United after William Nyuon Bany joined in 1992) held one card that made its neutralization or reintegration essential: dalliance with Khartoum.

Awaiting – and fomenting – Southern disunity had always been Khartoum's ultimate weapon, and the SPLM split was immediately exploited by the NIF régime. Having failed to oust Garang, and with no dependable source of funds or weapons, the Nasir Group contacted the government both publicly (as at Frankfurt in January 1992) and in secret. Khartoum supplied weapons and wielded the food weapon against Garang, ironically helped by Operation Lifeline's agreement to recognize the Nasir Group's own relief organization. The Nasir rebels won further legitimacy when, in May–June 1992 they were represented, along with the Torit faction, in talks with the Sudanese government under the Organization of African Unity (OAU) auspices in Abuja. These failed but ended with the two factions agreeing to a common position on self-determination for the South.

There ensued at various locations (Abuja, Barcelona, Amsterdam, Nairobi, London, Washington) at least three other sets of negotiations – between the two factions and between each of them and the Khartoum régime – sometimes facilitated by foreign governments (Nigeria, Egypt, Libya, Eritrea, Ethiopia, Uganda, Kenya; the US State Department, Congress and ambassador in Khartoum), organizations (the UN, the OAU and its successor, the African Union, Inter-Governmental Authority on Drought and Development (IGADD), Christian Solidarity) or individuals (Jimmy Carter, 'Tiny' Rowland, Sudanese living abroad). Involvement also of the NDA or a member illustrates the point that, whatever their announced purpose, in such negotiations the various parties were often jockeying for position rather than expecting – or attempting to reach – a lasting peace. Even in the late 1990s no party to negotiations was irrevocably committed to any particular point of agreement in previous talks, and the most that may be said is that such points eased the excruciating process that ended in the Comprehensive Peace Agreement of 2005.

The latter half of the decade witnessed moreover a calculated attempt by the NIF régime to achieve 'Peace from Within' – a separate deal with the Nasir Group or, as that faction split, with various individuals – even as it continued to pursue its war aims in the South. Those were simple enough: pacification and control of the oilfield areas and maintenance of the country's international borders through incessant violence, goals conducive to ethnic cleansing. The military position was thus ultimately one of deadlock, with disastrous consequences for civilians. Fighting between SPLA factions was complicated by defections or expulsions from each to the other – or to neither – of soi-disant commanders. Elements of 'Anya Nya 2' continued their own bloody operations, as did various tribal militias.

When in 1993 some rebel commanders joined the Nasir Group as 'SPLA-United', others broke away to re-join the SPLM/SPLA-Mainstream. In 1994 SPLA–United itself broke up: Riek Machar ordered the arrest of Lam Akol, who escaped, but John Luk and Gordon Kong were jailed. Riek thereupon changed the rump's name to South Sudan Independence Movement (SSIM); he and William Nyuon dismissed each other. Lam re-launched the SPLM/SPLA-United. Each of these factions in turn gained prominent members from – or lost them to – another or to Khartoum. In April 1996 Riak and Kerubino Kwanyin Bol signed a 'Political Charter' with Khartoum; others signed later. Lam Akol resurfaced there in 1998 as Minister of Transport. Frivolous differences failed to mask personal ambition and the consequent appeal to tribal loyalties in a political game of musical chairs.

Despite a characteristic fog of factionalism within both the South and the exiled Northern political establishment, two fundamentally opposed visions of the Sudan remained discernible. The NIF régime, with rhetoric sometimes reflected in public policy, held fast to the concept of the Islamic State. It thus comported essentially with its predecessors, military and civilian, in seeing the South as an integral part of the Sudan, and itself as bound to a civilizing mission of islamization. That it couched this fundamental view in the jargon of statecraft did not conceal an inherently colonialist, even totalitarian, attitude, but one that the old sectarian political parties were yet still unwilling to renounce. And while the mainstream SPLM continued to espouse a united – but democratic and secular – Sudan, others reflected more accurately (if opportunistically) Southerners' aspiration for outright independence from the Arab Muslim North.

Nevertheless, beginning in 1994, mediation by an East African regional body, IGADD,[4] clarified in carefully calculated language a convergence of the two main rebel factions over the necessity for a secular system in the Sudan, or at least in the South, pending Southerners' exercising a right of self-determination. It was over these two basic points, however, that Khartoum would not commit, and after four rounds of talks over many months the IGADD mediation too ended in failure. There followed in April 1997 a more general peace deal between Khartoum and several Southern leaders purporting to have significant followings. This affirmed continuing unity of the Sudan, with a federal structure, and the promise of a Southern referendum on secession. Principal signatories were rewarded with appointments: Riek Machar was named to head a new council for the South but, *ipso facto*, like past Southern politicians in Khartoum, he had no power nor, more importantly, would various Southern militants submit to his authority. True to form, most of them duly defected.

While old ethnic tensions were revived in support of each rebel faction and indeed degenerated even into *intra*-tribal civil war, notably among the Nuer, there was often nothing but egoism dividing various rebel leaders. The appearance of new military-political 'movements' with high-sounding names and issuing countless 'declarations', 'charters', 'accords' and 'protocols' seemed juvenile but for their fatal consequences.[5] A similar pattern emerged in the travelling road show of ageing expatriate 'leaders' of Southern opinion who claimed attention in pretentious symposia at European and American hotels. Evergreen political 'movements', some with their own military ambitions, likewise appeared within the neighbouring regions in revolt, including Darfur and the Eastern Sudan. Meanwhile in March 1994 a National Convention of the mainstream SPLM/SPLA had enhanced John Garang's legitimacy. It endorsed comprehensive reorganization of the movement, an amnesty for defectors and, importantly, establishment of an administrative infrastructure for occupied territory under the rubric of a 'New Sudan'. Because fighting intensified between the government's regular and militia forces and the mainstream SPLA, mass migrations, famine and civilian casualties in the hundreds of thousands briefly recaptured international attention. But the NIF régime was heartened by success in exploiting Southern rivalries in pursuit of goals less lofty than victory or peace. In 1993 the Arakis corporation won exclusive rights to exploit the oil reserves in the so-called Heglig and Unity fields, and Khartoum made common cause with the Nuer commander of Anya-Nya 2, Paulino Matip, to secure the area.

By the turn of the century the outcome of the civil war remained in doubt. That it had during the first decade of NIF rule in many ways followed a pattern set since independence gave little hope for political settlement and no reason to expect a military solution. The seeming impossibility of co-operation between a Southern rebel organization, even as sophisticated and determined as the SPLM/SPLA, and Northern-based parties, even when facing their own destruction at the hands of the NIF, betrayed the fundamental weakness of Sudanese politics. Agreements signed by the SPLM and the Northern parties in 1994 and 1995 provided a framework for settling constitutional questions after the overthrow of the NIF, but still only by skirting the issue of the role of Islam. International efforts continued to be used for tactical advantage. The Northern parties agreed only reluctantly in the mid-1990s to a Southern right to self-determination, and even then rendered it meaningless through various qualifications; disagreements arose over which groups and parties should be granted membership in the NDA. Elements of that umbrella group, moreover, showed willingness to abandon its protection, most notably the Umma, which withdrew in 2000 and whose leader, al-Sadiq al-Mahdi, returned from exile to Khartoum.

The Sudan's chaotic foreign relations during this period were directly tied to the war in the South and the emergence of rebel movements in other border areas. Given the ideological carapace of the régime, these were more than ever inextricable from both domestic politics and the Sudan's sorry economic state. Thus, for example, in the old Red Sea Hills, Kassala and Blue Nile provinces (several times re-named and reconstituted), Khartoum's inability to keep out refugees and others from Eritrea and Ethiopia, its support for foreign jihadist movements (including notoriously Usama b. Ladin) and assignment to them of land for bases and training camps, and its failure to relieve the local effects of drought and consequent impoverishment led to a recrudescence of militant Beja opposition movements, notably the Sudanese Allied Forces (SAF) established in 1994. The SAF and other groups got assistance from Eritrea and the SPLM but were unable seriously to threaten the régime's limited interests in the region. The rise of this and similar movements in the upper Blue Nile region, adjacent to Ethiopia, where cross-border involvement was even more complex, was symptomatic ultimately of Khartoum's loss of control. Thus while the specific causes of local disaffection varied, and the role of foreign elements – from both neighbouring states and further afield – similarly depended in part on discrete local interests, the ultimate conclusion to be drawn is not of rebellion radiating from the Southern Sudan but of the inability of the Sudanese state to hold together, at least so long as direction of its affairs was dictated by the interests of a Khartoum élite under cover of an Islamist ideology.

Nowhere was this clearer than in Darfur and the Nuba Mountains. By the NIF's tenth anniversary in power multiple crises were already pushing Darfur towards the brink of what would, a few years later, be called 'the world's worst humanitarian disaster'. Since its conquest by Anglo-Egyptian forces in 1916 Darfur had been largely neglected; the colonial objective was little more than maintenance of law and order. By 1956, therefore, Darfur lagged behind even parts of the South in measures of economic and social development. The post-independence régimes, military and civilian, had hardly broken with that pattern, and successive reorganizations of the country's local and provincial administrations had ironically made Darfur more dependent on Khartoum while weakening its ability to fill the vacuum created by continuing neglect. The effects of drought, over-grazing, internal (and cross-border) migration, over-population and economic backwardness now combined with similar conditions in neighbouring Chad and interference from Libya to bring matters to a head. Even before the 1989 *coup* the Khartoum régime of al-Sadiq al-Mahdi had armed tribal militias in Darfur and Kordofan in pursuit of the war against the SPLA. Thus equipped, these now took the law into their own hands and began to dispossess through organized violence and atrocities the Muslim – but non-Arab – Fur and Masalit.

With the advent of the NIF the level of violence in Darfur increased. The absence of government forces, or their inability or unwillingness to defend civilians, was ironically behind the 'rebellion' later assumed by foreigners to be the cause rather than the effect of Khartoum's policy. Fur and Masalit began to organize and arm themselves as the militias grew stronger with the support of the new régime. Violence against civilians became systematic, as a way of clearing land for resettlement by Arab tribesmen. In this the role of the *janjawid*, Arab tribesmen indistinguishable from bandits, became infamous, but it was their practical alliance with – rather than operation in defiance of – government forces that rendered their atrocities catastrophic for the province. Thus the descent of Darfur was under way long before international attention was paid to this phenomenon. The government, for its part, saw or professed to see in resistance first simple crime, then primordial inter-tribal warfare, sometimes the hand of the SPLM (as when, in 1991, an SPLA incursion from the Bahr al-Ghazal indeed took place and was quickly repulsed), and ultimately the usual foreign suspects in Arab and Muslim lore. The very success, however, of the unholy alliance Khartoum stitched together with local Arab groups, whether formal militias or *janjawid*, by 2002–03 had created conditions too horrific for the outside world to ignore.

In the Nuba Mountains the NIF similarly provoked desperate local resistance to ethnic cleansing. Long considered either a North–South borderland or an 'African' vestige in the steady march southwards of Arab-Islamic culture, the region had foiled Anglo-Egyptian attempts at ordered administration. By the late twentieth century the Nuba hills and peoples, now much more accessible than in the past, had indeed been gradually 'becoming Sudanese'; a majority of the people were Muslim, and acculturation was evident in many ways, not least the universal adoption of Arabic as at least a second language. Yet, under cover of civil war in the South the NIF régime continued to pursue, and accelerated, policies designed to displace even the Muslim Nuba and take over their best lands. Thus, when the SPLM/SPLA began to recruit disaffected Nuba, the government depicted its policies of repression and expropriation as a reaction rather than a provocation. Whereas al-Sadiq al-Mahdi's government had loosed Baggara filibusters upon the Southern border peoples of the Bahr al-Ghazal and Upper Nile, now Nuba civilians became a target of choice for them and regular army units; mass murder and rapine against fellow Muslims were duly legitimized as jihad. The whole region became a battlefield between the government and its proxies on the one hand and local Nuba and SPLA units on the other. Most ominous was the general agreement of the main Northern political forces – whether within the régime or in opposition – and indeed of some international peace-brokers, that the Nuba region was, and should remain, in 'the North' rather than within whatever was finally defined as the South.

Multiple rebel movements were not the only factor in determining the NIF's topsy-turvy foreign policy. The close relations that al-Sadiq al-Mahdi's government (1986–89) had forged with Libya were strengthened, and closer ties with Iran and Iraq were predictably won at the cost of those with Egypt and the West, especially the US. The Sudan's inept support for Iraq's annexation of Kuwait in 1990 precluded early resumption of aid from the Gulf states, while evidence that the NIF sought to 'export' its revolution turned passive antagonism elsewhere into hostility; relations with Tunisia, Algeria and the Gulf were adversely affected. The US and European Union ended their aid programmes in 1990. The US declared the Sudan a terrorist state in 1993, started military aid to Eritrea, Ethiopia and Uganda in 1995 and imposed (ineffective but embarrassing) economic sanctions in 1997; when in August 1998 the US bombed a pharmaceutical plant in Khartoum North, claiming that it manufactured illicit explosives, the régime ironically enjoyed a brief moment of sympathy. American support for the SPLM was at first suspected, then tacit; food aid began openly in 1999. The Sudan's relations with Britain were severed at the end of 1993 over the humanitarian disaster in the South, and not resumed until 1995. The all-important relationship with Egypt deteriorated alarmingly: a long-dormant border dispute was revived and festered, anti-Egyptian demonstrations were countenanced in Khartoum, commercial and cultural links were severed and Sudanese opposition groups headquartered in Egypt were largely left unchecked. In 1995 an unsuccessful attempt in Addis Ababa to assassinate the Egyptian president was blamed by Egypt on the NIF, and Hasan al-Turabi and other leading figures of the régime revived the age-old spectre of blackmailing Egypt through control of the Nile. In the so-called Tripoli Declaration of 1999 Egypt in turn won the NDA's public support of the Sudan's territorial integrity. Correct relations with Egypt were restored only in 2000.

Relations with Eritrea and Ethiopia, even after the fall of Mengistu, were complicated. Régime change in Ethiopia cost the SPLM/SPLA its principal foreign base, but serious irritants remained. In the late 1990s Ethiopia again openly supported SPLA efforts in the border regions, but diplomatic relations were restored in 2000. The Sudan's relations with Uganda were likewise severely strained, as each state reportedly supplied rebels in the other, and in 1995 diplomatic relations were broken off; the continuing war in the South made rapprochement impossible. Relations with Kenya, which had long provided safe haven for Southern Sudanese rebels, were similarly poor, although a mutually beneficial façade of civility was maintained. With the newest state in the region, Eritrea, relations deteriorated throughout the 1990s, as we have seen, and were complicated by the presence in the Sudan of a large number of Eritrean refugees and by the Eritrean régime's support for Sudanese opposition parties: the NDA was long headquartered there. In December 1994 Eritrea broke diplomatic relations, and the two countries came close to open war in 1998, when Khartoum accused Eritrea of involvement in the fighting in the Eastern Sudan and near Juba; relations were restored only in 2000. It is worth noting that these crises reflected continuing geopolitical competition, not radical Islamism.

The involvement of neighbouring states in the Sudan's civil war was never disinterested. All had security at stake and, except for Egypt and Libya, had insurrections of their own to deal with, which Khartoum in turn could support or not as it saw fit. Therefore even the IGADD-sponsored talks of the early 1990s, which clarified the main North–South issues for negotiation as self-determination and the character – Islamic or secular – of the Sudanese state, held dangers for the mediators. In any event, those talks ended with Khartoum's refusal to discuss the issues, and did not resume until 1997. By the end of the decade, moreover, Egypt and Libya, among others, began to sponsor talks with all the parties – the NIF régime, the Southern rebels and the NDA – which were inherently biased towards Khartoum for geopolitical reasons. In the end their proposals never included a right to self-determination for the South, without which, it was clear, negotiation would never succeed: the possibility of secession was the South's only trump card short of military victory. But while in international palavers the traditional parties in the NDA might grudgingly admit the principle of self-determination, when cornered (or in power) they always opted instead for 'unity', by which they meant subordination of peripheral regions to the will of the Khartoum élite.

The Sudan's relations with international agencies, crucial for economic revival and for the mere survival of people in the war zones, predictably deteriorated during the NIF régime's first decade in power. In 1989 the Sudan's external debt was already about $13 billion, inflation was out of control and the war in the South drained resources. Pressed by the IMF to take drastic measures, the régime demurred rather than risk disquiet. The Sudan's support for Iraq in the 1990–91 Kuwait crisis cost it dearly in expatriate remittances and bilateral aid. A National Economic Salvation programme announced in 1990 aimed at self-sufficiency in food, deficit reduction and privatization through sale of state-run enterprises – to NIF-connected businessmen – under the guise of economic liberalization. When drought resulted in poor harvests in 1990–91, the régime, which had exported the country's food reserves for hard currency, first denied then belittled the consequent famine, took insufficient steps in relief and indeed made things worse through back-handed attempts to control supply. A new currency was introduced, and was devalued within a few months, when steps were also taken to reduce subsidies, lest the Sudan face expulsion from the IMF, which had already formally declared the Sudan as non-cooperating. The national airline and other public corporations were privatized, the pound was allowed to float and taxes were increased. The inflation that ensued brought rioting in the streets, which was suppressed. The introduction of the dinar had political as well as economic motives, since the interests of prominent expatriate opponents of the régime would be adversely affected.

From the early 1990s onwards the Sudan experienced hyper-inflation in important commodities and a persistent lack of hard currency, with consequent shortages of essential goods and resort to bartering, black-marketeering and other devices by the hapless populace. Efforts at relief, as usual, were concentrated in the cities, especially the capital region. Whereas the official rate of exchange had been about 15 Sudanese pounds to the US dollar in 1991, by the end of 1993 it was over 300 pounds, and by 1996 1,000 pounds. Because of the country's chronic arrears, in 1993 the World Bank ceased payment on the Sudan's loans, the Arab Monetary Fund refused to grant new ones and the IMF threatened to expel the Sudan. Yet the régime continued to prosecute the war in the South, at a cost estimated at $1–3 million a day.

That it was able to do this was due, almost entirely, to revenue from the oil industry. Oil in exploitable quantities had been discovered in the South and North–South border regions in the 1970s. During the Nimeiri era a pipeline from the oilfields at Bentiu was laid to the Red Sea. Revenue from increasing export volume and, perhaps more importantly, the consequent interest of ill-assorted foreign governments and companies, insulated the Khartoum régime from outright pariah status; the régime stopped at nothing to defend this all-important asset, including ethnic cleansing of the oil-producing areas and employment of South African mercenaries. It also became a central issue in North–South relations, and hence figured in the war aims of both sides. From the Southern point of view, the region's oil (and, even more controversially, its water) should be primarily a regional resource exploited for the benefit of the people in whose territory it is found; successive Khartoum régimes as predictably claimed natural resources as national resources, the benefits of which belong to the whole country. The obvious compromise reached in similar circumstances elsewhere is sharing, but it can be argued that the South's continuing status as a war zone worked to Khartoum's advantage so long as the oilfields remained under its control: oil export began in 1999. All revenue accrued to the national treasury, whence expenditure allowed the continuation of the war: a vicious circle. Oil reserves, and North–South borders, became principal issues in the negotiations that finally ended the war.

Relations with international aid agencies and NGOs deteriorated throughout the NIF's first decade in power. This was inevitable owing to the deliberate policy of the NIF and all, or almost all, rebel groups to exploit civilian populations – and the foreign agencies wishing to help them – for their own political objectives. Worse, the conditions engendering the need for relief were often deliberately created in the knowledge that relief could be obstructed; the destruction of villages, crops and herds thereby made refugees of the civilian population, who for survival became cross-border migrants or settled in squalid camps. In those circumstances relief aid was the more easily controlled by one party or the other in the fighting, and international agencies had to accept the parties' conditions for aid delivery. The reaction of leading donor governments was skewed by their own interests in the outcome of the fighting, not the least of which was access to the Sudan's oil and defence of their national oil industries' investments in it. The Sudan's new importance was reflected, in turn, in the positions taken at the UN and its agencies.

In 1989 an umbrella organization, Operation Lifeline Sudan (OLS) was established to coordinate the distribution of food aid. Its official nature and bureaucratic structure made it particularly vulnerable to the interference of the new régime in Khartoum. Food aid meant for the South was appropriated for Northerners. The overthrow of the *Dergue* in 1991 created a massive return of Southern refugees from Ethiopia. This roughly coincided with the split within the SPLM/SPLA, which Khartoum sought to exploit by directing food aid to people living in areas under the Nasir Group's control and denying it to areas under the control of Garang's SPLA. As it gained confidence, the new régime was able increasingly to extort supplies for its own military as the price foreign agencies had to pay for permission to feed starving Southern civilians and refugees. Successive detailed agreements with the agencies restricted their room to manoeuvre. Similar agreements were reached with the Southern rebel organizations. But conflict within OLS over relief strategies played into the government's hands, as did aid agencies' need to observe sovereign rights. The curtailment or resumption of foreign food aid was thus a weapon the government wielded intermittently as the local military situation on the ground in particular areas dictated. A similar pattern emerged over the much publicized issue of enslavement, whereby foreign religious and other agencies sought to buy and then free Southerners enslaved by Arab tribesmen: that there was a recrudescence of slavery is undoubted, but whether the well-intentioned purchase of slaves reduced the number of victims or merely stimulated demand remains open to question. More pressing were the conditions that led to the massive voluntary servitude – slavery in all but a formal sense – of displaced Southerners.

By 2000 the NIF régime's main claim to success was that it had remained in power, against the virtually unanimous – but disunited and ineffective – opposition of all other major political groupings in the Sudan, North and South. The litany of charges against it – of 'ghost houses' and torture chambers, of disappearances and detentions without trial, of support for international terror, of association with the least acceptable régimes in the region, of economic mismanagement, of cynical zeal in prosecuting the civil war, to the point where genocide was seriously mooted as its object, and irrefutable evidence of slavery was brushed aside – lost much of its impact on a jaded world. Just as the nineteenth-century Scramble for Africa had brought with it a campaign to end the slave trade, so the Cold War had provided at least a pretext for foreign intervention; the collapse of the Soviet Union returned the Sudan to the periphery of the world's concerns, while the country's strategic value, as oil producer and participant in the shadows of the 'War on terror' after 2001, again drew in the outside world.

Meanwhile the incompetence of opponents railing from abroad or posturing in Khartoum gave little reason for hope of change. The return of al-Sadiq al-Mahdi and the kaleidoscopic fortunes of Hasan al-Turabi who, in no particular order, occupied the roles of *éminence grise*, strongman, Assembly speaker, putative imam, party leader, foreign minister, *coup* planner, prisoner and war-monger indicated (if nothing else) that a real change in Sudanese politics would never come from the religious right. As proponents of 'new forces' grew old in exile, the damage done by the NIF and its predecessors had a cumulative effect. Whether in war or peace, through economic development or starvation, with foreign aid or in the face of international opprobrium, they represented ultimately only their own interests.

By the turn of the century the evidence of new pragmatism was clear. The régime had patched up its relations with neighbouring states. It had seen off Usama b. Ladin and other foreign radicals (and would, after September 2001, offer its services to the US). It had entered into partnerships with foreign corporations, started to export oil to the world market and resumed relations with the IMF. It had, in a showdown, bested Hasan al-Turabi and begun to accommodate domestic opponents by legalizing political activity. It had engaged the NDA and weakened it. It had divided the leaders of Southern rebellion. It had bought time.

CHAPTER SIXTEEN

The Sudan and the New Millennium[1]

Three related issues dominated the second decade of President Bashir's rule, all of them arguably precipitated by the policies of a régime that by 2010 had been in power longer than any in the Sudan's independent existence. These are the civil war in the South and the manner in which, in 2005, it was finally brought to an end; the destruction of Darfur which, at the height of the crisis, was called the world's worst humanitarian disaster and threatened the régime with foreign intervention; and the social and economic pressures that, despite new oil wealth, have built up within a system lacking a basis of political legitimacy. What throughout the decade 2000–10 was essentially a general strategy of procrastination seemed, by the end of this period, to be facing its greatest tests: national elections in 2010; a Southern referendum in 2011 which, if held, would almost certainly result in an overwhelming vote for independence; and the unprecedented implications of a head of state under international indictment for crimes against humanity. How this triple threat – to the future of the Sudan as a sovereign state no less than to the régime – came about is the subject of this chapter.

At its inception it seemed unlikely that NIF rule could survive for long, or that its passing would be painless. Having come to power in a military *coup*, subjected the country to severe and bloody crackdowns on potential enemies within the army and civil society and broken with the NIF mastermind, Hasan al-Turabi, the Bashir government at the new millennium seemed to have run out of room to manoeuvre. Its steps to institutionalize control, through national and regional legislative bodies, were dilatory and jejune. For all the mumbo-jumbo with which the régime and its apologists had surrounded its enormities, it was not a commitment to rigorous Islam that kept it in power but the inefficacy of its opponents. Not the founding of an 'Islamic State' but the inability of the military to win the war in the South and to prevent or later contain rebellion elsewhere on the periphery, in the east and especially in Darfur, may indeed still be the epitaph of the Bashir régime.

Although, as we have seen, President Bashir, backed by the army, had stood up to Hasan al-Turabi and dissolved parliament in December 1999, their struggle for control had only entered a new phase. The new cabinet announced a few weeks later was top-heavy with Turabi's associates, and he continued to act with impunity. It was in this context that al-Sadiq al-Mahdi returned from exile, relations were patched up with Egypt and Ethiopia and Bashir made new overtures to the SPLM/SPLA. Elections in December 2000 were boycotted by all the traditional parties (including Turabi's new National Congress Party); Bashir's pre-ordained re-election as president was based on a low poll. After an agreement was reached with the SPLM/SPLA in February 2001 Turabi was arrested.

That agreement was one of several that indicated a new pragmatism of the régime even before September 2001, when the terrorist attacks in the US turned the Sudan's political kaleidoscope once again. By then the régime had already resumed correct relations with most of the Sudan's neighbours, had split the NDA by reaching a separate agreement with al-Sadiq al-Mahdi and the Umma and had successfully (from its point of view) pursued a divide-and-conquer strategy ('Peace from Within') with the Southern rebels that allowed it to exploit the Bentiu oilfields. Egypt and Libya had begun active media-tion efforts with the NDA on terms favourable to the régime, and President Bush had appointed a special envoy, a former senator, John Danforth, to engage the two sides in the civil war. When, therefore, after September 2001 Washington courted Khartoum's cooperation, it found a partner already well along the road towards normal diplomatic engagement. The value to the West of any assistance the régime was able to provide, especially in criminal intel-ligence, is impossible now to assess.

The long and complicated 'peace process' that culminated in the agree-ment of January 2005 bore little resemblance to the events leading up to the Addis Ababa Agreement of 1972.[2] Determination on the Southern side to avoid the mistakes enshrined in that agreement was indeed a factor in the insistence on an extraordinarily detailed instrument, while Khartoum, for its part, used the tortuous pace of the process itself to buy time and extort concessions from both its enemies and the mediators. International opprobrium engendered by the régime's actions in Darfur was, for example, tempered by the need to maintain working relations with Khartoum during the period of Southern peace negotiations. Thus, even before the peace process made headway the EU agreed to resume aid and the UN removed sanctions on the Sudan.

As during the genesis of the Addis Ababa Agreement, however, during the early part of the new decade there was a gradual coalescence of headstrong Southern rebel captains. As Khartoum's 'Peace from Within' was exposed as a pinguid rubric for failed Southern politicians' separate deals, the 'mainstream' SPLM/SPLA gained general acceptance, within and outside the Sudan, as the indispensable partner in any real peace. In the 'Nairobi Declaration' of January 2002 Riek Machar rejoined the SPLM/SPLA; Lam Akol followed in October 2003, precipitating a crisis between his followers and what was left of SPLM/SPLA-United. In fits and starts others followed suit, and talks between the SPLM/SPLA and various Northern parties and opposition entities ensued. While it may be said that a series of partial agreements and ceasefires between the government and SPLM/SPLA built confidence, it is also the case that these punctuated a continuing state of war.

In July 2002, under IGAD auspices, the two sides achieved a breakthrough in the Machakos Protocol, setting out the structure and principal points of a comprehensive agreement. The unity of the Sudan was affirmed, pending Southerners' exercise of a right to self-determination 'through a referendum' at the end of an 'interim period' of six years, during which the two sides would strive to make the unity of the Sudan 'attractive to the people of South Sudan'. The Protocol prescribed the further steps to be taken to flesh out the principals and terms it adduced. Roles were reserved for the IGAD partners and for observer states including Italy, Norway, the UK and the US. This agreement was momentous enough to occasion a meeting between Bashir and Garang in Uganda. But much remained to be done. Since the war continued, with varying degrees of intensity, Khartoum's agreement to the Machakos Protocol might merely tantalize its enemies and critics, split them anew or buy time even as the Darfur crisis loomed on the international horizon, for no Khartoum régime had ever before formally agreed to a Southern right to secede. That right, however, would now be exercised only if the two sides could agree in all the other areas touched upon in the Protocol.

Years would elapse before that result was achieved. Meanwhile the two sides negotiated, under the auspices of IGAD and its 'Partners Forum' of interested countries, six separate instruments dealing with a ceasefire, wealth-sharing, power-sharing, security and the future of border regions. The involvement also of the UN and of other governments, especially of the 'troika' (Norway, the US and the UK), maintained pressure on the two sides.[3] Before the formal signing of the aptly named Comprehensive Peace Agreement (CPA)[4] on 9 January 2005, however, the chance of scuttle remained, and this the Sudanese Government used to its advantage over other issues, notably Darfur.

The CPA was thus an omnibus of the Machakos Protocol and the separate agreements negotiated since then together with 'modalities' on implementation. Its extraordinarily detailed provisions reflect the suspicions engendered by and since the 1972 Addis Ababa Agreement; experience nonetheless would show that no degree of specificity provided immunity to lawyerly prevarication. But the promise of self-determination for the South was the irreducible desideratum of Southern parties and interest groups, and much deviation and even backtracking could be (and has been) excused because of that.

The CPA specified an 'interim period' of six years: critics found this dangerously long; it might yet be proven to have been too brief. During that period each side was to withdraw its forces from the other's territory, and joint armed units would be formed. Sharī'a would not be applied in the South. A new Government of South Sudan (by now habitually reduced to the acronym of GOSS) would be established, involving some of the attributes of sovereignty, and would be represented in the national government, with Garang as 'first vice president'. Wealth-sharing in practical terms meant oil revenue, which was to be evenly split between Khartoum and Juba. At the end of the interim period an internationally supervised referendum in the South would decide between continuing autonomy and independence.

Some issues were specifically reserved for negotiations during the interim period. These included the fate of the contested border regions of Abyei and the two states of Southern Kordofan (the Nuba Mountains) and Southern Blue Nile, for which mechanisms were prescribed for settlement. These – or, rather, the means for enforcing them – proved inadequate. The CPA required a separate referendum to decide whether the Abyei area would be part of the North or South, but owing to disagreement over what constituted that area the two sides agreed to be bound by an international Abyei Boundaries Commission; when Khartoum nonetheless rejected its decisions the issue was referred to the Permanent Court of Arbitration in The Hague. In a 2009 ruling accepted by both sides the tribunal defined most of the disputed region (but not its oil-producing territory) in a way thought favourable to the South; meanwhile, in 2008 the town of Abyei itself was destroyed in fighting between government and SPLA forces, and its population put to flight. The other two border issues were complex, the more so because the solutions arrived at might be considered templates for the country as a whole; both the Nuba Mountains and Southern Blue Nile had relatively small but ethnically diverse populations and suffered locally from the political problems at the root of Southern rebellion. The CPA's complicated step-by-step prescriptions, which involved precise proportions of power sharing at the state level and assumed an unrealistic degree of political and bureaucratic sophistication, almost guaranteed delay even if applied with goodwill. Details of state government structures, land commissions and censuses were prescribed, as were terms for referenda to be held after local and national elections.

An important element of the CPA was power sharing at the centre. A new Government of National Unity (GONU) – in fact neither national nor united – was duly formed, with General Bashir remaining as president and John Garang, as leader of the SPLM/SPLA, as first vice-president; cabinet positions were apportioned to Bashir's National Congress Party (NCP) and the SPLM. That this procedure effectively shut out unaligned Southerners and, more importantly, the opposition grouped in the NDA, was an obvious weakness, and gave rise to fears that arrangements for elections would be biased in favour of the two coalition partners. Worse, it would soon become clear that power sharing was effectively limited to the top of the administrative pyramid, and that the NCP retained operational control of the important ministries. In this sense the government resembled Khartoum régimes since independence, in which the traditional sectarian parties doled out a few third-tier ministerial positions to eager Southerners. This impression was reinforced after 30 July 2005 when, only weeks after assuming office in Khartoum, Garang was killed in a helicopter crash while returning to the South from Uganda. Salva Kiir, the deputy who assumed his positions, was widely thought more amenable than Garang to Southern secession. Destined now to be remembered as the father of Southern independence, Garang, had he lived, might have given substance to the SPLM rhetoric of a New Sudan.

Negotiation of the CPA took place in a context of burgeoning disaster in Darfur. The origins of that crisis have been largely misunderstood. Khartoum's empowerment of, and alliance with, Arab *janjawid* terrorists there was the response of a weak but brutal régime to the desperate self-defence of the long-suffering 'African' (Fur, Masalit) population. The worm had turned only after decades of inter-related and easily discernible social and economic crises worsened by the policies of a careless and inept Khartoum régime. Darfur, as much of the trans-African *sahel*, had for at least a century experienced a gradual desiccation owing to a decline in rainfall and changes in rainfall patterns. This coincided with an increase in the size of the region's population and, worse, of its herds, far greater than the fragile environment could support. Tribal migrations, in the past regular or occasional, became increasingly urgent and aggressive, as homelands dried up and encroachments, once accommodated, became permanent. Breakdown of government control, never strong, coincided with similar problems in neighbouring Chad, and was exacerbated by the easy acquisition of modern arms across international borders. Libya stirred the pot. Problems that had once been susceptible to traditional means of settlement – palavers, blood money, personal relations of tribal chiefs – took on new dimensions of international politics, ethnic identity, land-hunger and simple brigandage in a context of governmental abdication.

For Darfur the successive reforms of provincial and local administration of the Nimeiri era had resulted in theoretical devolution of authority from the centre without the means to carry it out at the periphery. The third parliamentary régime, dominated by the Umma, which looked to Darfur for its main electoral support, ironically continued the policies of neglect. Sedentary Fur and Masalit farmers, their crops trampled and herds rustled by local and Chadian tribesmen migrating from drought-stricken homelands, looked in vain to the government for protection. Fur self-defence units sprang up and, by 1988, the so-called War of the Tribes had already taken on aspects of a race war. A National Council for the Salvation of Darfur faced an Arab Alliance purporting to speak for the Arab tribes. The central government seemed at best powerless as the level of violence increased amid talk of an 'Arab Belt' and an 'African Belt' dividing Darfur; the massive refugee problem that would capture the world's attention fifteen years later had already begun. Nevertheless, in July 1989 a comprehensive Reconciliation Agreement was signed at El Fasher by tribal representatives which, had it been enforced by the central government, might have brought Darfur back from the brink. But by then the government of al-Sadiq al-Mahdi had been overthrown and the NIF was in power.

Like several of its predecessors, the new régime enacted reforms of provincial government plangent with ideological pretensions but in harmony with its own real interests. In 1991 re-centralization was undertaken, only to be reversed three years later when Darfur, the electoral stronghold of the Mahdist Umma, was divided into three states and Native Administration was revived. Transparent divide-and-rule was the object: state boundaries were drawn in such a way as to make the Fur a minority in each. Similarly Dar Masalit, in western Darfur, was divided into 'emirates', a majority of which were assigned to Arab tribesmen whose number had been swollen by in-migration from the North and Chad; the upshot was the eventual disenfranchisement of the Masalit in their own *dar*, a process already violently under way through Arab raids. The government, at first tacitly, later openly, sided with the aggressors now termed *janjawid*. A similar pattern emerged elsewhere in Darfur, fed by drought, famine, cheap weapons, local effects of similar conditions across the borders in Chad and the Central African Republic and a new invocation of racist ideology according to which the non-Arab Fur, Masalit and others were despised. It was under these circumstances that, in the mid-1990s, local self-defence units sprang up in desperate resistance to the *janjawid* and the NIF.

Although the unfolding disaster in Darfur was not caused by the continuing war in the South, the two crises had common elements. In both regions local peoples were arrayed against the repressive policies of the Khartoum régime, which sought for itself or its clients control of natural resources (land, water, oil) at any cost. In support of that basic goal the régime invoked nationalist, racial or ethnic and Islamic ideologies; dismissed as 'tribal warfare' the insurrections it provoked; mercilessly employed both the regular army and local militias; made food a weapon, and barred or harassed foreign aid efforts; and routinely violated ceasefires, truces and other agreements – all to the point where ethnic cleansing (which might simply mean removal of hostile populations, as in the Nuba Mountains or the Bentiu region) seemed increasingly to involve genocide.

The Darfur crisis attracted foreign attention to a degree unique in the Sudan's history and undoubtedly shocking to the Khartoum régime. This resulted from a confluence of factors. Revolt there was loosely directed by political entities, the Justice and Equality Movement (JEM), the Darfur Liberation Front and the Sudan Liberation Movement and Army (SLM/SLA), which all elicited foreign interest. That was channelled in Europe and North America mainly by a Save Darfur movement and countless associated or discrete groups, which through the Internet and other means soon resembled the anti-apartheid movement of the 1970s. As in that case, however, much denunciation was *pro forma*, and while international efforts brought unwanted attention to the Sudan, their effect in Darfur itself is difficult to assess. The spectacle of a warrant by the International Criminal Court in 2009 for the arrest of President Bashir on charges of war crimes and crimes against humanity only increased his popularity at home, where the image of the Sudan as unfairly maligned was ingrained, and he continued with impunity (if selectively) to travel abroad; the effect in Darfur was chaotic, however, as Bashir ordered the immediate eviction of aid organizations.

Denouncing foreign pressure with anti-colonial rhetoric, the régime had by 2005 presided over a 'humanitarian disaster' of enormous proportions: news of atrocities – widespread rape, torture, mass murder – were retailed in the international media; estimates of excess deaths were in the hundreds of thousands,[5] and the majority of Darfur's population had been put to flight across the international borders or to insecure camps dependent on imported food aid. Pressure groups forced Western governments to take up the cause, bilaterally and at the United Nations, but although direct military intervention was frequently mooted, none occurred. By 2006 the crisis had at least temporarily passed. International – mainly African – 'peace-keepers' were situated, and negotiations between the government and rebel organizations took place under various auspices. A Darfur Peace Agreement signed at Abuja in May 2006 was never implemented, and by the end of the decade, with the annual death toll having subsided, the Darfur crisis had been reduced to the status of a long-term refugee problem. The same fate seemed in store for refugees from revolt in the east.[6]

The world's failure adequately to address the crisis at its height was partly the result of unwillingness to jeopardize negotiations for the CPA; even in late 2004 there seemed a strong possibility that these might break down altogether, and after January 2005 the two crises remained in some ways connected. The Darfur rebel groups never seriously composed – or credibly defined – their differences. Overrating the significance of their ability to hold out, they gave openings to both their rivals and enemies to make separate deals. Early in 2010, as Khartoum and the fissiparous Darfur rebel groups held talks in Ethiopia, Chad and Qatar, jockeyed for position, reached tentative agreements then immediately broke them, the American envoy, General Scott Gration, stated – off-handedly or purposefully – that the world's patience and attention were running out. Ceasefire agreements between Khartoum and both the JEM and a new amalgam of rebel groups fell apart.

As the crisis in Darfur thus increasingly assumed the proportions of a long-term phenomenon – no peace, no war – international attention indeed swung away from it. To the extent it remained focused on the Sudan at all, now the national elections and Southern referendum scheduled for 2010 and 2011 respectively were its objects. But despite billions of dollars expended in various programmes, and the stationing in the South of a 10,000-strong United Nations Mission in Sudan (UNMIS), the overall impression is of neglect. The Government of National Unity's open violation of the terms by which UNMIS should operate went unpunished. The Assessment and Evaluation Commission created under the CPA failed to carry out its mission. During the interim period many of the CPA's other prescriptions were unfilled or openly flouted by both sides, though blame must be placed in proportion with each side's ability to carry them out. As the senior partner of the Khartoum coalition the NCP was required to take the lead in implementing the reforms at the heart of – indeed arguably the reason for – the 'interim period'. These included constitutional and legislative changes, at both the national and state levels, and the security arrangements. The overriding impression is of purposeful delay. Whether this had been the intention of the NCP all along or emerged as a strategy only when the elections and referenda loomed, is less important than the result – general dissipation of the goodwill that had attended the signing of the CPA in 2005 and fears, deep and wide, that some excuse would be found to scuttle the national elections or the Southern referendum, or both. It is worth noting, too, that the confidence that had built up during the post-Machakos period between the chief negotiators died with Garang, and that behind every complaint about even the technicalities of implementation lay the suspicion of bad faith.

In important areas covered in great detail by the CPA the Government of National Unity took little or no action. Perhaps the most important of these was evacuation from the South of most government forces and demobilization of most SPLA fighters. Demilitarization of the South fell behind schedule from the very outset, notably in the oilfield areas but elsewhere as well. Old hands recalled that failure to deal with disaffected – and unemployed – veterans of the first civil war had been a serious deficiency in implementing the Addis Ababa Agreement of 1972; now the number of SPLA fighters was as high as 200,000, but steps to demobilize, disarm and reintegrate them lagged; where were they to go, and what were they to do?

This issue was moreover a symptom of a more general problem dogging implementation of the CPA. We have seen that, even before the war the South was one of the least developed areas in the world. During two decades of fighting its puny infrastructure had been destroyed, a generation had gone uneducated and basic elements of more than a subsistence economy had ceased to exist. Huge practical problems had to be faced: roads and bridges were perhaps the easy part; what of hospitals and schools – and the personnel needed to staff them? Under the terms of the CPA the South had an interim constitution and an autonomous government. But time and again during the interim period problems arose because the South lacked trained manpower. Luckily, among the two million Southern refugees who by 2009 had returned to the South there were some with higher education and skills, but with those have come also expectations of a standard of living that the South is unlikely soon to support.

A scientific national census was crucial in preparation for elections in 2010. To be sure, the conduct of a census faced daunting challenges, as would consequent new electoral laws. Should a census record the ethnicity of Sudanese, or simply their numbers and places of residence? To which region – North or South – should the millions of Southerners living outside the South be assigned? Most were refugees from the fighting, but some were not; many ethnic Southerners had lived outside the South for decades, and many indeed had never been there at all. Was the all-important referendum of 2011 to poll Southerners, or residents of the South? Could elections be held at all in Darfur? Through its control of the purse strings and bureaucracy the NCP held back funds for demarcation of boundaries, and for the census, which was repeatedly delayed. Results released in mid-2008 were widely disparaged. A National Elections Act legislated in July 2008, two years behind schedule, called for a mixture of direct elections in constituencies and an overall proportional vote, with a threshold for party representation in the new parliament. Khartoum delayed voter registration. For these and other reasons the national elections prescribed by the CPA had to be delayed twice and were not finally held until April 2010.

In October 2007 the SPLM formally withdrew from the Government of National Unity in protest at the lack of progress in implementing the CPA. It returned in December after negotiations had hammered out new timetables for redeployment of government troops, delimitation of borders and funding of the census. But it was only at the end of 2009 that the national assembly enacted laws for the consultation process to take place in the 'Three Areas' (Abyei, the Nuba Mountains and southern Blue Nile) after the national elections. Other important laws had yet to be amended as required by the CPA to ensure fair elections.

On the eve of national elections and with the Southern referendum of 2011 looming ever larger on the horizon, the overarching themes of the interim period prescribed by the CPA were foot-dragging on the part of the NCP-dominated Government of National Unity in Khartoum, ineptness by the fledgling Government of South Sudan and neglect by the international community. But a breakdown of the CPA régime was as likely to result from one or another local problem – or a combination of local problems – left unattended in the South. Throughout 2007–10 incidents of local violence, involving SPLA fighters, remaining units of the national army, tribal militias, other local forces, returning refugees and local squatters increased in frequency and lethality. In some cases of active instigation before – and in more cases neglect after – violent episodes, the hand of the NCP was discerned; the destruction of Abyei has been mentioned. In a number of incidents between government forces and SPLA-affiliated Southerners, hundreds were killed and tens of thousands put to flight. In 2008–09, hundreds of thousands of Southerners were said to have been displaced. In early 2009 over 1,000 civilians were killed in inter-ethnic fighting in Jonglei. The inability or unwillingness of national or South Sudan forces – or UNMIS, which because of restrictions on its movements imposed by Khartoum was reduced almost to observer status – to intervene was highlighted when marauding elements of the Lord's Army from Uganda murdered civilians in central and western Equatoria. In 2009 alone the death toll in such violence – perhaps 2,500 – was judged higher than that in the simmering cauldron of Darfur. The fledgling South Sudan police force was ill-suited to control this level of violence, not least because post-war disarming of the civilian population had not been seriously undertaken.

Despite its daunting task the Government of South Sudan was hardly blameless for the difficulties besetting implementation of the CPA. Problems endemic to Southern Sudanese politics lived on in office-seeking, tribalism, nepotism, graft and other forms of corruption, the frittering away of NGOs' resources and goodwill, and a yawning divide between the tiny Western-educated élite and the mass of war-weary Southerners. The creation of an elaborate governmental and administrative superstructure bespoke a long-deferred division of spoils, even as a virtual state of Nature met returning refugees; in many respects the GOSS was a government in name only. Before the 2010 elections the extremely delicate task of demobilization had just begun; a sense of law and order had hardly survived decades of civil war, and reports were rife of arbitrariness in such enforcement as there was: civilians remained armed for self-defence. Foreign aid money earmarked for social services was held up by Khartoum and siphoned off by Juba. Public-health indicators showed the region worse off than Darfur, while the official budget of the GOSS remained heavily skewed towards the military. Dependent on its share of oil proceeds for almost all its revenue, the GOSS was by 2009 effectively bankrupt, unable to meet recurring commitments and even salaries. Official corruption tainted the entire CPA project, at home and abroad, and indeed became an election issue when the perennial rebel Lam Akol founded 'SPLM-Democratic Change', whose anti-corruption platform was the more ironic for support from the NCP. Jockeying for position for the 2011 referendum appeared to be the sole object of much electioneering.

Despite or indeed because of the crises and delays that punctuated the interim period, international attention to enforcement of the CPA increased as the elections drew near. In October 2009 the US announced what was evidently considered a new and comprehensive policy on the Sudan, involving active if limited engagement with the Khartoum régime and greater support for UN and other efforts aimed at reducing the level of violence, fully implementing the CPA and preventing the Sudan's becoming a haven for terrorists. A special IGAD summit on implementation of the CPA, held in Nairobi in March 2010, urged the finalizing of North–South borders and the passage of a referendum law before national elections. For its part, and despite a huge and multifarious presence in the Sudan, the UN's failure to impose sanctions over the Darfur issue raised doubts about the willingness of the Security Council to enforce provisions of the CPA.

The much anticipated national elections were held in April 2010. Much about these was extraordinary, not least the fact that the incumbent candidate for the presidency was under indictment at The Hague for war crimes. As an earnest of national ambitions the SPLM/SPLA nominated Yasir Arman, a Northern Sudanese Muslim, against President Bashir; the SPLM's own leader, Salva Kiir, instead ran for the presidency of South Sudan. (Turning the tables, Hasan al-Turabi's Popular Congress Party nominated a Muslim relative of John Garang, Abdullah Deng Nhial, who haplessly espoused unity in the upcoming referendum.) Much speculation attended the presumed quandary of Northern Sudanese as the parties of the Mahdi and Mirghani families, the phoenix-like Umma and Democratic Unionists, offered their respective dynasts (in the Umma's case al-Sadiq al-Mahdi, whose first term atop a Sudanese national government had been in 1966).

By the time of polling, however, the suspense had dissipated. Successive withdrawal of his leading opponents added to the aura of inevitability with which electoral irregularities had already imbued President Bashir's candidacy. Although these were serious, and included the impossibility of a fair poll in Darfur and elsewhere, unreliable rolls, obvious government interference and the incompetence of officials unused to unrigged elections, the conclusion was widespread that even an immaculate process would have given the same result. For to many Northern Sudanese it seemed obvious that the Bashir régime, for all its faults, was presiding over an oil-fed economic boom of unprecedented proportions, a spate of high-profile foreign-assisted development – from the massive Merowe Dam on the Nile to the transformation of Khartoum – and a degree of political stability that elections actually threatened to upset.

In concurring, a host of foreign observers contributed to the impression that the poll was but a prelude to the Southern referendum scheduled for January 2011, and that challenges to the legitimacy of the results, no less than pre-election complaints about corruption, might provoke or excuse postponement or cancellation of that all-important procedure. In this view only President Bashir, confirmed in office by the popular vote of Northern Sudanese, would have the authority to hold the referendum and, more to the point, to acquiesce in its seemingly inevitable result. In the event the official count gave him 68 per cent of the vote and his nearest rival, Arman, 22 per cent. Salva Kiir was returned as president of the GOSS with 93 per cent of the vote as against Lam Akol's 7 per cent, a lop-sided result open to interpretation.

In the aftermath of the election the attention of the outside world, which had been distracted by events elsewhere (and by the seeming interminability of Sudanese crises) belatedly turned to the 2011 referendum. Notwithstanding the relatively smooth conduct of the presidential poll, the prevailing view remained that only the incessant involvement of foreign powers, directly or under the auspices of the UN, could ensure that the 2011 referendum would take place and that its results would be honoured. Few observers, in or of the Sudan, expected a peaceful process, and speculation was rampant about which of a dozen possible scenarios – each ending in cancellation of the referendum and renewal of civil war – was most likely.

Amid that speculation little credence was given to the view, at least as plausible in the light of the Sudan's long history, that the ultimate goals, whether neatly formulated or only dimly perceived, of Sudanese nationalism in any of its several forms, might better be served by Southern independence than by a unity enforced by arms. The process that had culminated in the CPA, even if cynical and temporizing, had revealed the scope for compromise over the purely political issues in North–South relations. The Abyei case had shown a way to settle a disputed boundary. Resource sharing – the apportionment of water, the sharing of oil revenue and cross-border grazing rights – could be effected over the long term only through agreement. Recent, rapid, oil-fed development in the North – however uneven, inefficient and attended with its own problems – has put in stark relief the backwardness of the South and the enormous amount of time and money that a sovereign government, whether of a united Sudan or an independent South, must invest there; might the North be better off economically without it? History has shown that the broad influence of Northern Sudanese culture – including notably Islam and Arabic – has been neither stymied by international boundaries nor promoted by policies imposed by Khartoum. In this view the Sudan's division into two sovereign states might well be the prelude to new and stronger aggregations built upon common interests and evolving in peaceful ways.

Notes

Introduction: The Land and the People

1. In 1823, the *Defterdar* Muhammad Bey Khusraw was entitled 'commander-in-chief of the Sudan and of Kordofan'. Ten years later, 'Ali Khurshid Pasha was given the title of 'governor of the provinces of the Sudan', perhaps the first official usage of the term in something like its modern sense. The Ottoman sultan's *ferman* to Muhammad 'Ali Pasha in 1841 did not mention the Sudan as such (see p. 39).
2. Barabra, the plural of *Barbari* (in English, Berberine) is the name given to the Nubians of this region.
3. See below, Ch. 2, p. 24.
4. See below, Ch. 1, p. 20.
5. See below, Ch. 2, p. 25.
6. Arbaji was an important town from the sixteenth to the eighteenth century. It was visited by Bruce, the Scottish traveller, in 1772, and was devastated by its own ruler in 1783–84.
7. *Makk* was a title given to the vassal-kings under the suzerainty of the Funj sultan.
8. John Lewis Burckhardt, a Swiss by birth, visited Shendi in 1814. See below, Ch. 2, pp. 24, 30.
9. See 'Umar al-Naqar, *The Pilgrimage Tradition in West Africa* (Khartoum 1972), 104–13.

Part One Before the Turco-Egytian Conquest

1. The Eastern Bilad al-Sudan *in the Middle Ages*

1. French translations of Ibn Sulaym's account of Nubia, as transmitted by al-Maqrīzī (d. 1442), may be found in Et. Quatremère, *Mémoires géographiques et historiques sur l'Égypte et sur quelques contrées voisines* (Paris 1811), II, 1–126 (Mémoire sur la Nubie); and U. Bouriant (tr.), Maqrizi, *Description topographique et historique de l'Égypte* (Paris 1900), II, 549–53.
2. The text of the oath is given by the contemporary Arabic chronicler, Ibn al-Dawādārī, *Kanz al-durar wa-jāmi' al-ghurar*, VIII (ed. U. Haarmann, Freiburg 1971), 185–6.
3. Ibn Khaldūn, *Kitāb al-'ibar* (Beirut n.d.), v, 922–3.
4. Gaston Wiet (ed.), [al-Maqrīzī], *El-Mawâ'iz wa'l-i'tibâr fî dhikr el-khitat wa'l-âthâr*, iii (Paris 1922), 263–4. By Jacobite Christianity is meant the Monophysite doctrine, held by the Coptic Church in Egypt.
5. The accepted view that 'Aydhab was destroyed by an expedition sent by the Mamluk Sultan Barsbay in 1426 is effectively challenged by Jean-Claude Garcin, 'Jean-Léon l'Africain et 'Aydhab', *Annales Islamologiques*, xi, 1972, 189–209.

2. The Eastern Bilad al-Sudan *from the early Sixteenth to the early Nineteenth Century*

1. A critical edition has been published by Yūsuf Faḍl Ḥasan, *Kitāb al-ṭabaqāt fī khuṣūṣ al-awliyā' wa'l-ṣāliḥīn wa'l-'ulamā' fi'l-Sūdān* (second edition, Khartoum 1974). A summary translation (not always accurate) with useful notes was made by Sir Harold MacMichael, *A History of the Arabs in the Sudan* (Cambridge 1922), II, 217–323. See also S. Hillelson, 'Tabaqât Wad Ḍayf Allah: studies in the lives of the scholars and saints', *Sudan Notes and Records*, VI, 1923, 191–230.

2. No full critical edition has yet appeared, but Katib al-Shuna's basic text with some collation with other MSS. was published by al-Shāṭir Buṣaylī 'Abd al-Jalīl, *Makhṭūṭat kātib al-Shūna fī ta'rīkh al-salṭana al-Sinnāriyya wa'l-idāra al-Miṣriyya* (Cairo 1963); while the final recension was edited by Makkī Shubayka, *Ta'rīkh mulūk al-Sūdān* (Khartoum 1947). An annotated summary translation from a MS. of this recension is given in MacMichael, *History of the Arabs*, II, 354–430. A translation from a collation of various texts is provided by P.M. Holt, *The Sudan of the Three Niles: The Funj Chronicle 910–1288/1504–1871* (Leiden 1999).
3. For a survey of Arabic sources see R.S. O'Fahey, comp., *Arabic Literature of Africa: Vol. I, The Writings of Eastern Sudanic Africa to c. 1900*, Leiden 1994.
4. For a critique, see S. Hillelson, 'David Reubeni, an early visitor to Sennar', *Sudan Notes and Records*, XVI, 1933, 55–66.
5. Maria Teresa Petti Suma, 'Il viaggio in Sudan di Evliyā Čelebī', *Annali dell'Istituto Orientale di Napoli*, N.S. XIV, 433–52.
6. James Bruce, *Travels to Discover the Source of the Nile* (second edition, Edinburgh 1805), VI.
7. John Lewis Burckhardt, *Travels in Nubia* (London 1819).
8. See P.M. Holt, 'The coming of the Funj', *Studies in the History of the Near East* (London 1973), 67–87.
9. J.L. Spaulding, 'The Funj: a reconsideration', *Journal of African History*, XIII/1, 1972, 39–53.
10. Wendy James, 'The Funj mystique: approaches to a problem of Sudan history', in Ravindra K. Jain (ed.), *Text and Context: The Social Anthropology of Tradition* (Philadelphia 1977), 95–133.
11. Bruce, *Travels*, VI, 372.
12. *Ṭabaqāt*, 41. '*Idda*: the period during which, under the Sharī'a, a divorced woman may not remarry.
13. *Ṭabaqāt*, 345.
14. P.M. Holt, 'The Sons of Jābir and their kin: a clan of Sudanese religious notables', *Studies*, 88–103.
15 P.M. Holt, 'Holy families and Islam in the Sudan', *Studies*, 121–34.
16. An extract from this notice in the *Ṭabaqāt* is given and translated by S. Hillelson, *Sudan Arabic Texts* (Cambridge 1935), 194–9.
17. See Hillelson, *Sudan Arabic Texts*, 174–93.
18. W.G. Browne, *Travels in Africa, Egypt, and Syria, from the Year 1792 to 1798* (London 1799).
19. Muḥammad b. 'Umar al-Tūnusī, *Tashhīdh al-adhhān bi-sīrat bilād al-'Arab wa'l-Sūdān* (ed. Khalīl Maḥmud 'Asakir and Muṣṭafā Muḥammad Mas'ad: Cairo 1965). French translation by Dr Perron, *Voyage au Darfour* (Paris 1845).
20. Translated by Allan G.B. Fisher and Humphrey J. Fisher, *Sahara and Sudan*, IV (London 1971).
21. Na'ūm Shuqayr, *Ta'rīakh al-Sūdān al-qadīm wa'l-ḥadīth wa-jughrāfiyatuh* (Cairo 1903), II, 111–47.
22. See Rex S. O'Fahey and Jay L. Spaulding, 'Hāshim and the Musabba'āt', *Bulletin of the School of Oriental and African Studies*, XXXV/2, 1972, 316–33.
23. Cf. Holt, *The Sudan of the Three Niles*, 9.
24. Cf. Holt, *The Sudan of the Three Niles*, 19.
25. Cf. Holt, *The Sudan of the Three Niles*, 70–1.
26. Browne, *Travels*, 212.
27. Browne, *Travels*, 215.
28. *Pièces diverses et correspondance relatives aux opérations de l'Armée d'Orient en Égypte* (Paris An IX [1800–1801]), 187, 216, 217.
29. On Ahmad al-Tayyib al-Bashir, see P.M. Holt, 'A Sudanese saint: Aḥmad al-Ṭayyib b. al-Bashīr (1155–1239/1742–1824)', Otakar Hulec and Milos Mendel (eds), *Threefold Wisdom – The Arab World and Africa* (Prague 1993), 107–15.
30. On the career and significance of Ahmad ibn Idris al-Fasi, see R.S. O'Fahey, *Enigmatic Saint: Ahmad Ibn Idris and the Idrisi Tradition* (London 1990).

Part Two The Turco-Egyptian Period: 1820–81

3. The Inauguration of the Turco-Egyptian Régime: 1820–25

1. [G.B. English], *A Narrative of the Expedition to Dongola and Sennaar* (London 1822), 21.
2. The name of Berber was at this time applied only to the district inhabited by the Mirafab. The complex of villages on the right bank, the predecessors of the modern town of Berber,

had no common name. At the time of the conquest the village of Nasr al-Din was the effective capital of the district. Fifty years earlier, at the time of Bruce's visit, the capital had been Gooz (*al-Quz*), another village in the complex.
3. English, *Narrative*, 140.
4. This was the two-horned *taqiyya umm qarnayn*, the symbol of authority in the Funj state.
5. English, *Narrative*, 159–60.
6. The date (17 Rajab 1136) is given by Jabarti (*'Ajā'ib al-āthār*, IV, 318) who also makes it clear that the objective of the expedition was Darfur, not merely Kordofan.
7. John Petherick, who visited Kordofan in 1847, recounts an anecdote 'among others of a similar kind' of the *Defterdar*'s capricious justice; *Egypt, the Soudan and Central Africa* (Edinburgh and London 1861), 121–2.
8. *Mu'allim* (Arabic: 'teacher') was the regular title of Christian and Jewish officials in this period.
9. Sir Harold MacMichael, *History of the Arabs in the Sudan* (Cambridge 1922), II, 420.
10. The name of Khartoum (*al-Khurtum*) means 'the elephant's trunk'.

4. Settlement and Stagnation: 1825–62

1. Translated from Shubayka's edition of the Funj Chronicle. The passage is omitted in MacMichael's translation. The presentation of Shaykh 'Abd al-Qadir to Khurshid is probably not only symbolical but also mythical. It is not mentioned in the contemporary account by Katib al-Shuna; cf. P.M. Holt, *The Sudan of the Three Niles: The Funj Chronicle 910–1288/ 1504–1871* (Leiden 1999), 95–6.
2. Kanfu was the paternal uncle of the future King Theodore, who made himself ruler of Ethiopia in 1855 and committed suicide at the time of Sir Robert Napier's expedition to Magdala in 1868.
3. Khurshid was appointed governor of Adana, a province at this time controlled by Muhammad 'Ali. He died in 1845, in the post of governor of the Egyptian province of the Sharqiyya.
4. During the winter of 1838–9, Muhammad 'Ali Pasha visited the Sudan. His principal object was to inspect the gold-producing region of Fazughli. Disappointed with what he saw, he returned to Egypt. His visit is devoid of significance for Sudanese history.
5. Kanbal was the son of *Makk* Jawish, who had resisted the advance of Isma'il Pasha. After his death, Kanbal became a legendary figure: 'he is described, on account of his cruelty and savage deeds, constantly wandering round, without grave, rest, or peace, as the punishment of his crimes' (F. Werne, *African Wanderings* (London 1852), 177–8).
6. Muhammad wad Dafa'allah's wife, Nasra, was a person of even greater consequence than he himself. She was the daughter of the Regent 'Adlan by a Funj princess and held her court at Surayba, near Wad Medani, where she was visited by Lepsius in 1844, and by Bayard Taylor in 1852.
7. These measures should undoubtedly be linked with decrees of the Ottoman Sultan 'Abd al-Majid, who in October 1854 prohibited trade in white slaves, and in February 1857 trade in black slaves.

5. The Era of Khedive Isma'il: 1863–81

1. See above, p. 59.

Part Three The Mahdist State: 1881–98

6. The Mahdist Revolution: 1881–85

1. The original Ansar were the 'Helpers' of the Prophet Muhammad in Medina. In this, as in other instances, the Mahdi patterned his movement on early Islamic history.
2. The name is often given in English as Osman Digna. His Beja followers were the 'Fuzzy-Wuzzies' of Kipling's poem.
3. Later the first Earl of Cromer.
4. *Al-Siddiq, al-Faruq* and *al-Karrar* are names traditionally given to Abu Bakr, 'Umar and 'Ali respectively.

7. The Reign of the Khalifa 'Abdallahi: 1885–98

1. See G.N. Sanderson, *England, Europe and the Upper Nile 1882–1899* (Edinburgh 1965).
2. So-called in most contemporary and later British accounts.

Part Four The Anglo-Egyptian Condominium: 1899–1955

8. Pacification and Consolidation: 1899–1913

1. The Capitulations were treaties by which the Ottoman sultans had conceded special rights to Europeans. With the decline of Ottoman power they had become in effect charters of extra-territoriality for anyone who could claim citizenship of a signatory state.
2. Cromer, *Modern Egypt*, II (London 1908), 549.
3. The Mixed Tribunals, set up in the reign of Khedive Isma'il to try civil suits in which Europeans were concerned, were independent of the Egyptian government.
4. The incident in which the three Ashraf were killed has been the subject of a controversy as to whether they were shot while trying to escape, or executed after failing.
5. See Gabriel Warburg, *The Sudan under Wingate, Administration in the Anglo-Egyptian Sudan, 1899–1916* (London 1971), 129–33.

9. Revolt and Reaction: 1914–36

1. See A.B. Theobald, *'Ali Dinar, Last Sultan of Darfur, 1898–1916* (London, 1965), 174–6.
2. Report of the Milner Mission, 1919.
3. The title of khedive was superseded by that of sultan at the beginning of the war. Sultan Ahmad Fu'ad became king after independence in 1922.
4. 'Minute by His Excellency the Governor-General', 1 January 1927, Sudan Government Archives, CIVSEC 1/9/33.
5. 'The educational experiment in the Anglo-Egyptian Sudan, 1900–1933', *Journal of the Royal African Society*, XXXIV, 1935, 49.
6. R. Bence-Pembroke, 'Proposals for the introduction of the policy on native administration', 23 January 1927, Sudan Government Archives, CIVSEC 1/20/60.
7. *Khalwa* (literally, 'a place of seclusion') means primarily a retreat for Sufi initiates. The Sudanese usage, to signify a place for religious instruction, is a surviving trace of the Sufi character of the islamization of the Sudan. During the early Condominium period, the government subsidized *kuttabs* (elementary schools), employing government-trained teachers, in an attempt to improve standards.
8. 'Graduate' meant one who had completed study at the Gordon College or an intermediate school.

Chapter Ten The Development of Sudanese Nationalism: 1937–52

1. Meaning in modern Arabic 'nation', *umma* carries overtones of its original significance as the community of Islam in the time of the Prophet and subsequently.
2. See Conrad C. Reining, *The Zande Scheme* (Evanston, Illinois 1966).
3. See Gabriel Warburg, *Islam, Nationalism and Communism in a Traditional Society, the Case of Sudan* (London 1978), 96–8.
4. See Saad ed din Fawzi, *The Labour Movement in the Sudan, 1946–1955* (London 1957).

Chapter Eleven The Achievement of Independence, 1953–56

1. An interesting account is in the memoirs of Anthony Eden, *Full Circle* (London 1960), 272–4.

2. An official enquiry determined that the disturbances had been caused by the results of sudanization, interference in politics of Northern administrators and circulation of provocative rumours concerning the disposition of Southern army units. See Sudan Government, *Southern Sudan Disturbances*, August 1955 (Report of the Commission of Enquiry) (Khartoum 1956).

Part Five The Independent Sudan

12. Parliamentary and Military Government: 1956–69

1. See G.N. Sanderson, 'Sudanese nationalism and the independence of the Sudan', in Michael Brett (ed.), *Northern Africa: Islam and Modernization* (London 1973), 97–109.
2. The Sudanese pound (£S), divided into one hundred piastres and one thousand milliemes.
3. See Peter Bechtold, *Politics in the Sudan* (New York 1976), 195.
4. The agreement of the major parties to consider federal status had led to the Southern MPs' support for the declaration of independence in 1955.
5. Government of the Sudan, Ministry of Irrigation and Hydro-Electric Power, *The Nile Waters Question* (Khartoum 1955).
6. For details of the settlement see Hassan Dafalla, *The Nubian Exodus* (London 1975).
7. See Gabriel Warburg, *Islam, Nationalism and Communism in a Traditional Society, the Case of Sudan* (London 1978), 93–140.

13. The Era of Jaafar Nimeiri: 1969–85

1. For a discussion of communist involvement in the *coup*, see Warburg, *Islam, Nationalism and Communism*, 132–4.
2. For a discussion of local government reforms, see John Howell (ed.), *Local Government and Politics in the Sudan* (Khartoum 1974).

14. The Transitional Government and the Third Parliamentary Régime: 1985–89

1. This chapter is based on press reports and private information.
2. See especially, Millard Burr "Quantifying genocide", U.S. Committee for Refugees Issue Paper, October 1993.

15. The National Islamic Front in Power, 1989–99

1. See Abdullahi A. Gallab, *The First Islamic Republic. Development and Disintegration of Islamism in the Sudan*, Aldershot 2008, 77ff. This account of the NIF régime relies upon private information, unpublished documents, periodical literature and published accounts as noted. For the NIF in power see also Abdel Salam Sidahmed, *Politics and Islam in contemporary Sudan*, Richmond, Surrey 1997; Abdelwahab El-Affendi, *Turabi's Revolution: Islam and Power in Sudan*, London 1991.
2. For convenience we refer throughout to Turabi's party as the NIF.
3. An insider's account is Lam Akol, *SPLM/SPLA: The Nasir Declaration*, New York 2003.
4. The name changed in 1996 to International Authority on Development (IGAD).
5. E.g. SPLA-Bahr al-Ghazal, Independent Bahr al-Ghazal Group, Sudanese Allied Forces, South Sudan Defence Force (SSDF), 'SSDF-2', 'SSDF-United', 'SSDF-Friendly to the SPLA', West Bank Nile Front, South Sudan Liberation Movement/Army, Imatong Liberation Front, South Sudan Independence Movement/Army, South Sudan Freedom Front, United Democratic Salvation Front, Independent Bor Group, Equatoria Defence Force, SPLA Independent Group (Nuba Mountains) and South Sudan United Army.

16. The Sudan and the New Millennium

1. This chapter is based mainly on unpublished documents, private information and articles in the periodical press.
2. I am grateful to Hilde F. Johnson for access to her MS on the negotiations.
3. The signing was witnessed by the presidents of Kenya and Uganda, the American and Egyptian foreign ministers and representatives of the UK, Norway, the Netherlands, Italy, the UN, the IGAD Partners, the African Union, the Arab League and the EU.
4. Also known as the Naivasha Agreement after the town in Kenya where most of the negotiations took place.
5. Interest groups' estimates of excess deaths during the Darfur crisis, as in the civil war in the South, are unreliable. For Darfur the number up to 2010 is usually given as 300,000; for the South, two million.
6. An East Sudan Peace Agreement was signed in October 2006 by the Sudanese Government and Eastern Sudan Front.

Maps

180

Maps

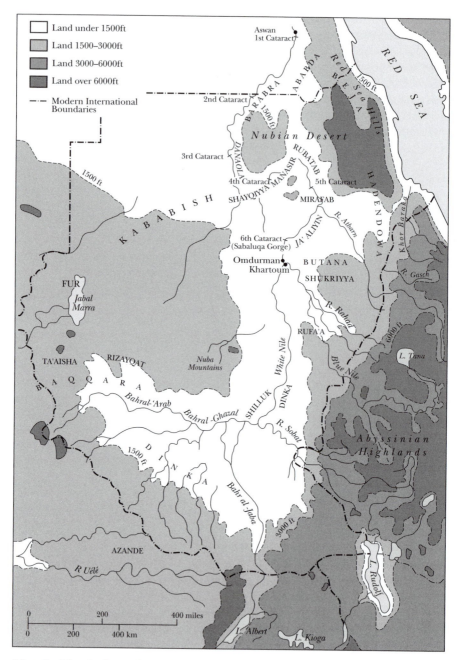

Map 1 The Sudan: physical and tribal

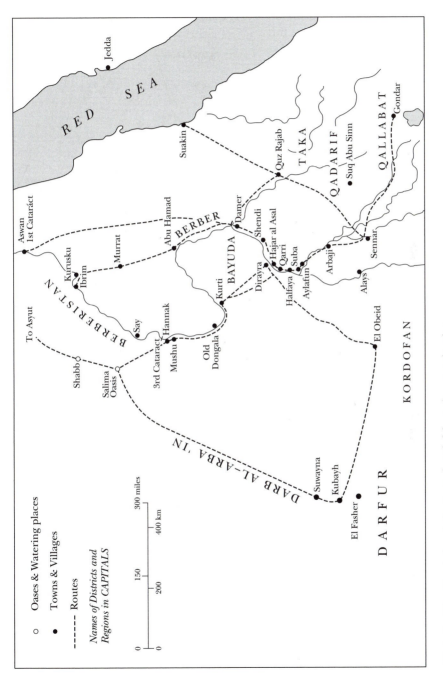

Map 2 The Funj dominions and neighbouring territories

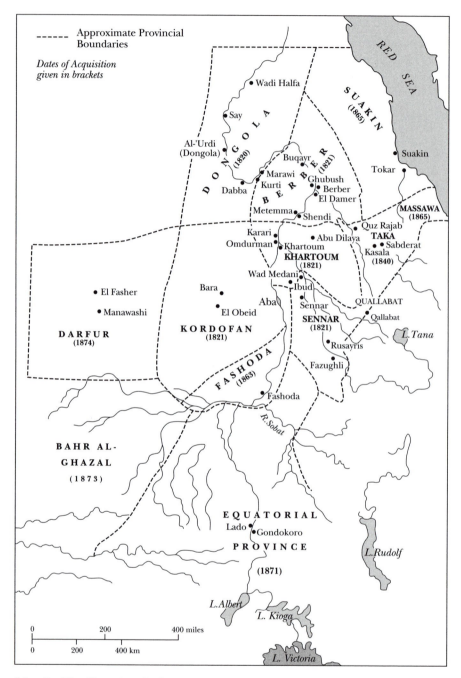

Map 3 The Egyptian Sudan

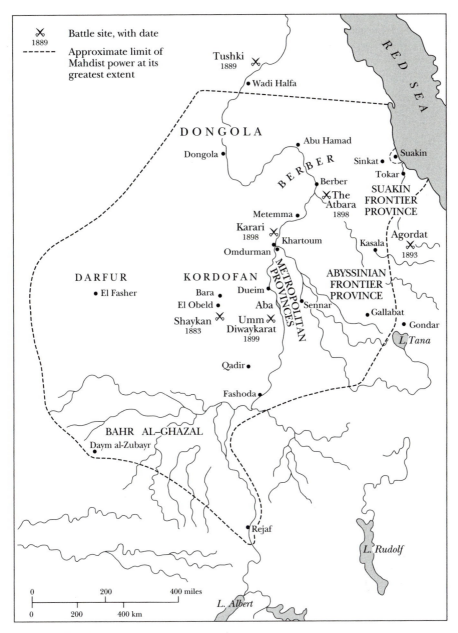

Map 4 The Mahdist state

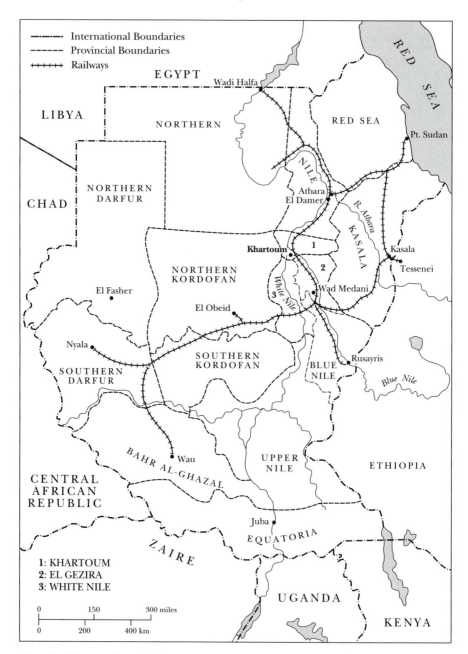

Map 5 The modern Sudan

Select Bibliography

Introduction: The Land and the People

Two essential and comprehensive bibliographical works, R.L. Hill, *A Bibliography of the Anglo-Egyptian Sudan from the Earliest Times to 1937* (London 1939) and Abdel Rahman el Nasri, *A Bibliography of the Sudan 1938–1958* (London 1962), are largely out of date. The relevant sections of J.D. Pearson, *Index Islamicus 1906–1955* (Cambridge 1958) and its *Supplements* (Cambridge 1962–), now online, list materials in periodicals, *Festschriften* and similar works. Extant Arabic MS materials are comprehensively listed by R.S. O'Fahey (compiler), *Arabic Literature of Africa*: Vol. I, *The Writings of Eastern Sudanic Africa to c. 1900* (Leiden 1994). *Sudan Notes and Records* (Khartoum 1918–) is a mine of information on all aspects of Sudanese studies, but its articles vary in quality. *Sudan Texts Bulletin*, edited by Ali Osman and Robin Thelwall (annually, 1980–86) and presenting the text and translation of documents from the pre-Islamic period onwards, continued as *Sudanic Africa: A Journal of Historical Sources* (Bergen, annually 1990–2005). There are relevant articles in the *Encyclopaedia of Islam* (second edition, Leiden and London 1960–2001), and a short general survey of Sudanese historiography in the *Supplement* to the *Encyclopaedia of Islam* (second edition, Leiden and London 2004). The geography of the Sudan is still fully treated only in K.M. Barbour, *The Republic of the Sudan: A Regional Geography* (London 1961). Terje Tvedt, *The Nile: An Annotated Bibliography* and *Southern Sudan: An Annotated Bibliography* (both London 2004) are useful. Richard Hill, *A Biographical Dictionary of the Sudan* (second edition, London 1967) remains indispensable.

A general history in English is Robert O. Collins, *A History of Modern Sudan*, (Cambridge 2008). Ali Salih Karrar, *The Sufi Brotherhoods in the Sudan* (London 1992) explains popular Islam. H.A. MacMichael, *A History of the Arabs in the Sudan* (Cambridge 1922), reprinted most recently in 2010, is a collection of materials from classical, Arabic and Sudanese sources, and incorporates much genealogical and tribal tradition. Of more limited scope is the same writer's *The Tribes of Central and Northern Kordofan* (Cambridge 1912). Among other tribal histories are A. Paul, *A History of the Beja Tribes of the Sudan* (Cambridge 1954), Aḥmad ʿAbd al-Raḥīm Naṣr, *Taʾrīkh al-ʿAbdallāb min khilāl riwāyātihim al-samāʿiyya* (Khartoum 1969), Ādam al-Zayn, *al-Turāth al-shaʿbī li-qabīlat al-Musabbaʿāt* (Khartoum 1970), and Muhammad Aḥmad Ibrāhīm, *Malāmiḥ min turāth Ḥamar al-Shaʿbī* (Khartoum 1971), Talal Asad, *The Kababish*

Arabs (London 1970), Ian Cunnison, *Baggara Arabs* (Oxford 1966), Abd al-Ghaffar Muhammad Ahmed, *Shaykhs and Followers* (Khartoum 1974) and Abbas Ahmed Mohamed, *White Nile Arabs* (London 1980). Two small peripheral kingdoms, Dar Masalit and Taqali, influenced respectively by Darfur and the Funj kingdom, are investigated in detail by Lidwien Kapteijns, *Mahdist Faith and Sudanic Tradition: The History of the Masālīt Sultanate, 1870–1930* (London 1985), and Janet J. Ewald, *Soldiers, Traders, and Slaves: State Formation and Economic Transformation in the Greater Nile Valley* (Madison, Wisconsin 1990).

Part One: Before the Turco-Egyptian Conquest

The pre-Islamic past is surveyed in A.J. Arkell, *A History of the Sudan to 1821* (second edition, London 1961, repr. 1974). The standard work on Christian Nubia is Ugo Monneret de Villard, *Storia della Nubia cristiana* (Rome 1938). A more recent study incorporating archaeological data is Giovanni Vantini, *Christianity in the Sudan* (Bologna 1981). The arabization of the Northern Sudan is studied in Yūsuf Faḍl Ḥasan, *The Arabs and the Sudan from the Seventh to the Early Sixteenth Century* (Edinburgh 1967). O.G.S. Crawford, *The Funj Kingdom of Sennar* (Gloucester 1951) assembles valuable data, and is still important. The Funj and Kayra sultanates are the subject of R.S. O'Fahey and J.L. Spaulding, *Kingdoms of the Sudan* (London 1974). A more specialized account of the Funj is given in Jay Spaulding, *The Heroic Age in Sinnār* (East Lansing, Michigan 1985). Detailed studies of aspects of the Kayra sultanate are provided by R.S. O'Fahey, *The Darfur Sultanate: A History* (New York 2008) and R.S. O'Fahey and M.I. Abu Salim, *Land in Dār Fūr* (Cambridge 1983). For a critique by a social anthropologist of the vexed question of Funj origins, see Wendy James, 'The Funj mystique: approaches to a problem of Sudan history', in Ravindra K. Jain (ed.), *Text and Context. The Social Anthropology of Tradition* (Philadelphia 1977). Several relevant articles are collected in P.M. Holt, *Studies in the History of the Near East* (London 1973). The 'Abdallabi shaykhdom is the subject of an Arabic monograph by Muḥammad Ṣāliḥ Muḥyi al-Dīn, *Mashyakhat al-'Abdallāb* (Beirut and Khartoum 1972). Editions and translations of the Arabic primary sources are given in the notes to Chapters 1 and 2 above. An important pioneer study of trade in the late Funj period is Terence Walz, *Trade between Egypt and Bilad as-Sūdān 1700–1820* (Cairo 1978).

For European travellers in the Sudan before the Turco-Egyptian conquest see Hill, *A Bibliography* (above). The journey of Charles Jacques Poncet, who visited Sennar at the end of the seventeenth century, has been reprinted by Sir William Foster (ed.), *The Red Sea and Adjacent Countries at the Close of the Seventeenth Century* (London 1949). The classical description of the Funj sultanate in its decline is James Bruce, *Travels to Discover the Source of the Nile* (Vol. VI, second edition, Edinburgh 1805). The earliest English traveller in Darfur was W.G. Browne, *Travels in Africa, Egypt, and Syria, from the Year 1792 to 1798* (London 1799). Conditions on the main Nile before the Turco-Egyptian conquest are described in John Lewis Burckhardt, *Travels in Nubia* (London 1819).

Part Two: The Turco-Egyptian Period: 1820–81

The only general account in English is still Richard Hill, *Egypt in the Sudan, 1820–1881* (London 1959), largely based on unpublished materials including the Egyptian archives. Parts of the period are treated in full by G. Douin in *Histoire du Soudan égyptien*, I (Cairo 1944 – all published), and in *Histoire du règne du Khédive Ismaïl*, III (Cairo 1936–41). An Arabic work covering the period is Muḥammad Fu'ād Shukrī, *Miṣr wa'l-Sūdān* (Cairo 1963), who examined a more limited topic in [M.F. Shukry], *The Khedive Ismaïl and Slavery in the Sudan (1863–1879)* (Cairo 1938). The opening-up of the South in this period is described by Richard Gray, *A History of the Southern Sudan 1839–1889* (London 1961). Anders Bjørkelo, *From King to Kashif. Shendi in the Nineteenth Century* (Bergen 1983) examines the impact of the Turco-Egyptian régime on the principal town of the Ja'aliyyin.

Accounts by travellers become increasingly numerous in this period. *A Narrative of the Expedition to Dongola and Sennaar* (London 1822), by 'an American in the service of the viceroy', was written by G.B. English, an officer in the Egyptian artillery at the time of the conquest. The Turco-Egyptian invasion coincided with 'an antiquarian visit to Egypt and Nubia, and an attempt to penetrate as far as Dóngola' by George Waddington and Barnard Hanbury, described in *Journal of a Visit to Some Parts of Ethiopia* (London 1822). Two other early travel accounts are those of L.M.A. Linant de Bellefonds, *Journal d'un voyage à Méroé dans les années 1821 et 1822*, ed. Margaret Shinnie (Khartoum 1958), and G.A. Hoskins, *Travels in Ethiopia* (London 1835). Manuscript source materials by contemporary European visitors and residents have been translated and edited by Richard Hill, *On the Frontiers of Islam* (Oxford 1970), and Paul Santi and Richard Hill, *The Europeans in the Sudan 1834–1878* (Oxford 1980). John Petherick, *Egypt, the Soudan and Central Africa* (Edinburgh and London 1861), describes early travels in the Bahr al-Ghazal. Two books by Sir Samuel W. Baker, *The Nile Tributaries of Abyssinia* (London 1874) and *The Albert N'yanza* (London 1877) are records of exploration that throw some light on conditions in the Sudan, while his *Ismailïa* (London 1874) is an account of his mission to the Southern Sudan on behalf of Khedive Isma'il. There is interesting material in T. Douglas Murray and A. Silva White, *Sir Samuel Baker, a Memoir* (London 1895), while a modern biography has been written by Dorothy Middleton, *Baker of the Nile* (London 1949).

The immense and still growing literature about Charles George Gordon began in this period. Richard Hill, 'The Gordon literature', *Durham University Journal*, New Series, XVI/3 (1955), 97–103 therefore needs updating. The essential study of Gordon's work in the Sudan is Bernard M. Allen,

Gordon and the Sudan (London 1931). Material on Gordon's activities in the country before the Mahdia is found in G. Birkbeck Hill (ed.), *Colonel Gordon in Central Africa, 1874–1879* (London 1881) and M.F. Shukry (ed.), *Equatoria under Egyptian Rule* (Cairo 1953). The career of Gordon's lieutenant in the Bahr al-Ghazal is described in the autobiographical work of Romolo Gessi (ed. Felix Gessi), *Seven Years in the Soudan* (London 1892). Another Italian servant of the khedive described his adventures in Gaetano Casati, *Ten Years in Equatoria* (London 1891). A collection of the letters and journals of Emin Pasha (Eduard Schnitzer), the last khedivial governor of Equatoria, is offered in G. Schweinfurth, F. Ratzel, R.W. Felkin and G. Hartlaub (eds), *Emin Pasha in Central Africa* (London 1888). For his biography, see Georg Schweitzer, *Emin Pasha, His Life and Work* (Westminster 1898). An important account of the Kayra sultanate in Darfur, shortly before its overthrow, was given by Gustav Nachtigal (tr. Allan G.B. Fisher and Humphrey J. Fisher), *Sahara and Sudan,* IV (London 1971). Materials left by two leading Europeans from the last phase of the Turco-Egyptian régime have been edited by M.W. Daly, *The Road to Shaykan: Letters of . . . Hicks Pasha* (Durham 1983), and Richard Hill, *The Sudan Memoirs of Carl Christian Giegler Pasha 1873–1883* (London 1984).

Part Three: The Mahdist State: 1881–98

A general history, which makes extensive use of the Mahdist archives, is P.M. Holt, *The Mahdist State in the Sudan, 1881–1898* (second edition, Oxford 1970). A study of events in the South is Robert O. Collins, *The Southern Sudan 1883–1898* (New Haven and London 1962). The diplomatic background to the 'reconquest' is examined in detail in G.N. Sanderson, *England, Europe and the Upper Nile 1882–1899* (Edinburgh 1965). Research in the Mahdist archives has resulted in a number of important Arabic monographs and collections of documents. Muḥammad Ibrāhīm Abū Salīm's *al-Ḥaraka al-fikriyya fi'l-Mahdiyya* (third edition, Khartoum 1989) is basically a study of the Mahdist chancery and documents, while the same author's *al-Arḍ fi'l-Mahdiyya* (Khartoum 1970) is an exposition of the land-law. The propaganda debate between the Mahdi and the orthodox *'ulamā'* who served the Turco-Egyptian administration is the subject of 'Abdallāh Alī Ibrāhīm, *al-Ṣirā 'bayn al-mahdī wa'l-'ulamā'* (Khartoum 1968). Three regional studies are Mūsā al-Mubārak al-Ḥasan, *Ta'rīkh Dār Fūr al-siyāsī* (Khartoum [1971]); Muḥammad Sa'īd al-Qaddāl, *al-Mahdiyya wa'l-Ḥabasha* (Khartoum 1973); and 'Awaḍ 'Abd al-Hādī al-'Aṭā, *Ta'rīkh Kurdufān al-siyāsi fi'l-Mahdiyya 1881–1899* (Khartoum 1973). Special mention should be made of the history written by a Lebanese officer in Egyptian military intelligence under Wingate, Na'um Shuqayr, *Ta'rīkh al-Sūdān al-qadīm wa'l-ḥadīth wa-jughrāfīyatuh* (Cairo [1903]), which is particularly valuable for the period of the Mahdia.

A major source, the entire corpus of the Mahdi's writings, has been published by Muḥammad Ibrāhīm Abū Salīm (ed.), *al-Āthār al-kāmila li'l-Imām al-Mahdī* (7 vols, Khartoum 1990–4). He earlier published a selection of documents including some from the Khalifa in *Manshūrāt al-Mahdiyya* (? Beirut 1969). Two other important sources edited by the same scholar are (1) three despatches of 'Uthman Diqna to the Mahdi, *Muzakkirat 'Uthmān Diqna* (Khartoum 1974); and (2) the hagiography by Ismā'il 'Abd al-Qādir al-Kurdufānī, *Sa'ādat al-mustahdī bi-sīrat al-Imām al-Mahdī* (Khartoum and Beirut 1972), of which a condensed English paraphrase is Haim Shaked, *The Life of the Sudanese Mahdi* (New Brunswick 1978). Abu Salim and Muḥammad Sa'id al-Qaddāl have jointly edited Ismā'īl 'Abd al-Qādir al-Kurdufānī's sequel (*al-Tirāz al-manqūsh bi-bushrā qatl Yuḥannā malik al-Ḥubūsh*) dealing with the Mahdist campaigns in Abyssinia, as *al-Ḥarb al-Ḥabbashiyya al-Sūdāniyya* (Khartoum 1972). Al-Qaddāl is also the author of a monograph on this subject, *al-Mahdiyya wa'l-Ḥabasha* (Khartoum 1973) and a biography of the Mahdi, *al-Imām al-Mahdī: Muhammad Ahmad ibn Abdallah, 1844–1885* (Khartoum 1985). The first of three volumes of autobiography by a Sudanese participant in the Mahdia, Bābikr Badrī, *Ta'rīkh ḥayati* ([?Khartoum] 1959–61), has been translated by Yousef Bedri and George Scott, *The Memoirs of Babikr Bedri* (London 1969). An important group of archives of the Mahdist treasury, the monthly accounts for Shawwāl 1314–Rajab 1315/22 March–24 Dec. 1897, were edited (Arabic text, English translation and introduction) by Ahmad Ibrahim Abu Shouk and Anders Bjorkelo, *The Public Treasury of the Muslims* (Leiden 1996).

Among contemporary works in English, three form a group on their own: F.R. Wingate, *Mahdiism and the Egyptian Sudan* (London 1891), *Ten Years' Captivity in the Mahdi's Camp, 1882–1892, from the Original Manuscripts of Father Joseph Ohrwalder* (London 1892), and Rudolf C. Slatin, *Fire and Sword in the Sudan* (London 1896). For a critique of these as war-propaganda, see P.M. Holt, 'The source-materials of the Sudanese Mahdia', *St. Antony's Papers, Number 4; Middle Eastern Affairs, Number One* (London 1958). An independent account by a European prisoner of the Mahdia is Charles Neufeld, *A Prisoner of the Khaleefa* (London 1899). For an account of events in the South in addition to those mentioned in the previous section, see A.J. Mounteney-Jephson, *Emin Pasha and the Rebellion at the Equator* (London 1890). A modern study is Iain R. Smith, *The Emin Pasha Relief Expedition 1886–1890* (Oxford 1972). Published primary sources on the siege of Khartoum and the relief expedition are A. Egmont Hake (ed.), *The Journals of Major-Gen. C.G. Gordon, C.B., at Kartoum*, covering only part of the siege, and Lord Wolseley's journal in Adrian Preston (ed.), *In Relief of Gordon* (London 1967). The Reconquest produced a great amount of journalistic narrative, of which G.W. Steevens, *With Kitchener to Khartoum* (Edinburgh and London 1898) and Winston Churchill, *The River War* (2 vols, London 1899) are the best-known examples.

Biographies of persons important during and after the Mahdia include H.C. Jackson, *Osman Digna* (London 1926), which does not use the Arabic material cited above. The account of Kitchener in Sir George Arthur, *Life of Lord Kitchener* (London 1920) may be compared with the presentation in Sir Philip Magnus, *Kitchener, Portrait of an Imperialist* (London 1959). Cromer's attitude to the Mahdia and the Reconquest is revealed in his *Modern Egypt* (London 1908). Wingate's role during and after the Mahdia is appraised by M.W. Daly, *The Sirdar: Sir Reginald Wingate and the British Empire in the Middle East* (Philadelphia 1997).

Part Four: The Anglo-Egyptian Condominium: 1899–1955

Many accounts of the Condominium were written by former members of the Sudan Political Service and tend to lack detachment. Useful examples are K.D.D. Henderson, *Sudan Republic* (London 1965), Sir Harold MacMichael, *The Sudan* (London 1954) and J.S.R. Duncan, *The Sudan's Path to Independence* (Edinburgh 1957). Bibliographical surveys are accessible in works mentioned above. Details of catalogues and other search tools for the important Sudan Archive of the University of Durham Library are available at its website. Two volumes of photographs from that archive are M.W. Daly and L.E. Forbes, *The Sudan* (Reading 1994) and M.W. Daly and Jane R. Hogan, *Images of Empire: Photographic Sources for the British in the Sudan* (Leiden 2005).

Political developments of the period have in recent years continued to attract attention. M.W. Daly, *Empire on the Nile: The Anglo-Egyptian Sudan, 1898–1934* (Cambridge 1986) and *Imperial Sudan: The Anglo-Egyptian Condominium, 1934–1956* (Cambridge 1991) provide a general history. G.M.A. Bakheit, *British Administration and Sudanese Nationalism, 1919–1939* (Cambridge Ph.D. 1965) deals with the rise of Sudanese nationalism. The White Flag League is the subject of 'Abd al-Karim al-Sid, *Al-liwa al-abyad* (Khartoum 1970). Especially useful for political developments during and after the Second World War are Mudddathir Abd al-Rahim, *Imperialism and Nationalism in the Sudan* (Oxford 1969), Heather Sharkey, *Living with Colonialism: Nationalism and Culture in the Anglo-Egyptian Sudan* (California 2003), K.D.D. Henderson, *The Making of the Modern Sudan, the Life and Letters of Sir Douglas Newbold* (London 1953), Sir James Robertson, *Transition in Africa, from Direct Rule to Independence* (London 1974) and Peter Woodward, *Condominium and Sudanese Nationalism* (London 1979).

The Sudan's role in Anglo-Egyptian relations is covered in several of the works already noted. John Marlowe, *A History of Egypt and Anglo-Egyptian Relations, 1880–1956* (London 1965) provides an overview; surveys of critical periods are W. Travis Hanes, *Imperial Diplomacy in the Era of Decolonization: the Sudan and Anglo-Egyptian Relations, 1945–1956* (Westport, Connecticut 1995) and Hassan Ahmed Ibrahim, *The 1936 Anglo-Egyptian Treaty* (Khartoum 1976).

Memoirs and biographies contain much useful information. In addition to those cited above, Hasan Ahmad Ibrahim, *Al-Imam 'Abd al-Rahman al-Mahdi* (Omdurman 1998) and *Sayyid 'Abd al-Rahman al-Mahdi: A Study of Neo-Mahdism in the Sudan* (Leiden 2004); Richard Hill, *Slatin Pasha* (London 1965); C.A.E. Lea, *On Trek in Kordofan*, M.W. Daly (ed.) (Oxford 1994); Edward Atiyah, *An*

Arab Tells his Story (London 1946); and Fadwa 'Abd al-Rahman Ali Taha (ed.), *Al-Sudan al-Sudaniyyin,* a biography of the statesman and educator 'Abd al-Rahman 'Ali Taha (second edition, Khartoum 1992) are informative. The second volume of *The Memoirs of Babikr Bedri* (London 1980) deals with education and politics during the period. A collective survey in restrospect is provided by Francis M. Deng and M.W. Daly, *'Bonds of Silk': The Human Factor in the British Administration of the Sudan* (East Lansing, Michigan 1989). The experiences of wives of British officials are recorded in Rosemary Kenrick, *Sudan Tales* (Cambridge 1987).

In recent years increasing attention has been paid to the colonial history of the Southern Sudan, although much of this has necessarily been from afar. R.O. Collins's *Land beyond the Rivers, the Southern Sudan, 1898–1919* (New Haven 1971), and *Shadows in the Grass* (New Haven 1983) cover the period. L.S.P. and G.N. Sanderson, *Education, Religion, and Politics in Southern Sudan 1899–1964* (London 1981) is a mine of information and analysis. Among Douglas H. Johnson's growing body of work, *Nuer Prophets: A History of Prophecy from the Upper Nile in the Nineteenth and Twentieth Centuries* (Oxford 1994) and *Governing the Nuer: Documents by Percy Coriat on Nuer History and Ethnography 1922–1931* (Oxford 1993) are particularly valuable. A contemporary survey has been published: Douglas H. Johnson (ed.), C.A. Willis (compiler), *The Upper Nile Province Handbook: A Report on Peoples and Government in the Southern Sudan, 1931* (Oxford 1995). Stephanie Bestwick, *Sudan's Blood Mmemory: The Legacy of War, Ethnicity and Slavery in South Sudan* (Rochester 2004) is an account based largely on modern oral sources. Classic works on peoples of the South by a famous anthropologist are listed in *A Bibliography of the Writings of E.E. Evans-Pritchard* (Harper & Row 1974). Much anthropological and other relevant research may be found in *Sudan Notes and Records* and in specialized periodicals.

Important works on social, economic and educational developments during the Condominium period include the magisterial J.D. Tothill (ed.), *Agriculture in the Sudan* (London 1948), Arthur Gaitskell, *Gezira, a Story of Development in the Sudan* (London 1959) and H.C. Squires, *The Sudan Medical Service, an Experiment in Social Medicine* (London 1958). Conrad Reining discusses *The Zande Scheme, an Anthropological Case Study of Economic Development in Africa* (Evanston 1966). A study of urbanization in the Anglo-Egyptian era is Kenneth J. Perkins, *Port Sudan: The Evolution of a Colonial City* (Boulder 1993). Developments in Muslim law are outlined in J.N.D. Anderson, *Islamic Law in Africa* (London 1954). Educational development is covered in V.L. Griffiths, *An Experiment in Education* (London 1955), Ina Beasley, *Before the Wind Changed,* Janet Starkey (ed.) (Oxford 1992) and Mohamed Omer Beshir, *Educational Development in the Sudan, 1898–1956* (Oxford 1969). The history of trade unionism is studied in Saad ed Din Fawzi, *The Labour Movement in the Sudan, 1946–1955* (London 1957); a monograph is Ahmad Alawad Sikainga, *'City of steel and fire': A Social History of Atbara, Sudan's Railway Town, 1906–1984* (Oxford and Portsmouth, New Hampshire 2002). The same author's *Slaves into Workers. Emancipation and Labor in Colonial Sudan* (Austin 1996) is informative.

Part Five: The Independent Sudan

The political history of the early post-independence period is studied, by detailed reference to the development of political parties and to their electoral performance, in Peter Bechtold, *Politics in the Sudan* (New York 1976). The role of the army in the early republic is discussed in Ruth First, *The Barrel of a Gun: Political Power in Africa and the Coup d'Etat* (London 1970). Sectarian politics and the history of communism in the Sudan are dealt with in Gabriel Warburg, *Islam, Nationalism and Communism in a Traditional Society* (London 1978). Several provincial histories have appeared, among them Muhammad Ibrahim Abu Salim, *Ta'rikh al-Khartum* (Khartoum 1971). Local government since the inception of the Condominium is studied in John Howell (ed.), *Local Government and Politics in the Sudan* (Khartoum 1974). Collections of articles on the Sudan since 1985 are Peter Woodward (ed.), *Sudan after Nimeiri* (London 1991), John Voll (ed.), *Sudan: State and Society in Crisis* (Bloomington 1991) and Sharif Harir and Terje Tvedt (eds), *Short-cut to Decay* (Uppsala 1994). The ideology and policies of the NIF régime are discussed in Abdel Salam Sidahmed, *Politics and Islam in Contemporary Sudan* (Richmond, Surrey 1997); Human Rights Watch/Africa, *Behind the Red Line: Political Repression in Sudan* (New York 1996); and Abdullahi A. Gallab, *The First Islamic Republic: Development and Disintegration of Islamism in the Sudan* (Aldershot 2008). The NIF leader, Hasan al-Turabi, is the subject of Mohamed Elhachmi Hamdi, *The Making of an Islamic Political Leader* (Boulder 1998) and Abdelwahab El-Affendi, *Turabi's Revolution: Islam and Power in Sudan* (London 1991). A survey, with documents, is Peter Nyot Kok, *Governance and Conflict in the Sudan, 1985–1995* (Hamburg 1996). The websites of relevant governments and their departments, inter-governmental organizations, bodies such as the United Nations and its constituent institutions and non-governmental organizations, special interest groups and political parties and groupings have largely super-seded even periodical literature as media for the dissemination of relevant information and documents and thus for the study of contemporary history.

The two North–South civil wars have been the subject of many recent studies, and have indeed blossomed into an academic specialty. Human Rights Watch/Africa, Amnesty International and African Rights are among many groups that have produced work on the wars and related atrocities. Douglas H. Johnson, *The Root Causes of Sudan's Civil Wars* (second edition, Oxford and Bloomington 2004) is a detailed summary of events. Ruth Iyob and Gilbert M. Khadiagala, *Sudan: The Elusive Quest for Peace* (London and Boulder 2006) is a useful overview. Benaiah Yongo-Bure, *Economic Development of Southern Sudan* (Lanham, Maryland 2007), Alex de Waal, *Famine Crimes: Politics and the Disaster Relief Industry in Africa* (Oxford and Bloomington 1997) and African

Rights, *Food and Power in Sudan: A Critique of Humanitarianism* (London 1997) cover relevant issues. M.W. Daly and Ahmad Alawad Sikainga (eds), *Civil War in the Sudan* (London 1993) is a collection of articles. Among Francis Mading Deng's relevant works are *Protecting the Dispossessed* (Washington 1993) and, with Larry Minear, *The Challenge of Famine Relief* (Washington 1992). The subject of J. Millard Burr and Robert O. Collins, *Requiem for the Sudan: War, Drought and Disaster Relief on the Nile* (Boulder 1995) is explained by its title. Reliable statistics have been a casualty of war; J. Millar Burr, *Quantifying Genocide in the Southern Sudan, 1988–1998* (Washington, DC 1998) is instructive. A study on a related subject is Alexander De Waal, *Famine that Kills: Darfur, Sudan, 1984–1985* (Oxford 1989). Donald Petterson, *Inside Sudan* (Boulder 1999) is an account of an American diplomat's involvement. Steven Wondu and Ann Lesch, *Battle for Peace in Sudan. An Analysis of the Abuja Conference, 1992–1993* (Boston, 2000) is a detailed study. Sudanese memoirs relate events through the lens of interested parties. These include Lam Akol Ajawin, *SPLM/SPLA: Inside an African Revolution* (Khartoum 2001) and *SPLM/SPLA: The Nasir Declaration* (New York 2003); Peter Adwok Nyaba, *The Politics of Liberation* (Richmond 1996); Arop Madut-Arop, *Sudan's Painful Road to Peace. A Full Story of the Founding and Development of SPLM/SPLA* (np, 2006); and Jok Madut Jok, *Sudan. Race, Religion, and Violence* (Oxford 2007). A journalist's useful account from behind the lines is Deborah Scroggins, *Emma's War* (New York 2002).

The Darfur crisis, long ignored, has recently received enormous attention. The websites of governments, international agencies, NGOs and interest groups provide massive up-to-the-minute but unfiltered material. A Social Science Research Council site, 'Making Sense of Darfur', presents the views of its expert moderator, Alexander De Waal, and a wide variety of contributors. Among published works for non-experts, M.W. Daly, *Darfur's Sorrow. The Neglected History of a Humanitarian Disaster* (second edition, Cambridge and New York 2010) is a first attempt at a survey of Darfur's modern history to the present. Julie Flint and Alex De Waal, *Darfur: A New History of a Long War* (London 2008) and Gerard Prunier, *Darfur: A Twenty-first Century Genocide* (third edition, Ithaca 2008) are useful. Human Rights Watch/Africa is a reliable source: the subjects of its *Darfur in Flames: Atrocities in Western Sudan* (Washington, DC 2004) and *Darfur Destroyed: Ethnic Cleansing by Government and Militia Forces in Western Sudan* (Washington 2004) are obvious.

Government control of the Sudanese press has very lately (2010) been relaxed. For recent events periodical literature and published secondary sources have largely been superseded by the plethora of documentary sources and opinion online. These must be treated with care as to their provenance, purpose and accuracy. In addition to the sites of organizations already mentioned, those of governments and international organizations are especially useful for recent history, current events and official versions of documents.

Index

The index is in word order with references to notes following page numbers with an italic n, e.g.: Arbaji 173*n6*. Names starting with al- have been filed according to the first letter of the following word, e.g.: al-Turani is filed under T.